First
Chronicles

Paul O. Wendland

The interior illustrations were originally executed by James Tissot (1836–1902).

Commentary and pictures are reprinted from 1 CHRONICLES (The People's Bible Series), copyright © 1994 by Northwestern Publishing House. Used by permission.

Copyright © 1995 Concordia Publishing House
3558 S. Jefferson Avenue, St. Louis, MO 63118-3968
Manufactured in the United States of America

1 2 3 4 5 6 7 8 9 10   04 03 02 01 00 99 98 97 96 95

CONTENTS

CONTENTS

PREFACE

The People's Bible Commentary is just what the name implies—a Bible and commentary for the people. It includes the complete text of the Holy Scriptures in the popular New International Version. The commentary following the Scripture sections contains personal applications as well as historical background and explanations of the text.

The authors of *The People's Bible Commentary* are men of scholarship and practical insight, gained from years of experience in the teaching and preaching ministries. They have tried to avoid the technical jargon which limits so many commentary series to professional Bible scholars.

The most important feature of these books is that they are Christ-centered. Speaking of the Old Testament Scriptures, Jesus himself declared, "These are the Scriptures that testify about me" (John 5:39). Each volume of *The People's Bible Commentary* directs our attention to Jesus Christ. He is the center of the entire Bible. He is our only Savior.

We dedicate these volumes to the glory of God and to the good of his people.

The Publishers

INTRODUCTION

The Author and Date of Writing:

The most likely author of the book of Chronicles is Ezra, the scribe and teacher of Israel. Early Jewish tradition says as much, and this is further corroborated by the similarity in style and content between the books of Chronicles and Ezra. The book of Ezra begins where the book of Chronicles ends: with the edict of Cyrus that allowed the exiled Jews to return to their homeland. This would seem to suggest that a single author saw the two books as parts of one complete work.

Since Ezra was active around 450 B.C., we could accept that year as an approximate date for the writing of the book.

The Book's Importance:
A Chronicle of the Kingdom of God

When people select a biblical book for study, Chronicles may not appear at the top of most of their "must read" lists. That daunting register of names at the very beginning appears like a bramble thicket—something a person has to hack through before he even gets to the start of the story!

Such a perception of the book is not something new. Already back in the time when Chronicles was being translated from Hebrew into Greek, the translators gave it the unhappy title: *The Things Left Out.* By this they may have meant that the books of Samuel and Kings pretty well took care of this portion of Israel's history and that the book of Chronicles merely served to fill in the gaps.

In more recent days—beginning in the 1800s—the book of Chronicles has been mocked and ridiculed by negative Bible scholars as being a hopelessly inaccurate patchwork of myths and legends, written by a man who had no real sense of history. Since World War II, however, this extremely negative view has changed somewhat. More recent commentators show greater respect for the Chronicler both as an historian and as a literary stylist.

So where does this leave us? Is Chronicles merely a book that fills in the gaps left blank by Samuel and Kings? Is our opinion of Chronicles to be held hostage to the most recent theory of the critics and commentators?

Not at all! We discover a more accurate perception of the book's importance and the holy author's reason for writing it in the book's Hebrew title, *The Annals of the Days* (literally: the things or events of the days). While we do not know whether the author himself called his book by this name, we can safely say that this title does capture his true intent in writing it. What the author clearly has in mind for his book is to recap for the people of his day the entire history of God's dealings with humanity up to the time in which he lived.

Every writer of history has a bias or a point of view from which he writes. This writer of sacred history is no different. He also has a definite point of view, and he approaches his work with it in mind. However, since the Chronicler is a child of God, he sees history in a far different light than a worldly historian might. For him history is not a meaningless jumble of unrelated events or a matter of evolution working out some unknown purpose for the universe or merely a succession of great men and big events. Nor does he attempt to trace all that happens to some source in class conflict, population pressure, or the economic conditions of the time. All these points of view are ones worldly historians adopt as they seek to interpret the past. On the other hand, a child of God, like the Chronicler, can only see history as HIS story, that is, the story of God working in the lives of men and nations to save HIS elect.

This idea of God working in the events of history and in the hearts of people is often referred to in Scripture as *the kingdom of God.* In that phrase the word kingdom does not refer so much to a place, like heaven, or a piece of earthly real estate with borders like the kingdom of Great Britain. Rather, the kingdom of God is *God's royal rule*—the working out of God's gracious, saving purpose in our lives and in all that happens.

The Chronicler traced *God's kingdom* from Adam to Abraham, from Saul to David, from Solomon to Zerubbabel. He showed how God promised to be found by his people *at the temple.* And since proper worship is an essential way for a believer to participate in the rule of God, the Chronicler described in detail the organization and functions of those who worked at the temple: *the priests and the Levites.* God clearly did not want his people to approach him in worship in just any way that they might please—but rather through his appointed priests. The priests, in turn, were helped in their work by the Levites. Far more than simply being hewers of wood and drawers of water, the Levites, with their singing and playing of sacred instruments, made God's worship beautiful. They also played a crucial role in keeping the whole temple complex running smoothly.

Finally, the holy writer showed how God ruled, guarded, warned, and preserved his people through *kings and prophets.* If a king did not act like a true shepherd of God's flock, the Lord responded in judgment. On the other hand, when the kings listened to the prophetic Word and served God wholeheartedly, God blessed his people.

Once we believe that history is HIS story, then the past can never be just a dry recounting of names and facts and dates.

Rather, it is the record of the living God, who is living and active in this present moment. And if God's people recall his works and ways of times past, they will know that he is active in their lives in the present and what his purpose for them is in the future.

The People for Whom the Book Was First Written

The Chronicler recounted the past so that God's people of that time could apply the Word to their own situation. And if we understand the spiritual difficulties that confronted those people of God who first received that Word, that will help us apply the holy writer's words to ourselves today. The biblical books of Ezra, Nehemiah, Haggai, Zechariah, and Malachi give us this necessary background.

Two great historical events shaped the thinking of God's people in the fifth century before Christ. The first occurred a thousand years before; the second was still green in their memory. The first had confirmed the children of Israel in the truth that they were God's chosen people; the second made them wonder whether that were still true. The first event was *the exodus from Egypt.* The second was the *exile into Babylon.*

A) The Exodus

It was about 1450 B.C. when Moses received his commission to lead the people of Israel out of their slavery in Egypt to the land that God had promised to Abraham and his descendants. By mighty acts of power and grace God overwhelmed the earthly glory of Pharaoh, set his people free from their harsh taskmasters, and brought them to himself on Mt. Sinai, where he gave them the covenant of the law. From that mountain God led his people—under Moses and later under Joshua—into the land of Canaan, a land he gave them as their possession.

Once in Canaan the people grew and flourished, especially under their two great kings, David and Solomon. Canaan became Israel. The heathen nations, both within and without Israel's borders, were either destroyed or subdued. The temple was built as the only legitimate place on earth to approach the true God. The house of David was in full flower in the tenth century before Christ, and during that period God's people saw their greatest earthly power and glory. Many prophecies about Christ were written at this time. Those prophecies—using the power and glory the people saw in David and Solomon as points of reference— quite naturally described the power and glory of the coming Messiah.

B) The Exile

The earthly power of the house of David did not last, however, and the exile into Babylon dashed whatever hope the Israelites might still have had for a return to those glory days. By the time of the exile in 586 B.C., much had already changed.

Because of their unfaithfulness, God's people had seen their kingdom divided into the northern kingdom of Israel and the southern kingdom of Judah. Then in 723/722 B.C. they had seen the northern kingdom destroyed by the Assyrian armies and the people of Israel dispersed among the nations of the Near East. Not much was left of the once proud empire of David and Solomon except for the towns and villages of little Judah huddling around Jerusalem.

The people of Judah, unfortunately, did not learn from what had happened to the northern kingdom. They, too, persisted in their unfaithfulness and became more and more corrupt. God's judgment fell upon them, and they found themselves helpless in the face of a new threat: the great city-state of Babylon. Babylon attacked Judah and no less than three times in the space of nineteen years (605-586 B.C.) carted off many of its most substantial citizens into exile. There, far from Zion, they were forced to live in the homeland of their conquerors between the Tigris and Euphrates rivers. Once they were settled in Babylon's empire, the people of Judah had to deal with the culture shock of living in a foreign kingdom with foreign gods, foreign customs, and foreign laws. And there they were confronted with the temptation to adopt the customs, cultures, and false gods of their conquerors.

Meanwhile, the city of Jerusalem had been destroyed, and God's temple lay in ruins. A descendant of David no longer ruled on the throne of a recognizable kingdom. No priests offered sacrifice to God in the appointed way. With the pillars of government, commerce, and religion in exile, the territory of Judah simply ceased to exist. Politically, the land itself was absorbed into the province of Samaria where it became just another administrative unit of the Babylonian Empire.

But God in his mercy preserved a remnant of his people. After seventy years in exile, they were allowed to return to their homeland. This came about as the result of a gracious edict issued by a Persian king named Cyrus. The year was 537 B.C.

The exiles returned with high ideals and hopes. They soon found out, however, how difficult it would be to start over. When the foundations for a new temple were laid, for example, many of the older people burst into tears. What they saw looked so pathetic compared to the glory of the temple they remembered (see Ezra 3:12,13).

This pretty well sums up the attitude of the people who first received the book of Chronicles. They were discouraged and downhearted because what they saw bore so little resemblance to the glory that once had been theirs. In their despair they were inclined to question everything, including their identity as God's people. Even the temple was losing its vital significance for them. Their faith in the coming of God's promised Messiah was at low ebb. Many succumbed to the temptation of forging a compromise with the heathen people around them. After all, why fight to preserve or rebuild what seemed lost and gone forever? In short, God's people were at risk of losing both their heritage and their hope.

The book of Chronicles was written to build up these discouraged believers. To restore their wavering confidence in themselves and their institutions, the Chronicler recounted for them their glorious history under David and Solomon. He reminded them how God's unfailing love had been at work in the events of the past, so as to awaken trust in that same love active in their present situation. He also wanted to warn the believers against making the same spiritual mistakes their fathers had made. Those sins, the Chronicler told them, were the precise reason why God had permitted the judgment of the exile and the fall of Jerusalem to occur. As Nehemiah had rebuilt the physical walls of Jerusalem, so the Chronicler was engaged in rebuilding the spiritual walls of Zion.

How did the Chronicler succeed in his God-given task? That can best be seen in the way God's people endured in the Promised Land throughout all the difficulties that confronted them in the centuries that remained before the coming of Jesus. Worship of the true God at his temple through priest and Levite continued. By the power of his Word, spoken through the Chronicler, God preserved the Jews as a people distinct from the godless nations round about them, until that day when the Lord himself "suddenly . . . [came] to his temple" and filled it with his glory (Malachi 3:1).

In a similar way, we who live in these troubled last days can take comfort from this account of God's kingdom, built on the enduring Word of our faithful God. We find ourselves living more and more in what some have called a "global village"—a world where we are bombarded on every side with customs and cultures much different from our own. In this environment we, like the Jews from Babylon, may be tempted to question our identity as God's people.

In this environment the people of this world seek to identify the common thread in all religions and seek to harmonize them all into one single faith. They accuse Christians, who still hold to Jesus as the only way to heaven, of being intolerant and judgmental. Faced with such accusations, we may become confused and wonder, "Are we causing unnecessary divisions? Is the gospel in Word and sacrament still the only certain way for God to come to us? Are there perhaps other ways to approach God—different, but still valid?" If such thoughts ever trouble us, then the Chronicler's insistence that man must seek God where he has promised to be found will help clear our heads, too.

Finally, for us who live at a time when the visible Christian church is in a state of collapse, the great comfort the Chronicler gave his people can ease our fears as well. In this history he records for us, we see many concrete examples of how, while everything might seem to be falling apart, the promise of God still endures forever. His great promise of a Savior, around which all history revolves, is the matter we take up next.

The Righteous King: Israel's Enduring Hope

Up to this point we have not yet discussed an important side of the Chronicler's message to the believers of his generation. He set out to keep alive in them the hope that God's Messiah, a royal descendant of David, was still going to come to his people. Remember that at the time the book was written, there was no son of David ruling on the throne. In fact, there was no king at all in Israel. After governor Zerubbabel passed from the scene, the house of David ceased to exert any political influence whatever. David's house had become—as the prophet Isaiah had predicted—a dead stump (Isaiah 11:1). And Judah itself was just one little backwater province in the huge Persian empire.

In view of all these things, the idea that King Messiah was still going to come must have seemed to be almost unbelievable. To counteract this kind of thinking, the Chronicler simply reasserted the promise made to David that one of his sons would not only build a temple, but would also rule over God's kingdom forever (1 Chronicles 17:14). By comparison and contrast he then showed what God's Righteous King would be like.

In dealing with the rule of David and Solomon, the Chronicler is selective in choosing his material. He passes over some negative incidents in the lives of these two kings, such as David's sin with Bathsheba and Solomon's many wives and practice of idolatry. The Chronicler is not pretending that these things never happened. He knew that his readers were familiar with the accounts in Samuel and Kings. But the Chronicler chose to concentrate on and emphasize the positive, because he wanted to use the godly qualities of David and Solomon to give his readers a picture of what the Righteous King would be like.

David and Solomon organized God's people around the temple. In so doing, they played a unique role in the Old Testament kingdom of God. In that role they were types of what the Messiah would do in gathering his elect from every nation to himself and in building them into a "holy temple . . . in which God lives by his Spirit" (Ephesians 2:21,22). By way of contrast, all the wicked kings of Judah are characterized with statements like this: "He did not do what was right in the eyes of the LORD" (2 Chronicles 22:4; 28:1; 33:2; 36:5,9,12). As a person reads about the wicked things these evil kings did, his heart begins to yearn for a King who "will judge [his] people in righteousness" (Psalm 72:2).

In these ways the writer of Chronicles kept alive the hope of God's people that the Messiah would come and that he would establish God's righteous rule in a way that would go far beyond anything David or Solomon had ever done. In these last evil days, may his words also increase our hope and longing for the return of our King!

Theme and Outline:

"YOURS, O LORD, IS THE KINGDOM!"
(1 Chronicles 29:11)

I. An Overview of God's Kingdom from the Beginning to the Restoration (1 Chronicles 1-9)

   A. From Adam to Abraham (1)

   B. The Twelve Sons of Israel (2:1,2)

   C. The Royal Tribe of Judah (2:3—4:23)

   D. The Outer Edge of Israel: Simeon and the Tribes of the Transjordan (4:24—5:26)
      1. The Tribe of Simeon (4:24-43)
      2. The Tribe of Reuben (5:1-10)
      3. The Tribe of Gad (5:11-22)
      4. The Half-Tribe of Manasseh (5:23-26)

   E. The Priestly Tribe of Levi (6)

Parts III and IV will be treated in 2 Chronicles

PART I

AN OVERVIEW OF GOD'S KINGDOM FROM THE BEGINNING TO THE RESTORATION

1 CHRONICLES 1-9

Meaning and Purpose of the Genealogies

It's easy to lose patience with the Chronicler right at the start. People usually don't look through their phone books for a little relaxing reading at the end of the day. And a phone book of names is what these first nine chapters of genealogies might at first appear to be. List after list, name after name—hardly the way to hold the attention of the modern reader!

If you share this view, then my advice to you is simply to read the next few paragraphs on the purpose of the genealogies and then move on to page 125. However, it would be a shame if a few names stood between you and the Chronicler's message, and I am sure you will find these genealogies worth whatever effort you put into them.

Even in our culture a list of names can have greater power to move the soul than we might at first think. Consider, for example, that long black wall of stone in Washington, with the names of those who fell in Vietnam etched on it. Those names clutch at the heart and strike the chords of memory. Or consider the New Year's Eve custom some churches have of reading off the names of those who died during the past year. Just hearing the names spoken, one right after another, often brings tears to peoples' eyes. It reminds the people of the congregation of all that the departed saints had meant to them and how God had enriched their lives through them.

In a similar way, the Chronicler wrote these genealogies to remind the Israelites of the past and how God had woven his plan of salvation into the history of men and nations. Reeling off these familiar names—familiar to the Israelites if not to us—permitted him to compress eons of history into a few words. At the same time it allowed him to give a helpful overview of all that had happened before the main period of history he wished to cover. Far from wanting to waste anyone's time with his seemingly endless list of names, the holy writer was setting the stage for his later discussion of the kingdom of God in Israel. He could have chosen no more effective way of saying to his people, "The God in charge of all nations is the same saving God who was at work in our history."

Keep in mind the situation to which the Chronicler was speaking. The people of Judah were wondering if they still were God's people. Their faith in the validity of their institutions was wavering. Their temple, compared to the one Solomon had built, was not much to look at. Could God still dwell in it? Could they still be the kingdom of God if no descendant of David ruled as king on a visible throne?

By means of the genealogies the Chronicler replied, "Yes, God is still with us, just as he was with our forefathers! We are the legitimate successors to the Israelites of old. Our temple with its priests and Levites still has the command and promise of God attached to it. God's plan to bless all nations through Abraham's descendants has not been derailed. We may, therefore, wait in hope for King Messiah, the Son of David, to come."

From Adam to Abraham:

The Genealogy of Adam

1 **Adam, Seth, Enosh, ²Kenan, Mahalalel, Jared, ³Enoch, Methuselah, Lamech, Noah.**

⁴**The sons of Noah:**
Shem, Ham and Japheth.

The Chronicler begins at the dawn of history, outlining the development of God's dealings with the human race from Adam to Abraham. He is drawing from the genealogies in Genesis 5, 10, and 11:10-27. Omitting the names of Cain and Abel, he restricts himself to the godly line sprung from Seth. Notice how abruptly he begins, how tersely he continues. In the first four verses he simply mentions the names of successive generations down to Noah without inserting phrases such as "X was the father of" or "Y was the son of." It's as if he was marking the measured tread of God's footsteps from generation to generation.

He shows the connection between Adam, to whom God first made the promise of a Savior, and Noah, who carried God's promise into the world after the great flood.

The Genealogy of Japheth

⁵**The sons of Japheth:**
Gomer, Magog, Madai, Javan, Tubal, Meshech
and Tiras.
⁶**The sons of Gomer:**
Ashkenaz, Riphath and Togarmah.
⁷**The sons of Javan:**
Elishah, Tarshish, the Kittim and the Rodanim.

The Chronicler now traces the threefold division of the human race after the flood from the three sons of Noah: Shem,

Ham, and Japheth. Readers of Genesis will be familiar with these names as the Table of Nations found in Chapter 10 of that book. Following a pattern we will notice time and again, the Chronicler begins with the less important lines of descent so that he can come to a climax with the most important—in this case the line of Shem. The fact that Shem is presented last highlights the position of his descendant, Abraham, in God's plan of salvation.

It is hard to identify and locate with any certainty the Japhethite names and tribes. Gomer seems to be the name of the ancestral founder of the Cimmerians, who lived north and east of the Black Sea. Javan has been considered by most scholars to be a Hebrew spelling of "Ionia," the land on the western coast of Asia Minor inhabited by the ancient Greeks. As for the other sons of Javan, Tarshish has been identified with Tartessus in Spain, the Kittim with the people of Cyprus, and the Rodanim with the people of Rhodes.

One more brief point before we move on. It is clear that we are not dealing here with genealogies in the strict sense of that term. Some of these names (e.g., "the Kittim") refer, not to a person, but to a tribe of people. Some, like Javan, may refer to places or settlements. In many cases there no doubt may have been a well-known ancestor who founded a place and gave his name to it. We need to be aware that the Chronicler is making historical connections between people, places, and nations; he is not simply tracing a strict family tree.

The Genealogy of Ham

  ⁸ The sons of Ham:
      Cush, Mizraim, Put and Canaan.
  ⁹ The sons of Cush:
      Seba, Havilah, Sabta, Raamah and Sabteca.

16

The sons of Raamah:
Sheba and Dedan.
[10] Cush was the father of
Nimrod, who grew to be a mighty warrior on earth.
[11] Mizraim was the father of the Ludites, Anamites,
Lehabites, Naphtuhites, [12]Pathrusites, Casluhites
(from whom the Philistines came) and Caphtorites.
[13] Canaan was the father of Sidon his firstborn, and of
the Hittites, [14]Jebusites, Amorites, Girgashites,
[15]Hivites, Arkites, Sinites, [16]Arvadites, Zemarites
and Hamathites.

As their names indicate, the Hamitic descendants lived in
north Africa, the Arabian peninsula, and the land of Canaan.
Most scholars locate the territory of Cush in the upper Nile
region and identify it as either Nubia or Ethiopia. "Mizraim"
is the Hebrew word for Egypt. The son of Ham no doubt settled there.

The Chronicler pinpoints the origins of some early enemies of Israel in this list. From Mizraim came the Casluhites
and Caphtorites, inhabitants of Mediterranean islands. These
"people from the sea" invaded the coast of Canaan. After
they had intermarried with the indigenous inhabitants of that
area, organized themselves, and built cities, they posed a serious threat to Israel. We are more familiar with them as the
Philistines (see also Amos 9:7 and Jeremiah 47:4).

In looking over Canaan's descendants, Bible readers may
notice names familiar to them from other places in Scripture
as the "legion of the damned," that is, those early inhabitants
of Canaan that the Israelites were told to drive out before
them as they took possession of the land (see Genesis 15:21,
Exodus 3:8, and Joshua 3:10).

[17]The sons of Shem:

Elam, Asshur, Arphaxad, Lud and Aram.

The sons of Aram:

Uz, Hul, Gether and Meshech.
[18]Arphaxad was the father of Shelah,

and Shelah the father of Eber.
[19]Two sons were born to Eber:

One was named Peleg, because in his time the earth
was divided; his brother was named Joktan.
[20]Joktan was the father of

Almodad, Sheleph, Hazarmaveth, Jerah, [21]Hadoram,
Uzal, Diklah, [22]Obal, Abimael, Sheba, [23]Ophir, Havilah
and Jobab. All these were sons of Joktan. [24]Shem,
Arphaxad, Shelah, [25]Eber, Peleg, Reu, [26]Serug, Nahor,
Terah [27]and Abram (that is, Abraham).

The Chronicler now makes the connection between Noah
and Abram through Noah's son Shem. His purpose is to trace
the spiritual line of descent of those who bore the promise of
the coming Savior. Eber had two sons, only one of whom
was a direct ancestor of the Savior. In keeping with the stylistic trait mentioned previously, the Chronicler dispenses with
the less important line of Joktan first so that he can focus on
the important line—the direct line to Abram through Peleg.

Peleg's name means "division," and as the Chronicler reminds us in verse 19, he got his name from the fact that the
earth was divided during his lifetime. This is a reference to
God's confusing men's languages at Babel, thereby compelling men to divide and separate into different tribes (see
Genesis 11).

The name of Peleg's father, Eber, is also interesting because it was this ancestor of Abram who gave his name to the
race we call the "Hebrews" (see Genesis 14:13).

Ten generations in all are listed from Shem to Abram in verses 24 to 27. In many places in Scripture ten is a number signifying completeness. That symbolism is probably derived from the thought that it takes ten fingers to make a complete set. Some scholars have thought that the listing of ten names was a deliberate stylistic choice made by the Chronicler. They have combined this feature with others in the chapter to present us with the following as the basic structure for the first 27 verses of Chronicles.

A Godly line:	Adam to Noah	*10 generations*
B Table of Nations:	Japheth 14 names	
	Ham 30 names	*70 names in all*
	Shem 26 names	
A Godly line:	Shem to Abram	*10 generations*

While this A—B—A pattern is interesting, we cannot be absolutely sure that it was a deliberate feature of the Chronicler's style, nor that he intended the names and the numbers to line up in precisely that way. But we can say that if it is a deliberate choice on the writer's part, it reinforces in a stylistic way the indisputable fact that God's saving plans are deliberate, measured, and sure.

Meaning of These Verses for Us Today:

Before continuing with Abram's descendants, let's take a break and ask ourselves what meaning we can take away for ourselves from these opening verses of Chronicles. Among other things, we can learn that God's plan of salvation embraces *all* the descendants of Adam, all nations. And that what God was planning to do through Israel, he was doing for *all,* ourselves included. We also learn that God cares about individuals and that people unknown to us are still well known to him. And while our names may never appear on the world's *Who's Who* list, as long as they are written in the Book of Life, it doesn't matter.

Lastly, these verses remind us of great turning points in ancient history, all of which were under the control of our mighty God. Noah reminds us of the flood. Peleg reminds us of Babel. *Our God is terrifying in his judgments!* Abram reminds us that God in his grace was pleased to set this man apart from the unbelieving mass of mankind in order to send the world a Savior through him. *Our God is amazing in his grace!*

The Genealogy of Abraham

The last half of the chapter traces Abraham and his descendants. The Chronicler begins with those descendants who did not constitute the line from which the Messiah would come. With the next chapter he will turn to those who did, the children of Israel. Once again we notice the pattern the Chronicler employed, dealing with the less important before the most important. Those who came from Abraham through Ishmael and Keturah are quickly dealt with before he mentions Isaac and his two sons, Esau and Israel. Then Israel is dropped from the discussion until Esau, as the son of the lesser importance, has had his line of descent traced. Esau's line completes the chapter.

The holy writer directs our attention first to Abraham's descendants through his two concubines, Hagar and Keturah, and his wife Sarah:

28The sons of Abraham:
Isaac and Ishmael.

29These were their descendants:
Nebaioth the firstborn of Ishmael, Kedar, Adbeel,
Mibsam, 30Mishma, Dumah, Massa, Hadad, Tema,

[31]Jetur, Naphish and Kedemah. These were the sons of
Ishmael.

[32]The sons born to Keturah, Abraham's concubine:
Zimran, Jokshan, Medan, Midian, Ishbak and Shuah.
The sons of Jokshan:
Sheba and Dedan.
[33]The sons of Midian:
Ephah, Epher, Hanoch, Abida and Eldaah.
All these were descendants of Keturah.

[34]Abraham was the father of Isaac.
The sons of Isaac:
Esau and Israel.

Twelve tribal princes are listed as having come from Abraham's son Ishmael. The number takes on greater significance when we read the words of the Lord's promise to Abraham, "And as for Ishmael . . . he will be the father of *twelve* rulers, and I will make him into a great nation" (Genesis 17:20). God keeps his promises. Names like Tema and Dumah are also associated in Scripture with settlements in the north of the Arabian peninsula. It is likely that Ishmael's sons lived there.

Abraham's children by his second wife Keturah also apparently settled in Arabia. Their names are associated with scattered places in the south and the north of that land mass. The Chronicler, rather than using the word "wife" as Moses does in Genesis 25:1, calls Keturah a concubine. In this way he draws attention to the truth that Sarah and her child Isaac had the place of prime importance in God's plan of saving humanity.

[35]The sons of Esau:
Eliphaz, Reuel, Jeush, Jalam and Korah.
[36]The sons of Eliphaz:
Teman, Omar, Zepho, Gatam and Kenaz;
by Timna: Amalek.

[37]The sons of Reuel:
  Nahath, Zerah, Shammah and Mizzah.

[38]The sons of Seir: Lotan, Shobal, Zibeon, Anah, Dishon,
Ezer and Dishan.

[39]The sons of Lotan:
  Hori and Homam. Timna was Lotan's sister.

[40]The sons of Shobal:
  Alvan, Manahath, Ebal, Shepho and Onam.
  The sons of Zibeon:
  Aiah and Anah.

[41]The son of Anah:
  Dishon.
  The sons of Dishon:
  Hemdan, Eshban, Ithran and Keran.

[42]The sons of Ezer:
  Bilhan, Zaavan and Akan.
  The sons of Dishan:
  Uz and Aran.

[43]These were the kings who reigned in Edom before any
Israelite king reigned:
  Bela son of Beor, whose city was named Dinhabah.

[44]When Bela died, Jobab son of Zerah from Bozrah succeeded him as king.

[45]When Jobab died, Husham from the land of the Teman-
ites succeeded him as king.

[46]When Husham died, Hadad son of Bedad, who defeated
Midian in the country of Moab, succeeded him as
king. His city was named Avith.

[47]When Hadad died, Samlah from Masrekah succeeded
him as king.

[48]When Samlah died, Shaul from Rehoboth on the river
succeeded him as king.

[49]When Shaul died, Baal-Hanan son of Acbor succeeded
him as king.

[50]When Baal-Hanan died, Hadad succeeded him as king.
His city was named Pau, and his wife's name was

Mehetabel daughter of Matred, the daughter of Me-Zahab. 51Hadad also died.

The chiefs of Edom were: Timna, Alvah, Jetheth, 52Oholibamah, Elah, Pinon, 53Kenaz, Teman, Mibzar, 54Magdiel and Iram. These were the chiefs of Edom.

The nation of Edom played a major role in the history of Israel. From David's time on they were under the thumb, first of the united kingdom of Israel, then of the southern kingdom of Judah. The Edomites never resigned themselves to being a conquered people. During the time of kings Solomon, Jehosaphat, Jehoram, and Ahaz, they staged rebellions against their overlords. The rule of the house of David over them seems never to have been absolute.

Relations between Edom and Judah took an even nastier turn when the house of David was under siege by the Babylonians. At the time the Edomites took savage glee in the destruction of Jerusalem. According to Psalm 137, they said, "Tear it down, tear it down to its foundations!" (verse 7). Since they were instrumental in the downfall of Jerusalem, they came under God's judgment. As Isaiah had predicted in his 34th chapter, the princes of Edom were driven out of their strongholds. This happened around the fifth century before Christ when the Nabatean Arabs swept across the Edomites' traditional lands to the south and east of the Dead Sea. The Edomites—or Idumeans as they were later called—were forced to migrate, and at the time of the Jews' return from exile, they were living directly to the south of Hebron in the pasture lands of the Negev.

By the time of the Chronicler, then, the Edomites had become Judah's nearest neighbors directly to the south. It would have, therefore, been important for the holy writer to make clear to his readers where these people had come from and what their relationship to the Jews was. That is why we see more space devoted to the genealogy of the Edomites than to any other nation in this chapter.

In verses 35-37, we have a list of Esau's sons. They acquired their original homeland by dispossessing the sons of Seir, mentioned in verses 38-42. It is clear from this section that the sons of Esau married the daughters of Seir (compare 1:36 with 1:39). The Edomites were the result of this intermingling.

A succession of their pre-Davidic kings follows in verses 43 to 51. The last two verses complete the list for Edom by naming their tribal chieftains.

Meaning of These Verses for Us Today:

What application can we make for ourselves of these verses? Parallel passages from Genesis and Romans provide the key to understanding. God is here clearly shown to be making good on his promise to Abraham, "You will be the father of *many* nations. No longer will you be called Abram; your name will be Abraham . . . I will make you very fruitful; I will make nations of you and kings will come out of you" (Genesis 17:4-6).

Those many nations, partially outlined in these verses, are perfectly fulfilled in us who are "of the faith of Abraham," as Paul says (Romans 4:16). Every time we baptize a baby, every time an adult comes to faith, the genealogy of Abraham has another name added to it! Write your own name in the margins of your Bible at this place, and you will fulfill the Chronicler's intention in giving us this genealogy.

Paul continues, "He is our father in the sight of God in whom he believed—the God who gives life to the dead and calls things that are not as though they were" (Romans 4:16,17). God had made this astounding promise to a man who had no children at all. He was to be, God told him, the father of many—whole nations would trace their descent back to him! He was to be, God told him, the father of kings and the forefather of the King of kings. The Chronicler reminds us that neither the faith of Abraham, nor ours, is ever misplaced when we rely on the promise of God.

The Sons of Israel:

2 **These were the sons of Israel: Reuben, Simeon, Levi, Judah, Issachar, Zebulun, ²Dan, Joseph, Benjamin, Naphtali, Gad and Asher.**

These names serve as the bridge between the genealogy of Abraham and the genealogies of the tribes of Israel, beginning with Judah. God kept his promise to Abraham and made a great nation out of these twelve brothers. It is helpful to remember that we have here a listing of Israel's *sons*. When we come to lists of the twelve *tribes,* we will see differences, depending on where we look. The differences stem from the fact that not all of Israel's sons were included on every list as being the founder of a tribe. In addition, Israel's son Joseph had two tribes stem from him, the tribes of Ephraim and Manasseh.

The Chronicler was pointing out a truth to the Israelites of his own generation, a truth meant to sustain their hearts in troubled times. Out of all the nations of the world God had chosen them to be his very own. He had brought them out of Egypt, settled them in Canaan, and put his dwelling place among them. He did not choose them because they were worthy, righteous, or especially deserving. It was purely by grace (Deuteronomy 7:7-9 and 9:6).

Out of the sinful mass of mankind, God has chosen us in Christ to be his very own. He has set us free from sin and death and has built in our bodies his temple. He did not choose us because we were righteous or especially deserving.

It was purely by grace. In this truth we, too, rest our hearts in these troubled times (2 Timothy 1:9).

The Royal Tribe of Judah:

By now we have become accustomed to the Chronicler's pattern of dealing first with the genealogy of lesser importance and then moving on to the more important. Here he breaks his pattern and changes his method and shifts Judah to the front in order to give David's tribe even greater prominence. It's as if he can contain himself no longer. For nearly the next three chapters he deals with Judah, Israel's royal tribe.

Some commentators accuse the Chronicler of being hopelessly muddled in his presentation of Judah. That's because they do not see the two interlocking structures underlying the text. The first structure glues chapters two to four in such a way that David's clan, Hezron, appears in the center like a precious stone in a silver setting. The second structure arranges the clan of Hezron in such a way that the descendants of Ram (the sub-clan from which David came) are listed both at the beginning and at the end, like bookends holding everything together.

Have a look at these two tables by way of illustration:

A) The structure of chapters 2-4, the tribe of Judah

Clan Name	Reference	Structure
Shelah	2:3	A
Perez	2:4-8	B
HEZRON	2:9-3:24	C
Perez	4:1-20	B
Shelah	4:21-23	A

> ### B) The structure of the sub-clans under the genealogy of Hezron
>
> | Name of Sub-Clan | Reference | Structure |
> |---|---|---|
> | RAM | 2:10-17 | A |
> | Caleb | 2:18-24 | B |
> | Jerahmeel | 2:25-33 | C |
> | Jerahmeel | 2:34-41 | C |
> | Caleb | 2:42-55 | B |
> | RAM | 3:1-24 | A |

An arrangement like *A-B-C-C-B-A* may not hold much appeal for a modern commentator, but such an arrangement would have been very satisfying to an ancient Hebrew. And after all, the Chronicler was writing for them, not for the commentators. His purpose in this double and interlocking arrangement was, once again, to give the greatest possible prominence to the house and lineage of David. "Remember David," he was telling his original readers, "and the many promises he received from God." Thus the genealogies serve to emphasize and create an anticipation for material that the Chronicler will develop more fully later.

Judah's Sons

³**The sons of Judah:**
   Er, Onan and Shelah. These three were born to him by a Canaanite woman, the daughter of Shua. Er, Judah's firstborn, was wicked in the LORD's sight; so the LORD put him to death. ⁴Tamar, Judah's daughter-in-law, bore him Perez and Zerah. Judah had five sons in all.

Of Judah's three sons by his Canaanite wife, only one survived. Shelah is mentioned here and then dropped from discussion until the end of the Chronicler's treatment of the tribe. Er and Onan both were destroyed by God for living in defiance of God's commands (see Genesis 38:8-10).

From the beginning, as Paul says, "not all who are descended from Israel are Israel" (Romans 9:6). Mere physical descent from Abraham and Israel was no guarantee of eternal safety, eternal salvation. If a son of Judah rejected his Savior and demonstrated it in his life, he was cut off. On the other hand, as we shall see later, people from other nations also would be grafted into the tribe.

The reference to Tamar points back to an unsavory episode in the life of Judah. She had been married first to Er and then to Onan, but she had no children. When she began to despair of Judah's ever carrying out his lawful responsibility and giving her Shelah as a husband, she hatched a plot to deceive her father-in-law. She dressed up as a prostitute and enticed Judah to sleep with her. Judah willingly complied, not knowing who she was. Perez and Zerah were the result. The whole seedy affair is described in Genesis 38. Such was the stock from which David—and great David's greater Son—were born.

Is it really necessary to go into all this? Aren't some things better left unsaid? But what better way to emphasize that God likes to make something out of nothing! God's choice of Judah as the royal tribe was also a matter of pure grace—and not because there was anything special about the bloodline.

It is a great comfort to me to know that Jesus was born from a tribe of sinners. I learn from it how much that innocent Man wanted to be one with a wretch like me. Even in his ancestry, he identified himself completely with the lost, so that the lost might be found in him.

The Descendants of Perez and Zerah

⁵The sons of Perez:
Hezron and Hamul.
⁶The sons of Zerah:
Zimri, Ethan, Heman, Calcol and Darda—five in all.
⁷The son of Carmi:
Achar, who brought trouble on Israel by violating the
ban on taking devoted things.
⁸The son of Ethan:
Azariah.
⁹The sons born to Hezron were:
Jerahmeel, Ram and Caleb.

Our chief interest here is to follow the line that leads from
Judah to David through Perez and his son Hezron.

In passing, the Chronicler also mentions Zerah's descendants: four good, one bad, and one unknown. The *unknown* is
Zimri. Not much can be said about him except to say that he
was the father of Carmi (verse 7), who, in turn, was the father of Achar (see Joshua 7:1).

The four *good* descendants are Ethan, Heman, Calcol, and
Darda. The word son must be taken loosely here, since these
men were contemporaries of David and Solomon. Ethan and
Heman are also listed as Levites in 6:33-42. They served
David with distinction as temple musicians (see titles of
Psalms 88 and 89). It may be somewhat confusing to learn
that these men could trace their line back to two different
tribes. We might wonder how they can be considered both
members of the tribe of Judah and Levites at the same time.
This is best explained by saying that they were undoubtedly
Levites by pedigree whose ancestors had lived for a while
among the Zerahites before moving to Zuph in Ephraim
(compare 1 Chronicles 6:28,33 with 1 Samuel 1:1). While

among the Zerahites, they had become associated with that clan in a way that their connection with the Zerahites of Judah persisted. (It is helpful to remember that these lists are not "genealogies" in the strict sense of the word and that the word *son* or *father* often establishes a broader connection than one of strictly physical descent). In any case, Ethan and Heman could claim ties to Judah as well as Levi. The Chronicler highlights their lineage because anything connected with the temple is of great interest to him.

Calcol and Darda are included with Heman and Ethan as being men famous for their wisdom in the days of Solomon the king (1 Kings 4:31). Yet they did not outshine their master, Solomon. He surpassed them all. For a little shoot off Judah's stem, Zerah has not been doing too badly so far.

All that changes with Achar. His birth name was probably Achan, as Joshua tells us in chapter 7 of his book. He was such a scoundrel that his name became synonymous in Israel with trouble. This is why the Chronicler renames him Achar—"Trouble" in the Hebrew language. And trouble is what he caused for Israel. He deliberately defied God's ban on taking any booty from the city of Jericho. In his greed he selected some choice pieces of plunder and secretly buried them under his tent. There are no secrets to God, however, and after Israel had suffered an inexplicable defeat at the hands of the men of Ai, the "Trouble" was exposed. Achar confessed and was promptly executed. The Chronicler is reminding his readers here that willful sin and unfaithfulness to God will surely be punished. God is not mocked (Galatians 6:7).

In verse nine, the Chronicler begins to trace the lineage that is of greatest importance to him. He picks up Hezron, whose clan he will be describing to us until the end of chapter 3. The rest of chapter 2 and all of chapter 3 is built around

Hezron's three chief sons and their descendants: Ram, Jerahmeel, and Caleb.

A. *Hezron, Son of Perez, and His Descendants Through Ram:*

¹⁰**Ram was the father of Amminadab, and Amminadab the father of Nahshon, the leader of the people of Judah. ¹¹Nahshon was the father of Salmon, Salmon the father of Boaz, ¹²Boaz the father of Obed and Obed the father of Jesse.**

¹³**Jesse was the father of Eliab his firstborn; the second son was Abinadab, the third Shimea, ¹⁴the fourth Nethanel, the fifth Raddai, ¹⁵the sixth Ozem and the seventh David. ¹⁶Their sisters were Zeruiah and Abigail. Zeruiah's three sons were Abishai, Joab and Asahel. ¹⁷Abigail was the mother of Amasa, whose father was Jether the Ishmaelite.**

We enter some familiar territory here as we encounter many names known to us from other parts of the Bible. Nahshon was a leader of the tribe of Judah during the Exodus (Numbers 1:7). Boaz is known to us from the book of Ruth. From there it is but a small genealogical hop over Obed to Jesse and his sons. To this destination the Chronicler has been leading us ever since he began with the tribe of Judah. To give him honor, David is listed here as Jesse's seventh son—position number seven was the one of completeness and fulfillment. A fuller account of Jesse and his sons is found in 1 Samuel 16. David holds pride of place as the most illustrious, not only in Jesse's family, but in all Israel.

David's step-sisters are also mentioned: Abigail and Zeruiah. These women gave birth to warriors who served with distinction in David's army.

After this one brief mention of David, the Chronicler resumes his catalog of the descendants of Hezron by his other two sons. He will come back to David in chapter 3.

B. Hezron, Son of Perez, and His Descendants Through Caleb:

¹⁸Caleb son of Hezron had children by his wife Azubah (and by Jerioth). These were her sons: Jesher, Shobab and Ardon. ¹⁹When Azubah died, Caleb married Ephrath, who bore him Hur. ²⁰Hur was the father of Uri, and Uri the father of Bezalel.

²¹Later, Hezron lay with the daughter of Makir the father of Gilead (he had married her when he was sixty years old), and she bore him Segub. ²²Segub was the father of Jair, who controlled twenty-three towns in Gilead. ²³(But Geshur and Aram captured Havvoth Jair, as well as Kenath with its surrounding settlements—sixty towns.) All these were descendants of Makir the father of Gilead.

²⁴After Hezron died in Caleb Ephrathah, Abijah the wife of Hezron bore him Ashhur the father of Tekoa.

A short list of Caleb's descendants is given here. The Chronicler will be much more complete later on in the chapter. Right now his consuming interest is to introduce us to Bezalel, the man whom God equipped with his good gifts and Spirit to be the master craftsman for the Tabernacle (see Exodus 31:1-5). It is no accident that by verse 20 our writer has found in Judah's genealogy a way to foreshadow themes he will be returning to throughout his books. Ethan and Heman—Zerahites, ah, but also *Levites,* as his readers well knew. David the *king.* Now we meet Bezalel, the craftsman of the "wilderness *temple.*" Temple, king, and Levites all serve as points around which the books of Chronicles revolve. It seems as if the author is a pretty good craftsman himself.

It is a little more difficult to see the reason why the writer included verses 21-23. Makir and Gilead, his son, are well-known members of the Manassehite tribe (see Numbers 26:29). Once in the land of promise, they settled across the Jordan river in a region that became known as Gilead. It is in Gilead where the settlements collectively known as Havvoth Jair were found (see Numbers 32:41).

Perhaps by making this connection between the tribes of Judah and Manasseh, the Chronicler wanted to assure his readers that all Israel was still present in the tribe of Judah, even though Manasseh had largely been wiped out as a tribe in the Assyrian conquest. The incident in verse 23 could have been mentioned by way of prelude to the far greater Assyrian devastation that happened later.

The concluding verse of the section introduces us to Ashhur, son of Hezron, whose genealogy will be further discussed in chapter 4:5-9. Tekoa was a village south of Bethlehem inhabited by the Jews who returned from exile.

C. Hezron, Son of Perez, and His Descendants Through Jerahmeel:

²⁵The sons of Jerahmeel the firstborn of Hezron:
Ram his firstborn, Bunah, Oren, Ozem and Ahijah.
²⁶Jerahmeel had another wife, whose name was Atarah; she was the mother of Onam.
²⁷The sons of Ram the firstborn of Jerahmeel:
Maaz, Jamin and Eker.
²⁸The sons of Onam:
Shammai and Jada.
The sons of Shammai:
Nadab and Abishur.

²⁹Abishur's wife was named Abihail, who bore him Ahban and Molid.

³⁰The sons of Nadab:

Seled and Appaim. Seled died without children.

³¹The son of Appaim:

Ishi, who was the father of Sheshan.

Sheshan was the father of Ahlai.

³²The sons of Jada, Shammai's brother:

Jether and Jonathan. Jether died without children.

³³The sons of Jonathan:

Peleth and Zaza.

These were the descendants of Jerahmeel.

³⁴Sheshan had no sons—only daughters.

He had an Egyptian servant named Jarha. ³⁵Sheshan gave his daughter in marriage to his servant Jarha, and she bore him Attai.

³⁶Attai was the father of Nathan,

Nathan the father of Zabad,

³⁷ Zabad the father of Ephlal,

Ephlal the father of Obed,

³⁸ Obed the father of Jehu,

Jehu the father of Azariah,

³⁹ Azariah the father of Helez,

Helez the father of Eleasah,

⁴⁰ Eleasah the father of Sismai,

Sismai the father of Shallum,

⁴¹ Shallum the father of Jekamiah,

and Jekamiah the father of Elishama.

We will take this section as a unit, even though markers in the text indicate a division at the end of verse 33. When the book of Chronicles was written, there were no punctuation, paragraph, or verse markings to make it clear to the reader where one section ended and another began. They did, however, have other ways to do the same thing. One of the more common methods they used to alert readers to the fact that they were moving on to something new or closing out something old was to insert little formulaic statements. We see two examples of this kind of thing in verses 25 and 33. *"The sons of"* and *"These were descendants"* are opening and closing *formulas* to a genealogy. It is helpful to know this, not so that we can fill ourselves full of useless bits of trivia, but to recognize the textual evidence for that structure we spoke of earlier (page 27). Jerahmeel's genealogy is treated in two back-to-back segments, sandwiched between two segments of Caleb's genealogy. The entire section is framed by two segments of Ram's genealogy. It is for this reason we can say with some confidence, "We have an A-B-C-C-B-A pattern here."

Aside from this, not much can be said with respect to Jerahmeel's descendants. Most of this material is unique to the Chronicler. We cannot identify these names with people, places, and towns mentioned elsewhere.

Our writer does make a point in verse 34 of Sheshan having no sons, only daughters. He adopted his Egyptian servant into his family through marriage and carried on the family name and inheritance rights through him. (Alert Bible readers will recall that Abram [see Genesis 15:2] once contemplated doing something similar. He, admittedly, was in a much worse position at the time, since he had no children at all. So he asked God whether Eliezer, his servant, would be the one to inherit his estate.) In any case, God blessed Sheshan's decision by giving him descendants down to at least the fourteenth generation.

How happy we are that our inheritance does not depend on flesh and blood or on being male or female, but on the power of God! In Christ he gives us an inheritance "that can never perish, spoil or fade—kept in heaven" (1 Peter 1:4).

D. Hezron, Son of Perez, and His Descendants Through Caleb: (continued from 2:18-24)

We can divide these genealogies into two parts. Verses 42-50a give us further information on Clan Caleb, and verses 50 to 55 highlight Hur, son of Caleb, whose descendants became a clan in their own right.

⁴²The sons of Caleb the brother of Jerahmeel:
> Mesha his firstborn, who was the father of Ziph, and his son Mareshah, who was the father of Hebron.

⁴³The sons of Hebron:
> Korah, Tappuah, Rekem and Shema. ⁴⁴Shema was the father of Raham, and Raham the father of Jorkeam. Rekem was the father of Shammai. ⁴⁵The son of Shammai was Maon, and Maon was the father of Beth Zur.

⁴⁶Caleb's concubine Ephah was the mother of Haran, Moza and Gazez. Haran was the father of Gazez.

⁴⁷The sons of Jahdai:
> Regem, Jotham, Geshan, Pelet, Ephah and Shaaph.

⁴⁸Caleb's concubine Maacah was the mother of Sheber and Tirhanah. ⁴⁹She also gave birth to Shaaph the father of Madmannah and to Sheva the father of Macbenah and Gibea. Caleb's daughter was Acsah. ⁵⁰These were the descendants of Caleb.

Many of Caleb's descendants mentioned in this first section must have settled in central and southern Judah, since names like Ziph, Hebron, Maon, and Madmannah are also towns that we can locate in that area. In addition, those names are familiar to us from the story of David and Saul. It was the Ziphites who treacherously tried to give their tribesman David up to Saul. Near Maon was a wilderness in which David and his men found refuge for a time (see

1 Samuel 23:15ff). The ancient city of Hebron was the place where the men of Judah publicly anointed David as their king (2 Samuel 2:4).

We can again observe from this passage that the phrase "father of" has to be capable of a broader meaning than simply "the physical father of." Beth Zur and Kiriath Jearim are places. When a person is called "the father of" Beth Zur (verse 45) or "the father of Kiriath Jearim" (verse 50), we are dealing with a founder or a leading citizen of that place.

We now come to a difficult passage to interpret. Caleb is mentioned in verse 49 as being the father of Acsah. In this context, the Caleb referred to must be the *son of Hezron,* Jerahmeel's brother (verse 42). In the fourth chapter of Chronicles, we will run across another Caleb who is the *son of Jephunneh* (1 Chronicles 4:15). These clearly are two different men. Caleb, *son of Jephunneh,* achieved great prominence at the time of the Exodus by being chosen as one of the scouts who went into the land of Canaan. It was he who, along with Joshua, encouraged Israel to possess the land without delay (see Numbers 13:30). What makes matters somewhat more complex for us is that Caleb the scout belonged to the clan of (you might have guessed it) Caleb, the *son of Hezron.* That much can be inferred from their common association with the town of Hebron (see 1 Chronicles 2:42,43 and Joshua 14:13). But again, Caleb the scout and contemporary of Joshua cannot be the same man as Caleb, son of Hezron. Caleb, son of Hezron, was long dead by the time Caleb the scout saw the light of day.

So what's the fuss? Well, Caleb the scout is also said to have had a daughter named Acsah (Joshua 15:16). Two Calebs are not a problem. Two Calebs, each with a daughter named Acsah, does seem a bit too coincidental. Negative Bible scholars pounce on verses like these and say, "A contradiction! The Bible contradicts itself! Forget about an *inspired,* inerrant Bible!"

We can, however, put forward two possible explanations of this and still be true to Scripture. The first is that the Chronicler could be saying nothing more than that Acsah was considered the "daughter" of Caleb the clan head, since her natural father, Caleb the scout, was a member of that tribe and clan. All the daughters of the clan could be considered "daughters" of the clan's founder. The Chronicler was simply singling out Acsah for special mention here. This explanation has the advantage of leaving us with only one Acsah.

The other way of explaining it would be to say that Caleb the scout named one of his daughters after the well-known daughter of Caleb, the clan founder. This explanation has the advantage of letting both Joshua 15:16 and 1 Chronicles 2:49 stand in their most natural sense. We are left not only with two Calebs, but two Acsahs as well.

It is enough for a Bible believer to give one plausible explanation for the difficulty. The burden of proof lies with those who insist that Scripture must have contradictions. Finally, nothing will satisfy those who don't share our view of Scripture. A person can always find contradictions if he is looking for them.

It is hoped that this discussion will, at the very least, help us better understand what our pastors and teachers mean when they tell us that *the Bible is a clear book.* When we say that the Bible is clear, we are talking about an objective clarity, not a subjective one. This clarity exists even if I do not personally perceive it. For example, the sun is always shining; yet from my point of view it may sometimes be hidden by clouds or by the earth's shadow. In a similar way, the Bible is clear in and of itself. Still, from my point of view, there may be many things in a particular portion of it that remain hidden to my understanding. This may be due to my sinful weakness or come about as a result of my ignorance concerning some aspect of the text before me. Nevertheless, just as clouds don't really stop the sun from shining, so my personal difficulties in understanding don't really make the Bible unclear. The problem lies with me, not the Bible.

Besides all this, the Bible assures me that it is especially clear in letting me know the way I can be saved and in letting me know how I can live a life that pleases God. Paul asserts that the Holy Writings are "able to make [us] wise for salvation through faith in Christ Jesus, . . . thoroughly equipping [us] for every good work" (2 Timothy 3:15,17). That's clear enough for me. Not only will the Holy Writings get me to heaven, they will also fit me out with everything I need for a life of good works here on earth. Whatever clouds I can't remove by careful and prayerful study, I'll leave for the day when clouds and darkness end, and I see God face to face.

> The sons of Hur the firstborn of Ephrathah:
>> Shobal the father of Kiriath Jearim, ⁵¹Salma the father of Bethlehem, and Hareph the father of Beth Gader.
> ⁵²The descendants of Shobal the father of Kiriath Jearim were: Haroeh, half the Manahathites, ⁵³and the clans of Kiriath Jearim: the Ithrites, Puthites, Shumathites and Mishraites. From these descended the Zorathites and Eshtaolites.
> ⁵⁴The descendants of Salma:
>> Bethlehem, the Netophathites, Atroth Beth Joab, half the Manahathites, the Zorites, ⁵⁵and the clans of scribes who lived at Jabez: the Tirathites, Shimeathites and Sucathites. These are the Kenites who came from Hammath, the father of the house of Recab.

We resume our study of the text. Caleb's son, Hur, is described in a section concluding the chapter. We recognize Kiriath Jearim and Bethlehem as towns later reoccupied by the returned exiles. It would be of interest to the Chronicler's readers to see information like this connecting them to their past.

The closing verses contain two hidden gems. We are told in verse 55 about clans of scribes who settled at Jabez. At an early time the people of Israel were interested enough in reading and writing that whole *guilds* of people sprang up who could earn their living from the transmission of the written word. People like the scribes of Jabez preserved our Old Testament Scriptures for us.

Finally, we are introduced in the last verse to some people called Kenites who are said to be descended from Hammath. Hammath is further identified as the father of the house of Recab. Kenites were ancient non-Israelite inhabitants of the land of Canaan. They date back to Abraham's day (Genesis 15:19). Later on, Moses invited Hobab, son of Reuel the Kenite, to accompany Israel on their journey to the promised land. He promised Hobab a share in the good things God would give to Israel (Numbers 10:29-32). It is clear from Israel's later history that Hobab must have accepted Moses' invitation, for Kenite descendants of Reuel are found living in Israel at the time of the Judges (see Judges 1:16). What is especially interesting here is that Kenites are connected with the house of Recab.

The house of Recab is spoken of several times in Scripture, most notably as a group of people who remained faithful to the true God during Israel's great apostasy under Ahab (2 Kings 10:15). In Jeremiah 35, God holds up the Recabites as examples to Israel of what faithfulness means. They abstained from wine as a mark of their loyalty to a command

1 CHRONICLES 2:50-55

one of their forefathers gave to their family. This loyal adherence to the command of a dead ancestor showed how dark, by contrast, Israel's disloyalty had been to the covenant of the living God. Of particular interest to us here is that we see how even those who were not Israelite by physical descent were counted as part of God's people by the Chronicler. The Recabite line continued throughout the conquest and exile. One of their number helped Nehemiah restore the walls of Jerusalem (Nehemiah 3:14). Faithful they were; faithful they remained.

Sometimes we get the impression that the children of Israel were like some exclusive club. We suppose that if you were a Gentile in the time before Christ, you were pretty much out of luck as far as having any chance of being saved. Certainly God chose Israel out of all the nations of the world. "Salvation is from the Jews" (John 4:22). But even so, we see from examples like these that God never intended to save only the physical sons and daughters of Israel. He chose Israel in order to save all nations. That was as true in the Old Testament as it is today in the time of fulfillment in Jesus Christ.

E. Hezron, Son of Perez, and Descendants Through Ram (continued from 2:10-17)

The Chronicler picks up the thread of David's line once more. No other individual in Scripture has so much genealogical attention paid to him. Here an entire chapter is devoted to his descendants. Matthew and Luke trace additional strands of David's family in their Gospels (Matthew 1 and Luke 3:23ff). The Chronicler's purpose is to demonstrate the truth of God's promise to David: "I will provide a place for my people Israel and will plant them so that they can have a home of their own. . . . I will raise up your offspring to suc-

41

ceed you. . . . His throne will be established forever"
(1 Chronicles 17:9,11,14).

Our first section lists the sons born to David while he
ruled as king in Hebron (verses 1-4) and later at Jerusalem
(verses 4-9):

3 These were the sons of David born to him in Hebron:
The firstborn was Amnon the son of Ahinoam of Jezreel;
the second, Daniel the son of Abigail of Carmel; ²the
third, Absalom the son of Maacah daughter of Talmai
king of Geshur;
the fourth, Adonijah the son of Haggith;
³the fifth, Shephatiah the son of Abital;
and the sixth, Ithream, by his wife Eglah.
⁴These six were born to David in Hebron, where he
reigned seven years and six months.
David reigned in Jerusalem thirty-three years, ⁵and these were
the children born to him there:
Shammua, Shobab, Nathan and Solomon. These four
were by Bathsheba daughter of Ammiel. ⁶There were
also Ibhar, Elishua, Eliphelet, ⁷Nogah, Nepheg,
Japhia, ⁸Elishama, Eliada and Eliphelet—nine in all.
⁹All these were the sons of David, besides his sons by
his concubines. And Tamar was their sister.

For the Chronicler, the career of David at Hebron did not
hold much interest, though he was certainly aware of it, as
these verses indicate. He preferred to concentrate on the events
during David's reign in Jerusalem that led up to the building of
the temple. The list of sons born at Hebron is identical to the
list in 2 Samuel 3:2-5. The one exception is "Daniel" who is
identified as "Chileab" in the book of Samuel. For one individual to have more than one name may seem odd to us, but it
was perfectly normal in the ancient culture of the Near East.
The patriarch Jacob is one outstanding example.

As for the sons born in Jerusalem, this list, too, is substantially the same as the one found in Samuel (2 Samuel 5:13-16). The Chronicler adds two sons to the list: Nogah and Eliphelet, both found in verse 6. This same list reappears in 1 Chronicles 14:4 with some minor variations in spelling that need not trouble us. David's successor Solomon is found among the sons born in Jerusalem.

Interesting, too, are the two women mentioned here: Bathsheba and Tamar. Bathsheba (verse 5) was the wife of Uriah the Hittite. David slept with her and then killed her husband to cover up his crime of adultery. The rape of Tamar (verse 9) was the spark that eventually set off the fire of Absalom's rebellion against his father David. (Consult 2 Samuel 11-19 for the rest of the story.) Merely mentioning them by name in David's genealogy would be enough for an Israelite to recall all the unhappy events connected with them. Good king David surely needed a Savior, too.

The Chronicler's next section gives the royal succession:

[10]Solomon's son was Rehoboam,
> **Abijah his son,**
> **Asa his son,**
> **Jehoshaphat his son,**
[11]Jehoram his son,
> **Ahaziah his son,**
> **Joash his son,**
[12]Amaziah his son,
> **Azariah his son,**
> **Jotham his son,**
[13]Ahaz his son,
> **Hezekiah his son,**
> **Manasseh his son,**
[14]Amon his son,
> **Josiah his son.**

¹⁵**The sons of Josiah:**
Johanan the firstborn,
Jehoiakim the second son,
Zedekiah the third,
Shallum the fourth.
¹⁶**The successors of Jehoiakim:**
Jehoiachin his son,
and Zedekiah.

The Chronicler presents us with the names of all the kings who sat on the throne of Judah, down to the time of the Babylonian exile (586 B.C.).

The only difficulties occur in the last two verses of this section. After Josiah's death in 609 B.C., the kingdom of Judah went into sharp decline. Judah was caught in a squeeze between Egypt to the south and Babylon to the north. At one time the Pharaoh of Egypt marched into Judah, deposed a king, and set another in his place. At another time Nebuchadnezzar marched in, deposed a king for disloyalty, and set another in his place. To indicate that the new man was *his* man, the conquering king would give a new name to the king of Judah he had placed on the throne. For this reason, we need to keep our wits about us to match this list with the kings found at the end of 2 Kings and 2 Chronicles. Remember our previous observation that it was not unusual in this culture for one man to have two names.

The following is a list of the kings (in their proper order) who succeeded Josiah. I will first give the name as it is found in 1 Chronicles 3 and then follow it with other names for the same person found elsewhere. I offer it for the serious Bible student who wants to keep things straight.

THE LAST KINGS OF JUDAH

1. Shallum/Jehoahaz. He was elevated by the people after Josiah's death.

Three months later, he was deposed by Pharaoh Neco.

The fourth son of Josiah.

References: 2 Chronicles 36:2, 2 Kings 23:30.

See also Jeremiah 22:11.

2. Jehoiakim/Eliakim He was elevated by Pharaoh Neco, who gave him the name Jehoiakim. He reigned 11 years. He was the second son of Josiah.

References: 2 Kings 23:34-36 and 2 Chronicles 36:5.

3. Jehoiachin Son of Jehoiakim, grandson of Josiah. He was deposed after a three month rule and taken to exile in Babylon. The line of David during and after the exile is traced through him.

References: 2 Chronicles 36:9 and 2 Kings 24:8.

4. Zedekiah/Mattaniah He was elevated by Nebuchadnezzar, who gave him the name of Zedekiah. A son of Josiah and an uncle of his immediate predecessor Johoiachin, he was the last son of David to be called king of the Jews until the birth of Jesus.

References: 2 Chronicles 36:11 and 2 Kings 24:17,18.

An additional problem is raised by the mention of two Zedekiahs in verses 15 and 16. The NIV smoothes it out somewhat by translating verse 16 with "the successors of Jehoiakim" instead of the more literal "the sons of Jehoiakim." If we follow the NIV's interpretation, there was only one Zedekiah: the son of Josiah who was the last to sit on the throne of David. It is also possible, however, that there were two Zedekiahs and that the one in verse 16 was a son of Jehoiakim who never ascended the throne.

The Chronicler continues the line of David through the exile and beyond. His concern is to place David's line in the land of Judah after the return from Babylon. In this way he demonstrates from history that God's promise to David will not be bound, even though some of David's descendants may have been held in captivity by foreign enemies and their own sinfulness. God preserved the house of David and brought them back to the land of promise:

> [17]**The descendants of Jehoiachin the captive:**
> **Shealtiel his son, [18]Malkiram, Pedaiah, Shenazzar, Jekamiah, Hoshama and Nedabiah.**
> [19]**The sons of Pedaiah:**
> **Zerubbabel and Shimei.**
> **The sons of Zerubbabel:**
> **Meshullam and Hananiah.**
> **Shelomith was their sister.**
> [20]**There were also five others:**
> **Hashubah, Ohel, Berekiah, Hasadiah and Jushab-Hesed.**
> [21]**The descendants of Hananiah:**
> **Pelatiah and Jeshaiah, and the sons of Rephaiah, of Arnan, of Obadiah and of Shecaniah.**
> [22]**The descendants of Shecaniah:**
> **Shemaiah and his sons:**

**Hattush, Igal, Bariah, Neariah and Shaphat—six in
all.**
[23]**The sons of Neariah:**
Elioenai, Hizkiah and Azrikam—three in all.
[24]**The sons of Elioenai:**
**Hodaviah, Eliashib, Pelaiah, Akkub, Johanan, Dela-
iah and Anani—seven in all.**

We face a tricky bit for our understanding right at the beginning of these verses. A hasty reading of verses 17-19
seems to tell us that Zerubbabel was the son of Pedaiah,
who was the son of Jehoiachin the captive, along with
Shealtiel and others. That would make Shealtiel the uncle of
Zerubbabel.

This causes us to scratch our heads because Zerubbabel is
acknowledged elsewhere to be the *son* of Shealtiel (Ezra 3:2;
Nehemiah 12:1; Haggai 1:12). This man is so prominent because he is the leader of the first wave of returnees from exile. We need to take a closer look at the text to sort this out.
When we do, we notice that only Shealtiel is specifically
identified as being Jehoiachin's son. The others in verse 18—
including Pedaiah—are lumped together in a group. They
may be sons, or they may be more loosely descended from
the captive king.

If verse 18 continues to list the sons of Jehoiachin, then
we could solve the difficulty by saying that Pedaiah married
the childless widow of his brother Shealtiel and had sons by
her. According to levirate law (Deuteronomy 25:5,6), the *le-
gal* father would be Shealtiel even though Pedaiah was the
natural father. This explanation is certainly not outside the
realm of possibility. Stranger things have happened in Israelite family trees, as we are well aware by now. And yet
there is a far simpler resolution of the father/uncle issue. We
could simply understand the text to mean that Shealtiel was

the son of Jehoiachin. Verse 18, in turn, can be understood as giving us a list of Shealtiel's sons. Pedaiah, son of Shealtiel, then fathered Zerubbabel. This would mean that Zerubbabel received his patronymic from his grandfather instead of his father. The holy writer is giving us a bit more information here than at the other places mentioned. This explanation falls well within the common use of the Hebrew term "son of."

A second problem is raised by Jesus' genealogy in the Gospel of Luke. There Neri is listed as Shealtiel's father instead of Jehoiachin (Luke 3:27). Of several possible explanations, I prefer the one that simply says that Jehoiachin was also called Neri. If true, it certainly wouldn't be the first time we had come across the phenomenon of one man with two names. The other possibility takes its cue from Jeremiah 22:30 which may be interpreted as saying that Jehoiachin was to die without children. Neri, his relative, married his widow and raised up children who were legally considered Jehoiachin's by the levirate law referred to above.

The descendants of Zerubbabel listed in verses 19 and 20 are not mentioned in any genealogy of Jesus. Although Matthew and Luke both tell us that Jesus was a descendant of David by Zerubbabel, they give us completely different names to fill in the gap between Zerubbabel and Christ. If someone wishes to raise this as an issue, we could simply reply that the Chronicler nowhere says that he has listed every son of Zerubbabel. Besides this, there is good reason to believe that the Chronicler selected the names he did because they were particularly expressive of the hope that filled the hearts of the returning exiles. "Recompensed, Yahweh is Gracious, Peace, Considered (by God), Love Returns" are a representative sampling of what the names mean.

Before we move on to chapter four, we ought to discuss a question that has occupied the minds of many and forms the hook upon which scholars hang their various theories for dating the book of Chronicles. The question is: how many generations from Zerubbabel do we have listed from verses 21 to 24? Some say at least five. Some go as high as eleven. If either estimate is true, it would be difficult to date the book much earlier than 400 B.C. It would also make it very unlikely that Ezra the Scribe could have been the author.

The interpretation of verse 21 is crucial. Is this entire verse a listing of sons born to Hananiah? If so, then the direct line of Zerubbabel continues to the end of verse 24, and we can count at least five generations after him. Since we think that Ezra the scribe is the author of Chronicles, we believe that the list of Zerubbabel's descendants ends in the middle of verse 21 with Jeshaiah. *"And the sons of Rephaiah . . ."* in verse 21 begins a new listing of Davidic families who returned from exile along with Zerubbabel. We would then have only two generations after Zerubbabel: Hananiah, his son; Pelatiah and Jeshaiah, his grandsons. This view is entirely consistent with Ezra being the author, since the book then could be dated no later than 450 B.C.

While this explanation may seem to do violence to the verse in question, one ought to remember that the division of our Bible into verses is not part of the inspired text. In its favor we can also cite the fact that the editors of the Hebrew text made a minor break at Jeshaiah's name. Besides this, the words of the verse itself make it difficult to see the connection between Rephiah's *sons* (plural) and the two individual sons mentioned previously. Why the sudden change in the genealogical formula? It would seem to indicate that the writer intended to make a division of some type in the middle of the verse.

Whether these considerations convince you or not, a person can hardly reject Ezra as the author simply on the evidence of these verses. They do not render conclusive proof either way. Other evidence would have to tip the scales, and other evidence against Ezra's authorship is pretty sparse. In view of this, we see no reason to reject the long-held belief that he was, in fact, the one who wrote this portion of our sacred Scriptures.

Meaning of These Verses for Us Today:

Problems, difficulties, apparent conflicts—is it worth it all? This has been pretty heavy going, no doubt about it. Yet where else would we have found a better window to the soul of the early returnees from exile than by looking at those lovely names Zerubbabel gave his children? "Recompensed, Yahweh is Gracious, Peace, Considered (by God), Love Returns" (verses 19,20). Who has not gone through a dry spell of doubt or trouble and not breathed a similar prayer of thanks to God upon feeling the sunshine of his grace return?

In the midst of examining the trees, let's not forget the forest: the Chronicler is demonstrating the truth of God's promise to David. God said David's kingdom would endure. By tracing David's family down to his own generation, the Chronicler was giving concrete assurances to his readers that God had not forgotten them, nor his promises to them. The earthly kingdom of David may have ended, but the spiritual throne of David's son and successor, the Messiah, had not yet begun.

From our own vantage point as New Testament believers, David's line has come to an end, only to begin again. It ended in that it reached fulfillment in our Savior. It begins again in that all the gifts and graces of Jesus, the Son of David, belong to us now by faith. We rule along with him on David's throne (Revelation 1:6, 2:27).

The Descendants of Perez (continued from 2:4-8)

The Chronicler now returns to two sons of Judah briefly mentioned back at the beginning of Chapter 2: Perez and Shelah. Before winding up his discussion of the royal tribe of Judah, he wants to give us some additional information. This also completes his structural arrangement of Chapters 2-4 (see page 26).

In verse one he traces the genealogy of Perez to a depth of five generations:

4 **The descendants of Judah:
Perez, Hezron, Carmi, Hur and Shobal.**

The list is straightforward except for the mention of Carmi, elsewhere called a descendant of Zerah and a father of Achar (see 1 Chronicles 2:7). Since all the others are descendants from Perez in a direct line from father to son, it seems likely that Carmi is used here as another name for Caleb, son of Hezron. The last three generations serve as a rough outline for the chapter up to verse 20. The Chronicler deals with them in reverse order from youngest to oldest, beginning with *Shobal* in verse 2, continuing with *Hur* in verse 3, and concluding with *Caleb* (verse 11—a slightly different spelling of his name, but likely as not the son of Hezron all the same).

²Reaiah son of Shobal was the father of Jahath, and Jahath the father of Ahumai and Lahad. These were the clans of the Zorathites.
³These were the sons of Etam:
Jezreel, Ishma and Idbash. Their sister was named Hazzelelponi. ⁴Penuel was the father of Gedor, and Ezer the father of Hushah.

51

These were the descendants of Hur, the firstborn of
Ephrathah and father of Bethlehem.
⁵Ashhur the father of Tekoa had two wives, Helah and
Naarah.
⁶Naarah bore him Ahuzzam, Hepher, Temeni and Haa-
hashtari. These were the descendants of Naarah.
⁷The sons of Helah:
Zereth, Zohar, Ethnan, ⁸and Koz, who was the father
of Anub and Hazzobebah and of the clans of Aharhel
son of Harum.

⁹Jabez was more honorable than his brothers. His mother
had named him Jabez, saying, "I gave birth to him in pain."
¹⁰Jabez cried out to the God of Israel, "Oh, that you would
bless me and enlarge my territory! Let your hand be with me,
and keep me from harm so that I will be free from pain." And
God granted his request.

The Chronicler's chief purpose here is to help the restored
community recognize how they are connected to these ancient clans that existed before the exile. The Chronicler previously linked Shobal to the town of Kiriath Jearim and to
various other clans, including the Zorathites (2:50-53). Here
the Zorathites are divided into further sub-clans. From Nehemiah we recognize both Kiriath Jearim and Zorah as towns
inhabited by Jews who returned from exile (Nehemiah 7:29
and 11:29).

Hur's descendants are listed in verses 3 and 4, followed by
Ashhur's in 5-7. Ashhur we recall as the son born to Hezron
following his death (2:24). No further information was given
about him there. Here his line is more fully developed.
Among these names we recognize Bethlehem and Tekoa as
towns reoccupied after the exile (Nehemiah 7:26). The men
of Tekoa did yeoman's service under Nehemiah in rebuilding
the wall of Jerusalem (Nehemiah 3:5-27).

The section concludes with a lovely little story about a man named Jabez (possibly linked with the town by that name mentioned already in 2:55). It is built on reversals and wordplays and has a pointed lesson. The name "Jabez" sounds like the Hebrew word for pain. His mother gave him the name because he caused her a great deal of pain when she gave birth to him. In the culture of the Old Testament, names were far more than sounds used to identify a particular person. They summed up a person's character and pointed to his destiny. "As the man is named, so is he," a wise woman once said to David (1 Samuel 25:25). The future did not look bright for the man whose name was Pain.

Jabez was able to reverse his mother's dire prediction by calling on the God of Israel for help. If we wanted to preserve some of the original flavor of this section, we might paraphrase it this way: "Jabez turned out to be more distinguished than his brothers, even though his mother called him 'Pain,' saying, 'He gave me a lot of pain in birth!' But Jabez called out to the God of Israel saying, 'Oh that you would bless me . . . !' And God gave him what he asked."

The future did not look bright, either, for those tiny communities established by the Jews who returned from exile. Their enemies surrounded them. Rebuilding what had been was a slow and laborious process. It seemed as if the cards were stacked against them. But the God of Israel was with them, and, calling on his help, they could rest assured he would grant success. So, too, we can be sure that the kingdom of God will grow and prosper among us, however small its initial beginnings, however dim its earthly prospects seem to be. Anyone who feels the weight of the unbelieving world against him can take comfort from these words. Our God brings life from death, blessing from pain, and success from failure. Call on him!

¹¹Kelub, Shuhah's brother, was the father of Mehir, who was the father of Eshton. ¹²Eshton was the father of Beth Rapha, Paseah and Tehinnah the father of Ir Nahash. These were the men of Recah.

¹³The sons of Kenaz:
Othniel and Seraiah.
The sons of Othniel:
Hathath and Meonothai. ¹⁴Meonothai was the father of Ophrah.
Seraiah was the father of Joab,
the father of Ge Harashim. It was called this because its people were craftsmen.
¹⁵The sons of Caleb son of Jephunneh:
Iru, Elah and Naam.
The son of Elah: Kenaz.
¹⁶The sons of Jehallelel:
Ziph, Ziphah, Tiria and Asarel.
¹⁷The sons of Ezrah:
Jether, Mered, Epher and Jalon. One of Mered's wives gave birth to Miriam, Shammai and Ishbah the father of Eshtemoa. ¹⁸(His Judean wife gave birth to Jered the father of Gedor, Heber the father of Soco, and Jekuthiel the father of Zanoah.) These were the children of Pharaoh's daughter Bithiah, whom Mered had married.
¹⁹The sons of Hodiah's wife, the sister of Naham:
the father of Keilah the Garmite, and Eshtemoa the Maacathite.
²⁰The sons of Shimon:
Amnon, Rinnah, Ben-Hanan and Tilon.
The descendants of Ishi: Zoheth and Ben-Zoheth.

It is likely that "Kelub" of verse 11 is simply a variant spelling of the name "Caleb." We will make this assumption in interpreting these verses. Kelub/Caleb is the last one of

Perez's line whose descendants are brought up for review. We need to distinguish him from the Caleb/Kelub of verse 15. As we learned from our discussion of 2:49, these are two different men from two different generations. The Caleb of verse 11 was the clan head and son of Hezron. The Caleb of verse 15 was the contemporary of Joshua and one of the twelve tribal representatives who went to scout out the land of promise.

The genealogy mentions Othniel (verse 13), the nephew or younger brother of Caleb the scout, and some of his descendants. Othniel is familiar to us as the first of Israel's judges. His story is told in Judges 1 and 3:7-11.

The sons of Jehallelel are identified as the founders of Ziph (verse 16), while one of the sons of Ezrah is linked to Eshtemoa (verse 17). Neither of these towns existed in Judah after the exile, which is why we can be fairly certain that the entire genealogy preserves for us a picture of Judah prior to that cataclysmic event. We are told about a man named Mered, who had descendants from both an Egyptian ("Pharaoh's daughter" may mean no more than this) and a Jewish wife (verses 17,18). Since Ezra and the post-exilic community had so much trouble with Jews marrying foreign wives, a person might wonder why the Chronicler did not edit this out. Yet we can learn something from the fact that people like Mered still appear on the rolls of the royal tribe of Judah, even though he had been linked by marriage to Egypt. It teaches us that Ezra's concern over intermarriage in his day was not due to Jewish racial prejudice but to a desire to keep the commands of God.

The Descendants of Shelah (continued from 2:3)

²¹The sons of Shelah son of Judah:
Er the father of Lecah, Laadah the father of Mareshah and the clans of the linen workers at Beth Ash-

bea, ²²**Jokim, the men of Cozeba, and Joash and Sa-**
raph, who ruled in Moab and Jashubi Lehem. (These
records are from ancient times.) ²³**They were the pot-**
ters who lived at Netaim and Gederah; they stayed
there and worked for the king.

The Chronicler brings the genealogies of the royal tribe of
Judah to a close with Shelah, a son of Judah—mentioned
briefly at the beginning of chapter two and then dropped until
now. Shelah was the last surviving son of Judah's Canaanite
wife Shua. His records here are "from ancient times" (4:22).
His descendants developed into clans of linen workers (verse
21) and royal potters (verse 23).

It is possible that in verse 22 we have another reference to
early intermarriage between the tribe of Judah and a foreign
woman. An alternative rendering (taking "Jashubi" as a verb
instead of as a place name) would be: "Joakim, the men of
Cozeba, and Joash and Saraph, who married (women) from
Moab and returned to (Beth)lehem." If correct, this would be
an interesting parallel to the account of Elimelech's family in
Ruth 1.

Meaning of These Verses for Us Today:

We have made a few points for personal application along
the way. In ending our genealogical study of Judah, we can
once again remind ourselves of the Chronicler's chief purpose in writing it. For him and for his readers it was a
panoramic overview of God's kingdom under the house of
David. By tracing David's house from its roots all the way to
the exile and beyond, he proved to the Jews who had returned that they were one and the same people as those who
had lived in Judah during the glory days of David. David's
history was *their* history. David's promises were *their*
promises. David's God was *their* God.

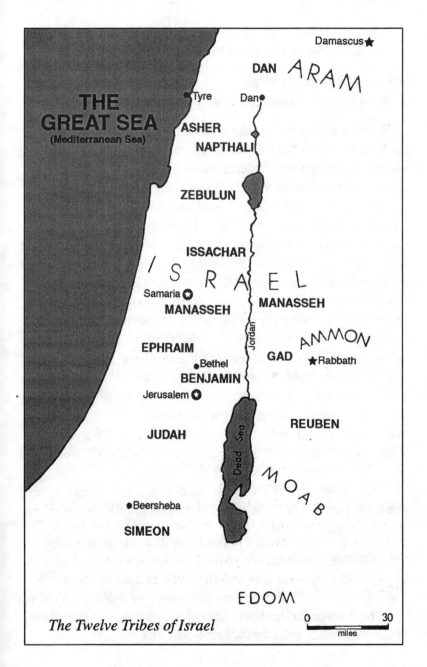

THE
GREAT SEA
(Mediterranean Sea)

Damascus ★

DAN ARAM

● Tyre   Dan ●

ASHER

NAPTHALI

ZEBULUN

ISSACHAR

I S R A E L

Samaria ✪   MANASSEH

MANASSEH

AMMON

EPHRAIM   GAD   ★ Rabbath

● Bethel

BENJAMIN

Jerusalem ✪

REUBEN

JUDAH   Dead Sea

M O A B

● Beersheba

SIMEON

EDOM

The Twelve Tribes of Israel

0   30
miles

57

Our God is the same. He shapes history generation after generation to work out for us his own saving purposes.

The Outer Edge of Israel:
Simeon and the Tribes of the Transjordan

We now take a tour of the outer edge of the kingdom of Israel. Pointing us first to the south of Judah, the Chronicler shows us around the settlements of Simeon (4:24-43). From there we cross the deep Rift Valley, where the Dead Sea and the Jordan River are located, and climb up to the heights of Moab on the eastern side. Just to the north of this tiny non-Israelite kingdom was the dwelling place of the transjordanian tribes of Israel. The Chronicler leads us from south to north. Beginning with the tribe of Reuben, located across the River Arnon from Moab, he moves north through Gad until he completes the tour with the half-tribe Manasseh (Chapter 5).

All these tribes had settled on the frontiers of Israel. They were exposed to the heathen influence of their neighbors to a greater degree than the rest of Israel. They either expanded their territory when they remained loyal to the true God (4:41-43; 5:19-22), or they were swept away completely when they worshiped heathen gods (5:25,26). "For the one who has nothing (spiritually), even what he has (physically) will be taken away" (Luke 19:26).

Simeon's listing is easily divided into three sections: his clans (verses 24-27), his settlements (verses 28-33), and his history (verses 38-43).

The Tribe of Simeon

Simeon's Clans

²⁴**The descendants of Simeon:**
Nemuel, Jamin, Jarib, Zerah and Shaul;

²⁵ **Shallum was Shaul's son, Mibsam his son and Mishma his son.**

²⁶**The descendants of Mishma:**

Hammuel his son, Zaccur his son and Shimei his son.

²⁷ **Shimei had sixteen sons and six daughters, but his brothers did not have many children; so their entire clan did not become as numerous as the people of Judah.**

The genealogical record of Simeon's clans is nearly the same as that found elsewhere in Scripture (Exodus 6:15, Numbers 26:12). Some names are spelled differently, and our writer has expanded on Shaul's clan down to Shimei, Shaul's great-grandson. From this we can deduce that the Chronicler had sources of information available to him independent of what we have elsewhere in Scripture.

Of particular interest to us is the Chronicler's comment, "his brothers did not have many children; so their entire clan did not become as numerous as the people of Judah." He is referring to the fact that Simeon, as a tribe, was almost completely absorbed into Judah. Just prior to his death, the great patriarch Jacob uttered certain prophecies concerning his twelve sons. In the Chronicler's statement, we see how Jacob's words came true. Of sons Simeon and Levi, Jacob had said, "Cursed be their anger, so fierce . . . I will scatter them in Jacob and disperse them in Israel" (Genesis 49:7).

Jacob spoke these dire words because of a vicious act of revenge committed by these two brothers against the men of Shechem. For the full story see Genesis 34. When we look at the tribe of Levi in the next chapter, we will see how, in his case at least, the curse was transmuted into a blessing.

Simeon's Settlements

²⁸**They lived in Beersheba, Moladah, Hazar Shual, ²⁹Bilhah, Ezem, Tolad, ³⁰Bethuel, Hormah, Ziklag, ³¹Beth Marcaboth,**

Hazar Susim, Beth Biri and Shaaraim. These were their towns until the reign of David. ³²Their surrounding villages were Etam, Ain, Rimmon, Token and Ashan—five towns—³³and all the villages around these towns as far as Baalath. These were their settlements. And they kept a genealogical record.

This register of Simeon's towns and villages dates back to the days of David and before (verse 31). It is similar to—yet clearly independent of—a list found in Joshua 19:2-9. Apart from one or two towns like Ziklag and Beersheba, it is difficult for us today to locate these places with any precision. In general we can say that Simeon lived in the dry southland or Negev of Israel. (Just for fun we can translate Beth Marcaboth and Hazar Susim. They mean "house of chariots" and "horse corral" respectively. Were these Simeonite frontiersmen from the Wild South of Judah people like the cowboys in the Wild West of America? Did they know their wagons and horseflesh? Maybe!)

On a more serious note, the Chronicler wants to be sure to inform us that these men of Simeon "kept a genealogical record" (verse 33). The tribe of Simeon may have been absorbed into Judah, yet they still retained some threads of their independence—enough to maintain separate records. Simeon was still a tribe of Israel, to whom "is the adoption as sons; theirs the divine glory, the covenants, the receiving of the law, the temple worship and the promises. Theirs are the patriarchs, and from them is traced the human ancestry of Christ, who is God over all, forever praised!" (Romans 9:4,5). God's promises did not and do not fail!

Simeon's History

³⁴Meshobab, Jamlech, Joshah son of Amaziah, ³⁵Joel, Jehu son of Joshibiah, the son of Seraiah, the son of Asiel, ³⁶also Elioenai, Jaakobah, Jeshohaiah, Asaiah, Adiel, Jes-

imiel, Benaiah, [37]and Ziza son of Shiphi, the son of Allon, the son of Jedaiah, the son of Shimri, the son of Shema- iah.

[38]The men listed above by name were leaders of their clans. Their families increased greatly, [39]and they went to the out- skirts of Gedor to the east of the valley in search of pasture for their flocks. [40]They found rich, good pasture, and the land was spacious, peaceful and quiet. Some Hamites had lived there formerly.

[41]The men whose names were listed came in the days of Hezekiah king of Judah. They attacked the Hamites in their dwellings and also the Meunites who were there and complete- ly destroyed them, as is evident to this day. Then they settled in their place, because there was pasture for their flocks. [42]And five hundred of these Simeonites, led by Pelatiah, Neariah, Rephaiah and Uzziel, the sons of Ishi, invaded the hill country of Seir. [43]They killed the remaining Amalekites who had es- caped, and they have lived there to this day.

This final section gives us some of the clan leaders of Simeon and their exploits in leading the men of Simeon into battle. The information we have here is more recent than that of the previous verses, advancing us in time about 300 years. It is dated to the reign of king Hezekiah (verse 41), who flour- ished around 700 B.C. At that time, the people of Simeon needed some living room, since their numbers were increas- ing. They expanded to the east toward Edom and Mt. Seir (verse 42). It is possible that there was tribal thrust westwards towards the coast as well. This interpretation depends on where a person locates the "Gedor" mentioned in verse 39.

The inhabitants they displaced are called Hamites (Egyp- tians or Canaanites), Meunites (dwellers in the land of Edom), and Amalekites. The Chronicler hints at the sudden nature (verse 40) and the devastating effects (verses 41, 42) of the Simeonite attacks. The word for "completely destroy" in verse 42 points to a religious as well as an economic motive underlying these wars. It literally refers to something placed under a religious ban, something totally devoted to the Lord, either for his use or his destruction.

The heathen nations inhabiting Canaan had all been placed under this ban in a general way (see Deuteronomy 20:17,18). The reason for it is mentioned in that same context. God knew that his people would be easily lured into vile heathen worship practices if these nations were to be allowed to live side by side with Israel. As for the Amalekites (verse 43), they had special cause to be placed under this interdiction, since they had launched an unprovoked attack on Israel. Early on during the Exodus, while Israel was on the road to Sinai and weary with travel, the Amalekites had culled out and killed the stragglers of the Israelite caravans. They did this in complete defiance of the one true God. In response, God decreed their complete destruction (see Exodus 17:14 and Deuteronomy 25:17-19).

Still operating under those decrees, the men of Simeon "completely destroyed" the Hamites and Meunites and "killed the Amalekites" who remained from the previous raids.

Some are shocked to find such things in the Old Testament Scriptures.. As a result they call the God of the Old Testament a vengeful tribal God, thirsting for blood. They see a great contrast between him and the God of love revealed in Jesus. What are we to say to such critics?

The God of both the Old and New Testament is the same God whom John calls "Love" (1 John 4:8). At the core of his being burns an unquenchable fire of love. He longs to save all people (1 Timothy 2:4). In love he preserved Israel as a nation distinct from the idolatrous nations around it. In love he sent a Savior to the world through Israel.

Yet even Christians who should know better are rapidly losing their sight these days of a truth found in both Testaments: God cannot be mocked (Galatians 6:7). Men still reap what they sow. When people willfully despise God's grace and defy his commands, they can expect a limit even to God's great patience. He will destroy those who live their lives in rebellious unbelief. It is an inevitable consequence of rejecting the true God who wants to—and who alone can—save all. Only those who reject clear Scripture will find this truth inconsistent with God's love.

Who will speak this truth in an increasingly defiant and godless age? The Christian must!

The great sin of Amalek was that "they had no fear of God" (Deuteronomy 25:18). May God preserve us from such presumption!

The Tribe of Reuben:

The tribes of the Transjordan were Reuben, Gad, and half of Manasseh. We might wonder why the Chronicler mentions them at all. By his day these tribes had ceased to exist as distinct groups, each settled within its own particular territory. Their separate social structures had been smashed in the Assyrian invasions of the eighth century B.C.

In places like this we can make out what one of the holy writer's purposes was in writing his book. He intended to show that true Israel—and all Israel—still existed in the people who returned from exile in Babylon. The history of all the tribes belonged to Judah now.

The tribe of Reuben lost its separate identity even earlier than the others. The Mesha inscription on the Moabite stone (c. 850 B.C.) seems to imply that the Reubenites had been absorbed into Gad, since it mentions Gad but not Reuben. The material in this section is very old and describes Reuben as it

63

existed at the time of Saul (see verse 10), about 200 years before the Mesha inscription.

In hearing the history of their people, a Jewish boy or girl might have asked, "Why was Reuben so small among the tribes of Israel? Wasn't he the firstborn and so the right one to succeed his father Jacob as leader of the family?" The Chronicler answers:

5 **The sons of Reuben the firstborn of Israel (he was the firstborn, but when he defiled his father's marriage bed, his rights as firstborn were given to the sons of Joseph son of Israel; so he could not be listed in the genealogical record in accordance with his birthright, ²and though Judah was the strongest of his brothers and a ruler came from him, the rights of the firstborn belonged to Joseph)—³the sons of Reuben the firstborn of Israel:**

Hanoch, Pallu, Hezron and Carmi.

⁴The descendants of Joel: Shemaiah his son, Gog his son, Shimei his son, ⁵Micah his son, Reaiah his son, Baal his son,

⁶and Beerah his son, whom Tiglath-Pileser king of Assyria took into exile. Beerah was a leader of the Reubenites.

Reuben lost his status as firstborn because he committed incest by sleeping with his father's concubine Bilhah (Genesis 35:22 and 49:4). Because of this, his rights as firstborn passed to two other brothers. Firstborn *rank* as leader went to Judah; the inheritance *rights* went to Joseph (verse 2)

The rights and privileges of being the firstborn were highly prized. Esau's act of selling his birthright to Jacob gives us an amazing example of a person who was unable to postpone gratification of his immediate needs. His contempt for his birthright was more than stupidity; it was a moral failure (Genesis 25:29-34). At the core of the birthright was the custom of giving two shares of the father's inheritance to the firstborn son. He not only got the choice portion of his father's estate, he also received an equal share of what was left to be divided among the others (see Deuteronomy 21:15-17). This virtually guaranteed that this son would be his father's successor in rank and power. From this we can see that the rights of the firstborn also included the idea of being the legitimate heir of the father's position as head of the family. The Elisha account is an illustration of this. When Elisha asked for a double portion of Elijah's spirit, he was not asking for twice as much spiritual power as Elijah had. He was asking to be Elijah's successor in the prophetic office (2 Kings 2:9).

In the case before us of Jacob's sons, Joseph received the double portion of the inheritance through his two sons Ephraim and Manasseh. Both of them obtained a share of the territory in the promised land. "But Judah was the strongest of his brothers and a ruler came from him" (verse 2). The rank as leader of the tribes went to Judah, and along with it went the promise of the Savior, who was to rule all Israel. When Reuben lost his rights as firstborn, he lost a great deal.

The sons and clan founders of Reuben are listed in verse 3. Then another son of Reuben is listed, along with his descendants in verse 4. What we have here is original to the Chronicler. He highlights Joel and his clan to show how the tribe of Reuben was carried off into exile in the person of Joel's descendant Beerah (verse 5). This happened in Tiglath-Pileser's invasion of the Transjordan around 740 B.C.

There is a message for us in this story of Reuben and his loss of firstborn status. We're not just talking about leadership status and inheritance rights. Ancient Israel was the people of God. Under God's rule in the Old Testament, earthly realities had a deeper spiritual significance. Reuben's willful sin demonstrated the unbelief of his heart. Because of it, God chastised him by taking away his earthly rights. If his descendants persisted in the unbelief of their father, they would lose both their earthly and their spiritual heritage. In the decline of Reuben's earthly fortunes, we are seeing a spiritual decline as well. First, they were absorbed by Gad, then they were obliterated under Tiglath-Pileser and the Assyrians. Unbelief leads to death.

By faith in Christ, we who were once slaves to sin, have received the full rights of sons. "Since you are a son, God made you also an heir" (Galatians 4:7). The forgiving love of Christ gives us firstborn rights and privileges before God. We have the *status* of full-fledged sons of God. We are *heirs* to all Christ has won for us by his death and resurrection. We have eternal life and all that goes with it. Through the Word, may God help us prize and hold fast to our inheritance.

May we avoid like the plague anything that might cause us to lose our grip on that heritage! It begins in the heart with unbelief. We start to prize our earthly goods more than our treasures in heaven. We pursue worldly goals and lose sight of the world to come. It ends in shameful sins and idolatry. Those who do such things will inherit death, not life. From this preserve us, dear Father in heaven!

While the tribe of Reuben as a whole came to a sad end, there were some in Reuben who were preserved in faith, a "remnant chosen by grace" (Romans 11:5). The Chronicler makes that point in the following verses:

⁷Their relatives by clans, listed according to their genealogical records:

Jeiel the chief, Zechariah, ⁸and Bela son of Azaz, the son of Shema, the son of Joel. They settled in the area from Aroer to Nebo and Baal Meon. ⁹To the east they occupied the land up to the edge of the desert that ex-

tends to the Euphrates River, because their livestock had increased in Gilead.

[10] During Saul's reign they waged war against the Hagrites, who were defeated at their hands; they occupied the dwellings of the Hagrites throughout the entire region east of Gilead.

Reuben's clan leaders and territory are preserved for us through verse nine. Numbers 32:34-38 is in substantial agreement with the settlements listed here for Reuben. Moab conquered Nebo and Baal Meon in the ninth century, as was mentioned previously. Gilead (verse 9) is probably a reference to the entire region on the east bank of the Jordan River, and not (as sometimes) to the smaller territory occupied by the clan of Gilead.

What is of prime importance here is the account of Reuben waging a war against the Hagrites and defeating them (verse 10). This was an act of faith and a spiritual victory as well as an earthly one. The Chronicler will make this clear when he discusses the same campaign more fully under Gad (verses 18-22). We, too, will talk more about it when we come to those verses.

The Tribe of Gad:

[11] The Gadites lived next to them in Bashan, as far as Salecah:

[12] Joel was the chief, Shapham the second, then Janai and Shaphat, in Bashan.

[13] Their relatives, by families, were:

Michael, Meshullam, Sheba, Jorai, Jacan, Zia and Eber—seven in all.

[14] These were the sons of Abihail son of Huri, the son of Jaroah, the son of Gilead, the son of Michael, the son of Jeshishai, the son of Jahdo, the son of Buz.

¹⁵ Ahi son of Abdiel, the son of Guni, was head of their family.

¹⁶ The Gadites lived in Gilead, in Bashan and its outlying villages, and on all the pasturelands of Sharon as far as they extended.

¹⁷ All these were entered in the genealogical records during the reigns of Jotham king of Judah and Jeroboam king of Israel.

Gad's territory is described as being "next to them" (the Reubenites). It extended to the north and east as far as Bashan. We should not think of these territories as being as strictly mapped out as county lines. This is especially true of the Transjordan tribes, whose occupation was following herds of livestock (see verses 9, 16, and 21). Herdsmen like to roam the open range. They don't like to be fenced in. So it comes as no surprise to see that there was considerable overlapping in the tribal allotments of Reuben, Gad, and half-Manasseh.

There are no sons of Gad mentioned. Instead, the Chronicler gives us a roster consisting of the tribal chief (Joel in verse 12) and various other clan and family heads (to the end of verse 13). This list is unique to the Chronicler, and he informs us that he copied it from records he had dating to the era of kings Jotham and Jeroboam (verse 17). We can date it approximately to 750 B.C. Since the Assyrian invasion under Tiglath-Pileser came shortly thereafter, it could well be that we have here the last genealogy recorded before the tribe as such passed into oblivion.

¹⁸ The Reubenites, the Gadites and the half-tribe of Manasseh had 44,760 men ready for military service—able-bodied men who could handle shield and sword, who could use a bow, and who were trained for battle. ¹⁹ They waged war against the Hagrites, Jetur, Naphish and Nodab. ²⁰ They were helped in fighting them, and God handed the Hagrites and all their allies

over to them, because they cried out to him during the battle. He answered their prayers, because they trusted in him. [21]They seized the livestock of the Hagrites—fifty thousand camels, two hundred fifty thousand sheep and two thousand donkeys. They also took one hundred thousand people captive, [22]and many others fell slain, because the battle was God's. And they occupied the land until the exile.

The Chronicler now records a military campaign dating back to Saul's era (compare verse 10) that was part of the glorious history of all three Transjordanian tribes. As such it formed one layer of the spiritual legacy that came down to the Jews after the exile. They were the legitimate heirs to the past and promises of all Israel.

After calling the tribal rolls of those fit and trained for battle, the Chronicler describes the war they fought. Many of the earthly details are obscure or unknown. The spiritual point is clear.

The Hagrites, Jetur, Naphish, and Nodab were probably clans of Arab origin. They may have traced their descent from Hagar, Abraham's concubine, and likely made their home in the deserts east of Gilead. These are just educated guesses. We also have no battle plans or campaign strategies given for the war itself. But we are told that the men of Israel were helped in their fight and that God handed their enemies over to them in battle. We are also told why: "(The men of Israel) cried out to him during the battle. He answered their prayers, because they trusted in him" (verse 20). As we said before, this was an act of faith, and the victory these tribes won was chiefly spiritual. They did not rely on their superior manpower or weaponry, but on the Rock of Israel. He was their God, and they trusted in him, uttering the prayer of faith in the thick of battle. For this reason God made their battle *his* battle (verse 22) and granted them the victory.

What a great comfort to know that God not only fights *alongside* us in our earthly and spiritual struggles, he actually makes our cause his own! When facing down the troubles of life, it is good to remember where our true strength lies and how we will achieve the victory.

By way of contrast, in the following account of the half-tribe of Mannaseh, the Chronicler also shows the reason for the downfall of these tribes.

The Half-Tribe of Manasseh:

²³The people of the half-tribe of Manasseh were numerous; they settled in the land from Bashan to Baal Hermon, that is, to Senir (Mount Hermon).

²⁴These were the heads of their families: Epher, Ishi, Eliel, Azriel, Jeremiah, Hodaviah and Jahdiel. They were brave warriors, famous men, and heads of their families. ²⁵But they were unfaithful to the God of their fathers and prostituted themselves to the gods of the peoples of the land, whom God had destroyed before them. ²⁶So the God of Israel stirred up the spirit of Pul king of Assyria (that is, Tiglath-Pileser king of Assyria), who took the Reubenites, the Gadites and the half-tribe of Manasseh into exile. He took them to Halah, Habor, Hara and the river of Gozan, where they are to this day.

At this point it seems as if our writer has lost interest in giving us extensive details concerning the sons, clan leaders, and territory of Manasseh. What information he does give serves merely to lead us into the terrible events described in the last two verses.

Manasseh's defeat could not be charged to weakness in numbers: the tribe was "numerous" we are told, spreading from Gad's allotment all the way north to Bashan and Mt. Hermon (verse 23). Nor could it be ascribed to any other earthly weakness: they were brave fighters, well-known and respected for their achievements, and they had a fine pedigree (verse 24).

Their failure was due to one thing only. They were spiritually bankrupt. They were unfaithful to the God whom their fathers had worshiped. They went whoring after the gods of foreign people. The Chronicler minces no words in describing the depths to which they had sunk and the true nature of their sin. The language he uses is meant to shock a spiritually torpid people to their senses. God was like a husband, lavishing his love on his people. But when Israel worshiped other gods, the nation was acting like an unfaithful wife who had prostituted herself to other men.

Manyika, manyika, ijulu ndelimwi. A village headman said those words to a missionary as they sat together outside his house in the shade of a mango tree. It's a proverb from the Tonga people of Central Africa. It means, "Many countries, but heaven is one." It signifies that different countries may worship God each in their own way, but in the end, they are all connecting up with the same God of heaven. This concept is not unique to Africa. It constitutes religion as we know it in America today. "Whether you worship the Triune God or Allah or Buddha or the god inside us all," we are told, "it makes no difference. The important thing is that you are exercising your spirituality."

The Chronicler speaks a firm "No!" to all who think this way. It does make a difference. There is only one true God and Savior. Those who know him and then reject him by permitting other gods to stand in his place as saviors are guilty of religious unfaithfulness and spiritual prostitution.

The utter foolishness of worshiping other gods is demonstrated by the fact that God had driven out before Israel the people who had been worshiping these other gods (verse 25). Yet later Israel went back to those same discredited gods. Such unbelief seems beyond belief; yet it happened.

The verdict on such apostasy is pronounced in verse 26. Since the people of Israel had deserted him for foreign gods, the God of Israel "stirred up the spirit" of a foreigner to come against his people and carry them off into exile. Reuben, Gad, and half-Manasseh were carried to the far north and east, away from their homeland, to places with such foreign-sounding names as Halah, Habor, and Hara. They would never come home again. Scripture records their names as a warning to any who trifle with grace.

The Priestly Tribe of Levi:

We have come to the second high point of the genealogies. After the royal tribe of Judah, the priestly tribe of Levi has more space allotted to it than any other tribe—eighty one verses in all! This fact is useful to know because it tells us how important the sons of Levi were to the Chronicler.

From the book of Ezra we get the impression that the priests and Levites were somewhat reluctant to leave the cities of Babylon and return to Judah. Perhaps they had lost their sense of being called by God. Or perhaps they had become too attached to their new lives in the secular city. To combat a situation like that, the Chronicler sought to exalt the ministry of the priests and Levites and the divine nature of their calling.

The Priestly House of Aaron

6 **The sons of Levi:**
Gershon, Kohath and Merari.
² The sons of Kohath:
Amram, Izhar, Hebron and Uzziel.
³ The children of Amram:
Aaron, Moses and Miriam.
The sons of Aaron:
Nadab, Abihu, Eleazar and Ithamar.

⁴Eleazar was the father of Phinehas,
  Phinehas the father of Abishua,
⁵Abishua the father of Bukki,
  Bukki the father of Uzzi,
⁶Uzzi the father of Zerahiah,
  Zerahiah the father of Meraioth,
⁷Meraioth the father of Amariah,
  Amariah the father of Ahitub,
⁸Ahitub the father of Zadok,
  Zadok the father of Ahimaaz,
⁹Ahimaaz the father of Azariah,
  Azariah the father of Johanan,
¹⁰Johanan the father of Azariah (it was he who served
  as priest in the temple Solomon built in Jerusalem),
¹¹Azariah the father of Amariah,
  Amariah the father of Ahitub,
¹²Ahitub the father of Zadok,
  Zadok the father of Shallum,
¹³Shallum the father of Hilkiah,
  Hilkiah the father of Azariah,
¹⁴Azariah the father of Seraiah, and Seraiah the father
  of Jehozadak.
¹⁵Jehozadak was deported when the LORD sent Judah and
  Jerusalem into exile by the hand of Nebuchadnezzar.

The first verse introduces us to the actual sons of Levi: Gershon, Kohath, and Merari. They gave their names to the three major clans in Levi. Later the Chronicler will spend more time tracing their development. Right now he wants to bring us quickly through Kohath to the priestly house of Aaron. From verse 4 to verse 14 we have a list of men who served in the office of high priest.

Before discussing the list any further, it might be helpful to understand a distinction between *Levite* and *priest*. All priests were Levites (from the tribe of Levi), but not all

Levites were priests. The Levites in general had been assigned various duties to perform in the house of God. Those duties were important—as we shall see later—and necessary, both for the good order of God's house and for the religious life of Israel. However, only one family out of the entire tribe of Levi had the right to serve as priests. "Aaron and his descendants were the ones who presented offerings on the altar of burnt offering and on the altar of incense . . . in the Most Holy Place" (1 Chronicles 6:49). Through Moses, God had directed that the only way to approach him in his holy dwelling was through the lawful priest. And the only lawful priest was one who could trace his line of descent back to Aaron (see also Exodus 28:1 and Leviticus 1:5-9).

We can see why it was so important for an Israelite believer to know where his priest had come from. We can also see why the Chronicler traces the genealogy of Aaron all the way down to Jehozadak and the exile (verse 15). Jehozadak was the father of Jeshua. Jeshua was the high priest who served at the time of the return from exile (Ezra 3:2; 5:2). The priestly line had remained intact. A true son of Aaron still served at the temple. Israel could still approach God.

What meaning does this have for Christians? We have no special priestly caste among us like the Old Testament Israelites. We recognize every believer as being a "priest[s] to serve his . . . God" (Revelation 1:6). Yet we still have one "great high priest" (Hebrew 4:14). Only in him do we have "access by faith into this grace in which we now stand" (Romans 5:2). He is the Lord Jesus Christ. No one can approach the Father except through him (John 14:6). It is still vitally important for the believer of today to know him, where he has come from, and what he has done for us.

Besides reminding the Israelites of the legitimacy of their priestly line, the Chronicler in these verses has a word or two to say to the priests within Israel. He does this by certain names he *includes,* and by other names that he *excludes* from his list.

By including Nadab and Abihu, he reminds any priest who might be reading this that it is important to worship God *in the correct way.* Nadab and Abihu were two sons of Aaron whom God put to death. Their offense may seem minor at first glance; yet it was a violation of a basic principle of worship that we would all do well to be aware of. Instead of burning the incense prescribed by God on the altar of incense, they cooked up their own batch and burned it instead. In destroying them, God indicated that he took a pretty dim view of setting aside his words and replacing them with human notions. For the full account read Leviticus 10.

Our culture today feels that it is everyone's right to worship God in any way a person might choose. Cults and exotic liturgies abound—each one offering some new way to come to God. The Lutheran confessions take a pretty dim view of self-chosen worship, that is, worship derived from man's own sinful opinions about the best way to approach God. It is not out of place to remind ourselves here that "God [is] pleased through *the foolishness of [preaching]* to save those who believe" (1 Corinthians 1:21). God comes to us through Word and sacrament. Any "worship strategy" which does not center in these is making a fatal error.

The Chronicler also pointedly *excludes* from further discussion the high-priestly line of Ithamar. From Ithamar's line sprang the house of Eli and his wicked sons, Hophni and Phineas. "His sons made themselves contemptible, and he failed to restrain them" (1 Samuel 3:13). Because Hophni and Phineas were blatantly sinning and because Eli failed to take effective measures to restrain them, God's holy house and his worship had come into disrepute. In response God said, "Those who honor me I will honor, but those who despise me will be disdained" (1 Samuel 2:30). Descendants of Ithamar are not found on this list, though many served as high priest.

It is a terrible thing when people serving in the public ministry today fall into open sin. The faith of God's people is often shaken, God's enemies are given the opportunity to blaspheme, and the unchurched are often further hardened in their unbelief. The community of Christ still has the right to expect that pastors and teachers will "be above reproach . . . hav[ing] a good reputation with outsiders, so that [they] will not fall into disgrace and into the devil's trap" (1 Timothy 3:2,7).

The Three Major Levite Clans:

¹⁶the sons of Levi:
> Gershon, Kohath and Merari.
¹⁷These are the names of the sons of Gershon:
> Libni and Shimei.
¹⁸The sons of Kohath:
> Amram, Izhar, Hebron and Uzziel.
¹⁹The sons of Merari:
> Mahli and Mushi.
> These are the clans of the Levites listed according to their fathers:
²⁰Of Gershon:
> Libni his son, Jehath his son, Zimmah his son,
> ²¹Joah his son, Iddo his son, Zerah his son and
> Jeatherai his son.
²²The descendants of Kohath:
> Amminadab his son, Korah his son,
> Assir his son, ²³Elkanah his son,
> Ebiasaph his son, Assir his son,
> ²⁴ Tahath his son, Uriel his son,
> Uzziah his son and Shaul his son.

²⁵The descendants of Elkanah:
  Amasai, Ahimoth,
    ²⁶Elkanah his son, Zophai his son,
  Nahath his son, ²⁷Eliab his son,
  Jeroham his son, Elkanah his son
  and Samuel his son.
²⁸The sons of Samuel:
  Joel the firstborn and
  Abijah the second son.
²⁹The descendants of Merari:
  Mahli, Libni his son,
  Shimei his son, Uzzah his son,
    ³⁰ Shimea his son, Haggiah his son and Asaiah his son.

Gershon, Kohath, and Merari were not only sons of Levi, they also became the founders of the three great Levitical clans listed here. As we learned earlier, the Chronicler's purpose in such an extensive clan listing is to "magnify the calling" of the sons of Levi for the people of his own generation.

The mention of Samuel in verse 28 catches our interest. He is the great prophet who saw the period of the Judges come to an end and who watched over the rise of the Hebrew monarchy. Here he is listed as a *Levite,* descended from the clan of Kohath. In 1 Samuel 1, however, Samuel's father is called an *Ephraimite.* The Levites (as we shall see later) were scattered over all the land of Israel. The difficulty of a Levite by descent also being called an Ephraimite is best explained by saying that, after Samuel's people had settled in Ephraim, they were regarded as Levites by tribe, Ephraimites by territory.

The Temple Workers

³¹These are the men David put in charge of the music in the house of the LORD after the ark came to rest there. ³²They ministered with music before the tabernacle, the Tent of Meeting,

until Solomon built the temple of the LORD in Jerusalem. They performed their duties according to the regulations laid down for them.

³³Here are the men who served, together with their sons:
From the Kohathites:

Heman, the musician,
the son of Joel, the son of Samuel,
³⁴the son of Elkanah, the son of Jeroham,
the son of Eliel, the son of Toah,
³⁵the son of Zuph, the son of Elkanah,
the son of Mahath, the son of Amasai,
³⁶the son of Elkanah, the son of Joel,
the son of Azariah, the son of Zephaniah,
³⁷the son of Tahath, the son of Assir, the son of Ebiasaph, the son of Korah,
³⁸the son of Izhar, the son of Kohath, the son of Levi, the son of Israel;

³⁹and Heman's associate Asaph, who served at his right hand:

Asaph son of Berekiah, the son of Shimea,
⁴⁰the son of Michael, the son of Baaseiah,
the son of Malkijah, ⁴¹the son of Ethni,
the son of Zerah, the son of Adaiah,
⁴²the son of Ethan, the son of Zimmah,
the son of Shimei, ⁴³the son of Jahath,
the son of Gershon, the son of Levi;

⁴⁴and from their associates, the Merarites, at his left hand:

Ethan son of Kishi, the son of Abdi,
the son of Malluch, ⁴⁵the son of Hashabiah,
the son of Amaziah, the son of Hilkiah,
⁴⁶the son of Amzi, the son of Bani,
the son of Shemer, ⁴⁷the son of Mahli,
the son of Mushi, the son of Merari, the son of Levi.

⁴⁸Their fellow Levites were assigned to all the other duties of the tabernacle, the house of God. ⁴⁹But Aaron and his descen-

dants were the ones who presented offerings on the altar of burnt offering and on the altar of incense in connection with all that was done in the Most Holy Place, making atonement for Israel, in accordance with all that Moses the servant of God had commanded.

⁵⁰These were the descendants of Aaron: Eleazar his son, Phinehas his son, Abishua his son, ⁵¹Bukki his son, Uzzi his son, Zerahiah his son,

⁵²Meraioth his son, Amariah his son, Ahitub his son, ⁵³Zadok his son and Ahimaaz his son.

We've come to a very interesting section in our chapter, interesting for several reasons. In verses 31 and 32, for example, we have the Chronicler foreshadowing themes on which he will be expanding throughout the rest of 1 Chronicles. King David will bring the ark to its permanent and proper resting place in Jerusalem (verse 31). David will organize the priests and Levites to serve before the Lord (verse 32). He will make things ready for Solomon to build a permanent temple in place of the tabernacle (verse 32). Some commentaries openly criticize the Chronicler for the bad outline of his work. Verses like these, however, show that the Chronicler knew exactly where he was going. He clearly signaled that direction to his readers.

For the first time in our book we meet David as the great organizer of Israel's temple worship. We will meet him again later in this same capacity. Noteworthy, too, is the high prominence given to music in the worship of the one true God. Of all the duties of the Levites, the ministry of music is listed first. There are many artistic gifts that God gives, and there are many forms of service. None serves the message of the gospel better than music.

It is worthwhile to note that the Levitical musicians were regarded as much more than simply blowers of horns, bangers of cymbals, and pluckers of strings. They were viewed, not as entertainers or performers, but as servants of the Lord. Under David they had a call into a type of public ministry. They delivered God's message to the people through words matched with music. As we glance at the titles over Psalms 39, 42, 44 through 49, and 73 through 88, we notice that many of the same names listed here reappear there as authors of those psalms. These musicians were inspired biblical poets as well as composers!

As Israel's king, David had the authority to carry out the will of God expressed in Numbers 3:5-9. There God said he was calling the Levites out of all Israel to perform the various duties of the tabernacle—with the exception of those reserved for the priests. David carried out that mandate by organizing the Levites into musical guilds "according to the regulations laid down for them" (verse 32).

The three clans are represented by three musical guilds. Heman (verse 33) comes from *Kohath*. Asaph, his right-hand man (verse 39), comes from *Gershon*. Ethan (also known as Jeduthun) comes from *Merari* (verse 44). The Chronicler then adds the comments in verses 48 and 49 to ensure that everyone understands the distinction between priest and Levite. He concludes by giving another listing of the high priests down to the time of king David. His purpose here is to put them into their proper place at the center of temple worship.

What can we take away for ourselves from all this? Certainly we are not bound by Old Testament forms and regulations. It would be a misapplication of Scripture to say that we must have called musicians just as David did. That was then. This is now. The Christian is free to choose, to select, to adapt, to create.

Yet isn't it a good idea to prize and develop musical talents among us? Rather than taking a low view of organists ("anyone will do; all they do is depress keys"), shouldn't we culti-vate an attitude among us that sees them as offering great ser-vice to the Lord? Are we quick to criticize our instrumental-ists because they hit a couple of wrong notes or play a hymn faster than we might like it? And are we slow to recognize the humble spirit of service that they display Sunday after Sunday? What kind of hymn writing is being done among us? Do we leave all that sort of thing to those whose doctri-nal pedigree is suspect? What place does music take in our church budgets? Somewhere behind office supplies and par-sonage upkeep? The prominence given to musicians in Israel suggests we ask ourselves questions like these.

Few things serve the gospel like good words matched to good music. God understood that. David understood that. It is good for us to understand that, too!

The Settlements of the Levites:

54These were the locations of their settlements allotted as their territory (they were assigned to the descendants of Aaron who were from the Kohathite clan, because the first lot was for them):

55They were given Hebron in Judah with its surround-ing pasturelands. 56But the fields and villages around the city were given to Caleb son of Jephunneh.

57So the descendants of Aaron were given Hebron (a city of refuge), and Libnah, Jattir, Eshtemoa, 58Hilen, De-bir, 59Ashan, Juttah and Beth Shemesh, together with their pasturelands. 60And from the tribe of Benjamin they were given Gibeon, Geba, Alemeth and Anathoth, togeth-er with their pasturelands.

These towns, which were distributed among the Ko-hathite clans, were thirteen in all.

61The rest of Kohath's descendants were allotted ten towns from the clans of half the tribe of Manasseh.

⁶²The descendants of Gershon, clan by clan, were allotted thirteen towns from the tribes of Issachar, Asher and Naphtali, and from the part of the tribe of Manasseh that is in Bashan.

⁶³The descendants of Merari, clan by clan, were allotted twelve towns from the tribes of Reuben, Gad and Zebulun.

⁶⁴So the Israelites gave the Levites these towns and their pasturelands. ⁶⁵From the tribes of Judah, Simeon and Benjamin they allotted the previously named towns.

⁶⁶Some of the Kohathite clans were given as their territory towns from the tribe of Ephraim.

⁶⁷In the hill country of Ephraim they were given Shechem (a city of refuge), and Gezer, ⁶⁸Jokmeam, Beth Horon, ⁶⁹Aijalon and Gath Rimmon, together with their pasturelands.

⁷⁰And from half the tribe of Manasseh the Israelites gave Aner and Bileam, together with their pasturelands, to the rest of the Kohathite clans.

⁷¹The Gershonites received the following:

From the clan of the half-tribe of Manasseh they received Golan in Bashan and also Ashtaroth, together with their pasturelands;

⁷²from the tribe of Issachar

they received Kedesh, Daberath, ⁷³Ramoth and Anem, together with their pasturelands; ⁷⁴from the tribe of Asher they received Mashal, Abdon, ⁷⁵Hukok and Rehob, together with their pasturelands;

⁷⁶and from the tribe of Naphtali

they received Kedesh in Galilee, Hammon and Kiriathaim, together with their pasturelands.

⁷⁷ The Merarites (the rest of the Levites) received the following:

From the tribe of Zebulun

they received Jokneam, Kartah, Rimmono and Tabor, together with their pasturelands;

⁷⁸from the tribe of Reuben across the Jordan east of Jericho

they received Bezer in the desert, Jahzah, [79]Kedemoth
and Mephaath, together with their pasturelands;
[80]and from the tribe of Gad
they received Ramoth in Gilead, Mahanaim, [81]Hesh-
bon and Jazer, together with their pasturelands.

All the other tribes had fairly discreet boundaries mentioned for their tribal allotments. Not so with Levi and the
house of Aaron. They were scattered in cities and villages
throughout the territory of the twelve tribes.

When we looked at Simeon in the last chapter, we learned
that he and Levi had been cursed by Jacob for the wholesale
slaughter of all the male inhabitants of the village of
Shechem (see 4:24-47 and comments). As a result, their father had said that Simeon and Levi would be dispersed in Israel (Genesis 49:7). Here we see that, so far as Levi was concerned, the curse was changed into a blessing.

We understand how that happened when we remember another incident from Bible history. After Moses had come
down from Mt. Sinai, he saw the children of Israel running
riot around a golden calf they had made. He asked who would
stand with him to quell the godless disorder. We read in Exodus that "all the Levites rallied to him" (Exodus 32:26). As a
result of this act of faithfulness, Moses said that they would be
set apart to the Lord, and receive the Lord's blessing.

That is why, in Levi's case, their scattering in Israel did not
lead to their destruction as a tribe. They retained their identity
in spite of it. God worked a blessing, not only for them, but
for all of Israel. As God's chosen servants, the priests and
Levites were given special cities to live in throughout the
kingdom. Those cities became centers of Bible learning, centers where each tribe would have an opportunity to learn about
the true God and the proper way to worship him.

The listing itself—with minor variations—is the same as that found in Joshua 21. Aaron and the priests were given cities among the tribes of Judah and Benjamin. The rest of the members of the Kohathite clan received towns in Trans-jordanian Manasseh (verse 61) and Ephraim (verse 66). Gershon was given cities in the north and northeast, among the tribes of Issachar, Asher, Naphtali, and half-Manasseh (verse 62). Clan Merari settled in Reuben, Gad, and Zebulun (verses 77-80).

Meaning of These Verses for Us Today:

The Chronicler is holding up the tribe of Levi for special honor, as we have said, because so few of them had responded to the call to return to Judah. They were needed there to reestablish the true worship of God. It seems they did not put a high value on their sacred callings as priests and temple workers. Perhaps their fellow Israelites did not either.

As we come to the brink of the third millennium after Christ, we have concerns similar to those of 450 B.C. The harvest is plentiful, the workers few. Where will we find pastors to fill our pulpits and teachers to serve in our classrooms in the years to come? Fewer and fewer young men and women are responding to the call. We can blame demographics and the "Baby Bust" of the 1970s. But surely part of the problem is that God's people no longer place as high a value on the public ministry as they once did. As our hearts become more and more entangled with the cares of the secular city, we place less and less value on the city whose builder and architect is God.

While we have the confidence that the risen Christ will still give his preaching and teaching gifts to the church, it remains for us to cultivate and value those gifts. The Chronicler's sentiment here is echoed by Paul in these words: "The elders who direct the affairs of the church well are worthy of *double honor,* especially those whose work is preaching and teaching" (1 Timothy 5:17).

The Tribes of Issachar, Benjamin, Naphtali, Manasseh, Ephraim, and Asher:

The Chronicler manages to squeeze the genealogies of six (and possibly seven) tribes into half the space he gave to the tribe of Levi, a mere two-fifths of what he allotted Judah. This reflects the greatly reduced status of these northern Israelite tribes at the time of the Chronicler. It is also an expression of his point of view that most of the members of these tribes were apostates in rebellion against God's true kings and priests (see 2 Chronicles 10:19, 11:14-16, and 13:8-12).

At the same time, he does not deal with his subject in a half-hearted way. Much of his material is unique. Clearly he had sources available to him that were independent of the biblical records preserved for us in Genesis, Numbers, and Joshua. This fact makes it difficult at times to harmonize the information we have here with other biblical genealogies. The difficulty is compounded when we have to struggle with differences in the spelling of names and with problems in the transmission of the sacred text.

Whatever problems we may have in discerning individual trees, the forest itself has a definite shape. The Chronicler, in outline form, is continuing the history of the kingdom of God. He wants to assure those who have returned from exile of their connection with the past and of God's faithfulness in preserving "all Israel" for his saving purposes in the future.

The tribes mentioned in this chapter are those that lived to the north of Judah and to the west of the Jordan river. The one possible exception to this is Manasseh, which had land on both sides of the Jordan.

The Tribe of Issachar

7 The sons of Issachar:
Tola, Puah, Jashub and Shimron—four in all.
²The sons of Tola:
Uzzi, Rephaiah, Jeriel, Jahmai, Ibsam and Samuel—
heads of their families. During the reign of David, the
descendants of Tola listed as fighting men in their genealogy numbered 22,600.
³The son of Uzzi:
Izrahiah.
The sons of Izrahiah:
Michael, Obadiah, Joel and Isshiah. All five of them
were chiefs. ⁴According to their family genealogy, they
had 36,000 men ready for battle, for they had many
wives and children.
⁵The relatives who were fighting men belonging to all the
clans of Issachar, as listed in their genealogy, were
87,000 in all.

This genealogy probably had its origin in a military muster
and gives us a snapshot of the tribe as it existed at David's
time. By David's era, Tola's descendants had multiplied to
become the dominant clan in Issachar. The main branch
could boast of 22,600 fighting men. The sons of Izrahiah
(verse 3) form another branch of Tola's family tree. By the
time of David they had become numerous enough to form
another clan in their own right with 36,000 fighters to their
credit. All the rest of Issachar's clans combined could muster
only 28,400 men, giving us a grand total of 87,000 for the
entire tribe (verse 5).

There is another man of Issachar with the name of Tola in
addition to the clan founder mentioned here. Judges 10:1
also speaks of a Tola who served as a leader of Israel. It
seems most likely that they were two different men of two
different generations.

The Tribes of Benjamin (Dan) and Naphtali:

⁶Three sons of Benjamin:
   Bela, Beker and Jediael.
⁷The sons of Bela:
   Ezbon, Uzzi, Uzziel, Jerimoth and Iri, heads of families—five in all. Their genealogical record listed
   22,034 fighting men.
⁸The sons of Beker:
   Zemirah, Joash, Eliezer, Elioenai, Omri, Jeremoth,
   Abijah, Anathoth and Alemeth. All these were the
   sons of Beker. ⁹Their genealogical record listed the
   heads of families and 20,200 fighting men.
¹⁰The son of Jediael:
   Bilhan.
   The sons of Bilhan:
   Jeush, Benjamin, Ehud, Kenaanah, Zethan, Tarshish
   and Ahishahar. ¹¹All these sons of Jediael were heads
   of families. There were 17,200 fighting men ready to
   go out to war.
¹²The Shuppites and Huppites were the descendants of Ir,
   and the Hushites the descendants of Aher.
¹³The sons of Naphtali:
   Jahziel, Guni, Jezer and Shillem—the descendants of
   Bilhah.

The Chronicler deals with genealogical material from the
tribe of Benjamin in three places: here, in 1 Chronicles 8, and
at the end of 1 Chronicles 9. Obviously, Benjamin was important to the holy writer. Of all the other tribes, Benjamin alone
sided with their brothers from Judah and remained loyal to the
house of David at the time of Jeroboam's rebellion. People
from Judah, Levi, and Benjamin formed the bulk of those who
returned from exile after the decree of Cyrus (see 1 Chronicles
9:3, 7-9; Ezra 4:1, and Nehemiah 11:7-9, 31-34). This is the
reason why little Benjamin is given such prominence.

In this section the Chronicler's immediate purpose seems to be to set Benjamin in its proper place among the tribes of Israel. In chapter 8 he takes up Benjamin's genealogy again—in that case to provide the background for Saul's lineage. In chapter 9 he repeats Saul's genealogy to lead into his description of the final unhappy days of that unfaithful first king of God's people.

With such a wealth of material, it comes as no surprise that Benjamin's genealogies present us with unique difficulties in understanding. Not the least of these is harmonizing the Chronicler's material with information on Benjamin given to us in Genesis, Numbers, and 1 Samuel.

Three sons of Benjamin are mentioned in verse 6. The clans that developed from them are taken up in verses 7, 8, and 10 in listings that appear to have come from a military census. The names of Bela and Beker also occur in Genesis 46:21. Jediael is mentioned only here, unless we are to consider him as being the same man as Ashbel, mentioned in Genesis 46:21, Numbers 26:38, and 1 Chronicles 8:1. If he is, it wouldn't be the first time we have run across a man with two different names.

In the list of the sons of Beker (verse 8), we note that most of the names refer to people. Anathoth, however, is familiar to us as the name of a city, quite likely founded by a descendant of Beker of the same name. We know it as the birthplace of the prophet Jeremiah and as one of the cities given by Joshua to the Levites as part of their allotment within the territory of Benjamin. Men of Benjamin settled there after the return from exile (see Nehemiah 11:32). A seemingly insignificant detail like this would speak volumes to those returnees for whom the book of Chronicles was written. It would assure them of their connection with the past and bolster their sense of being the legitimate heirs of the promises made to Israel.

Verse 12 presents us with some interesting questions in interpretation. The first set of questions arises in connection with the "Shuppites and Huppites." Are these the same as the "Muppim" and "Huppim" listed as sons of Benjamin in Genesis 46:21? If so, the account in Genesis is using "son of" in the sense of "descended from." Here they are described as descended from Ir, who himself was at the very least a grandson of Benjamin. Furthermore, are the "Shupham" and "Hupham" clans of Numbers 26:39 one and the same as our men here? Last, but not least, are the "Shephuphan" and "Huram" of 1 Chronicles 8:5 one more example of a different way to spell the same names? The answer to all these questions: probably! We might wish that some perfect master of spelling could have arisen to bring all these variations into one correct form used by all. But on second thought, if we consider the history and present practices of spelling in our own language, perhaps we shouldn't be too quick to cast stones.

Another question has to do with the interpretation of the second half of the verse. Some scholars have suggested that the phrase, "the Hushites the descendants of Aher" is a reference to the genealogy of Dan, who is otherwise not listed by the Chronicler. Here is their reasoning: in Genesis 46 and Numbers 26 Dan comes after Benjamin. Allowing for minor variations in spelling, the Hushites could well be the same "Hushim" listed in Genesis and the "Shuham" mentioned in Numbers as Dan's descendant. In addition the word "aher" is normally not a name, but the Hebrew word for "another." Their translation would then read, "and the Hushites the descendants of another (namely: Dan)." Such an off-hand reference to Dan could be accounted for as an expression of the Chronicler's distaste for the tribe. Dan was notoriously idolatrous. (Other scholars simply say the text has been mutilated through copying mistakes.) Further corroboration for this being a Danite listing is seen at the end of Naphtali's genealogy in the words, "the descendants (plural) of Bilhah" (verse 13). Dan and Naphtali both were sons of Jacob through his concubine Bilhah.

While some of these arguments may seem compelling, they are not conclusive. Zebulun has no listing either. Why shouldn't Dan be dropped? The omission could reflect the Chronicler's consistent lack of emphasis on the northern tribes of Israel. Besides this, the name "Hushim" crops up in the next chapter with reference to another person altogether (see 1 Chronicles 8:8,11). We have no way of knowing how common the name was. Therefore, its appearance at the end of Benjamin's genealogy can hardly be called iron-clad proof that we have here an obscure listing of Dan's tribe.

Naphtali's genealogy in verse thirteen poses no great problems. It is substantially the same as that listed in Genesis 46:24 and Numbers 26:48.

The Tribe of Manasseh:

¹⁴The descendants of Manasseh:

Asriel was his descendant through his Aramean concubine. She gave birth to Makir the father of Gilead. ¹⁵Makir took a wife from among the Huppites and Shuppites. His sister's name was Maacah.

Another descendant was named Zelophehad, who had only daughters.

¹⁶Makir's wife Maacah gave birth to a son and named him Peresh. His brother was named Sheresh, and his sons were Ulam and Rakem.

¹⁷The son of Ulam:

Bedan.

These were the sons of Gilead son of Makir, the son of Manasseh. ¹⁸His sister Hammoleketh gave birth to Ishhod, Abiezer and Mahlah.

¹⁹The sons of Shemida were:
 Ahian, Shechem, Likhi and Aniam.

The tribe of Manasseh was given land on both sides of the
Jordan River. The genealogy of that portion of the tribe living on the west bank is in the foreground here. Asriel is the
first clan mentioned. This name is familiar to us from Numbers 26:31 as a descendant of Gilead, the son of Makir. Here
the Chronicler makes a connection for us we otherwise could
not have known. Makir was born to Manasseh from his
Aramean concubine. Thus Asriel, too, can claim descent
from the same woman, since Asriel was Makir's offspring.
The book of Joshua informs us that clan Asriel received a
portion of the land allotted to Manasseh on the west bank
(see Joshua 17:1-3).

The Chronicler also asserts that there was a relationship by
marriage between the Makirites and the tribe of Benjamin.
He does this when he informs us that Makir took a wife for
himself from the Huppites and Shuppites (compare 7:15 with
7:12). Previously he had established a connection between
Makir of Manasseh and Hezron of Judah (see 1 Chronicles
2:21-23). It seems likely that his intent in making such asso-
ciations is to let the returned exiles know that they have relationships and blood ties to all Israel, even though for the
most part they may be descendants of Benjamin and Judah.

Another interesting feature of Manasseh's genealogy is the
number of women mentioned. Two "Maacahs" are listed, one
a sister and another a wife of Makir. The Chronicler's reference to Zelophehad "who had only daughters" (verse 15) is a
reminder to all his readers of the role these women played in
establishing the inheritance rights of women in Israelite law.
The descendants of Zelophehad's daughters were granted an
equal portion of the land along with the other clans of Ma-

nasseh living west of the Jordan (see Numbers 27 and Joshua 17:3-6 for the full story). In verse 18 we are told of a woman named Hammoleketh who was the mother of three clan-founders. Whether she is the sister of Gilead or Makir is hard to tell. In this entire section the connections in Hebrew are difficult to make out.

In verse 19 we come across some names we recognize: Shemida and Shechem. These are mentioned in Numbers 26:31,32 as Manassite clans descended from Gilead. Joshua informs us that they were given land west of the Jordan (Joshua 17:2). Interestingly enough, we also have information from outside the Scriptures corroborating their existence. Their names crop up on the Samarian ostraca, an impressive-sounding title for a collection of sixty-five potsherds dating from the eighth century B.C. In ancient times, before a person could go down to his local office supply store for a ream of paper, writing materials were at a premium. Merchants and military men would use broken bits of pottery to write little notes on. In the Samarian ostraca, we have preserved for us merchant's records of deliveries of oil, wine, and other items.

The fact that the names of Shechem, Shemida, Abiezer, and other Manassite clans appear on these ancient bits of clay does not "prove" the Bible to be true any more than any other archeological finding can be said to prove or disprove Scripture. But it does give us a sharp pin to burst the bubble of pride of those who treat the Bible with contempt as histori-cally unreliable.

Manasseh was known for its great bravery in battle. Gideon, the judge, was a Manassite from the clan of Abiezer. Our Sunday-school children hear of his exploits in delivering the Israelites from their Midianite oppressors. You can read his story for yourself in chapters 6 to 8 of Judges. Yet this great tribe, mighty in battle, had been reduced to nothing because it had forgotten the truth that guaranteed God's people victory in every battle, "Some trust in chariots and some in horses, but we trust in the name of the LORD our God. They are brought to their knees and fall, but we rise up and stand firm" (Psalm 20:7,8).

The Tribe of Ephraim:

²⁰The descendants of Ephraim:
Shuthelah, Bered his son,
Tahath his son, Eleadah his son,
Tahath his son, ²¹Zabad his son
and Shuthelah his son.

Ezer and Elead were killed by the native-born men of Gath, when they went down to seize their livestock. ²²Their father Ephraim mourned for them many days, and his relatives came to comfort him. ²³Then he lay with his wife again, and she became pregnant and gave birth to a son. He named him Beriah, because there had been misfortune in his family. ²⁴His daughter was Sheerah, who built Lower and Upper Beth Horon as well as Uzzen Sheerah.

²⁵Rephah was his son, Resheph his son,
Telah his son, Tahan his son,
²⁶Ladan his son, Ammihud his son,
Elishama his son, ²⁷Nun his son
and Joshua his son.

²⁸Their lands and settlements included Bethel and its surrounding villages, Naaran to the east, Gezer and its villages to the west, and Shechem and its villages all the way to Ayyah and its villages. ²⁹Along the borders of Manasseh were Beth Shan, Taanach, Megiddo and Dor, together with their villages. The descendants of Joseph son of Israel lived in these towns.

Here we have the most extensive genealogy for Ephraim found anywhere in the Scriptures. Yet considering its former glory as chief among the northern tribes of Israel, the material the Chronicler gives us on Ephraim is decidedly scanty. Of the three clans mentioned in Numbers 26:35, the Chronicler expands on only one, the clan of Shuthelah.

In verses 21 to 23 he records a tragic incident concerning two of Ephraim's sons. Apparently they were killed while making a cattle-rustling raid in the vicinity of Gath. Afterwards, Ephraim named a son "Misfortune" (Beriah) in memory of their deaths. Of all the great events and mighty victories the Chronicler might have mentioned in connection with this tribe, it is striking that he chooses this sad little story. The incident is also interesting to us for another reason. It gives us a snapshot of the early days of Israel's sojourn in Egypt. Ephraim, we know, was born and lived in Egypt with his children (see Genesis 41:50,52 and 50:22,23). Yet the stay of the Israelites in Egypt during those early days must have allowed for some migratory movement back and forth from Palestine. This story is one example of it.

It is also unusual in Scripture to read of a woman as a founder of cities. Yet that is exactly what we have in verse 24 where Beriah's daughter, Sheerah, has three communities chalked up to her credit. Two of them, Upper and Lower Beth Horon, are well known to us from the pages of Scripture. Uzzen Sheerah is mentioned only here.

The rest of the genealogical material is devoted to tracing the line of Joshua, the great successor to Moses and conqueror of Palestine. Ten generations in all are recorded from Ephraim to Joshua, and it could well be that this is a complete list covering the 430 years of Israel's stay in Egypt.

Thus—aside from the merest mention of a few of their settlements in the two concluding verses of this section—the Chronicler concludes his report on the "descendants of Joseph." It's almost as if the Chronicler regarded Ephraim's history as having ended with Joshua! In a way, perhaps, it did. The next great leader of Ephraim to rise up after Joshua would have been Jeroboam. But the Chronicler could hardly mention him, since he was the one who led the people in a revolt against God's anointed king and God's anointed priest.

We don't see this as being the Chronicler's peculiar bias—rather, it's a "God's-eye view" of history. Jeroboam and his successors may have built a strong and prosperous kingdom out of Ephraim and Manasseh. Their realm may have represented a great flowering of ancient culture. Secular historians may accord them whole chapters in their books. But they rate a bare sixteen verses in Chronicles. The kingdom of God does not look at outward achievements, but at the heart. It asks whether a heart is ruled by the one true God. If not, outward achievement is meaningless.

The Tribe of Asher:

³⁰The sons of Asher:
Imnah, Ishvah, Ishvi and Beriah. Their sister was Serah.
³¹The sons of Beriah:
Heber and Malkiel, who was the father of Birzaith.
³²Heber was the father of Japhlet, Shomer and Hotham and of their sister Shua.
³³The sons of Japhlet:
Pasach, Bimhal and Ashvath.
These were Japhlet's sons.
³⁴The sons of Shomer:
Ahi, Rohgah, Hubbah and Aram.
³⁵The sons of his brother Helem:
Zophah, Imna, Shelesh and Amal.
³⁶The sons of Zophah:
Suah, Harnepher, Shual, Beri, Imrah, ³⁷Bezer, Hod, Shamma, Shilshah, Ithran and Beera.

³⁸The sons of Jether:

Jephunneh, Pispah and Ara.

³⁹The sons of Ulla:

Arah, Hanniel and Rizia.

⁴⁰All these were descendants of Asher—heads of families, choice men, brave warriors and outstanding leaders. The number of men ready for battle, as listed in their genealogy, was 26,000.

This minor tribe, situated along the northern seacoast, rates as many verses as Ephraim. The Chronicler seems to be reinforcing the same point he made above. Asher may not have been much in the eyes of the world, but because God had chosen *all* of Israel to be his own, this tiny tribe was still precious on that account.

The genealogy presents us with few difficulties. The major clans correspond to the other biblical records in Genesis 46:17 and Numbers 26:44-46. The account in Numbers omits Ishvah from the list, but this may be due to a copying mistake brought on by such similar names occurring in succession. In verse 31 Birzaith is the name of a city. Malkiel is being described as its founder with the expression, "He was the father of Birzaith." We have seen this before, and so it is familiar to us.

Beriah's son Heber had three sons whose children are listed for us in verses 33 to 35. It is best to take the "Helem" of verse 35 as one and the same man as the "Hothem" of verse 32. Helem has his family tree taken two generations further through his son Zophah (verses 36 to 38). Note that the "Jether" of verse 38 is probably just an alternate spelling for the "Ithran" of verse 37.

The number of fighting men—26,000—is quite a bit smaller than the 41,500 men mentioned at the time of the Exodus (Numbers 1:40,41). Since our figure comes from a later date, we can deduce that the tribe of Asher had suffered over the years from war. Yet in spite of the fact that they had fallen on hard times (as these numbers indicate), and in spite of the fact that they were later uprooted from their homeland by the Assyrians, they were not entirely lost. Among those waiting for the Messiah in the days of Mary and Joseph is one "Anna, the daughter of Phanuel, of the tribe of Asher" (Luke 2:36). Unfaithful though these northern tribes were, God remained faithful. A remnant, chosen by grace, was preserved to greet the Messiah.

The Genealogy of Saul the Benjamite:

It may strike some people as odd that the Chronicler launches into another genealogy for Benjamin in chapter 8. Is this a vain repetition? An example of what Paul meant by "endless genealogies"? In view of what we've already learned about the Chronicler's skill as a stylist, we should rather assume that he has a reason for everything he does. It appears as if the Chronicler has two distinctly new reasons for placing Benjamin's genealogy here. The first is to provide a setting for King Saul, Benjamin's greatest son. The second is to lead up to his description of the restored community.

8 **Benjamin was the father of Bela his firstborn,**
Ashbel the second son, Aharah the third,
  ²Nohah the fourth and Rapha the fifth.
  ³The sons of Bela were:
    Addar, Gera, Abihud, ⁴Abishua, Naaman, Ahoah,
    ⁵Gera, Shephuphan and Huram.

Five sons of Benjamin are mentioned in the first two verses. If we take "Aharah" in verse one as being the same person as "Ahiram" in Numbers 26:38, then the first three listed here are identical to the first three listed in Numbers. After that, we run into problems. The last two on our list, Nohah and Rapha, are only found here. Nothing more can be said about them. They pass from here into obscurity.

A listing of Bela's descendants commences in verse three. If the text is correct, we learn here that possibly six of the ten "sons" of Benjamin listed in Genesis 46:21 are more exactly to be considered sons of Bela. Putting corresponding names from the two lists side by side will make this more clear:

GENESIS 46:21	1 CHRONICLES 8:3-5
Gerah	Gera
Naaman	Naaman
Ehi	Ahoah
Muppim	Shephuphan
Huppim	Huram
Ard	Addar

The differences appear greater in English than they do in the Hebrew. When we make allowance for minor spelling differences and small copying errors, the likelihood of these two lists referring to the same people becomes all the greater.

The listing of Gera twice among Bela's sons alerts us to the probability that there have been mistakes made in the transmission of the Hebrew text we are reading. It could well be that the reading suggested in the NIV footnote after the first mention of Gera's name is the correct one: "Gera, the father of Ehud." This would make sense, particularly in view of the fact that the Chronicler goes on to discuss the descendants of Ehud in verses six and following.

Before we go on to that, however, it is probably high time we discussed the matter of copying errors in the text of

Scripture, since the possibility has been mentioned several times. Let no one be disturbed at the thought that there are tiny differences in the reading of manuscripts of the Old Testament that have come down to us from the ancient world. It does not affect the doctrine of inspiration and inerrancy one bit, since that doctrine applies to the original documents penned by the holy writers. The fact that there are copying mistakes tells us that those who *transmitted* the text were capable of error. It does not say that those who *composed* the text under inspiration of God made mistakes.

In most cases where we have variant readings for the same passage, it is not hard to determine what the original text said. The text with the wrong reading is very obvious. In the few percentage of cases where we are unsure what the original text said, not one single doctrine is affected. The example above is a case in point. The text may be: "Gera, the father of Ehud" or "Gera, Abihud." Either way, the teaching of Scripture remains sure, and our grip on eternal life secure.

It used to be that the average Christian did not have to concern himself much with such matters. But we live in a time when our newsmagazines and newspapers publish attacks on the reliability of Scripture as if they were gospel. Many sectarian groups find grist for the mills of their false doctrine here as well. If the Bible is a flawed book, someone seeking truth from its pages would then require an interpreter with an inside track to God—a prophet or guru—to unlock its meaning or fix up its mistakes. The tragedy is: this view has become so prevalent today that few bother to read the Bible, even though they may feel the hungry emptiness of having no real God to rely on. That is why it is good for us to be able to give some answer to the Bible's critics when they raise these issues. They all are making mountains out of molehills.

The facts are that we have more evidence for the text of Scripture than for any other book handed down to us from ancient times. Scholars don't question the fact that we have the text of other ancient books. Nobody would argue that we have a different *Odyssey* than that composed by Homer. Why should anyone question the reliability of the Bible? If we no longer have the original autograph manuscript of Genesis, signed by Moses himself, we ought not be surprised. We live in a world where moth corrupts and thieves break in and steal. Books wear out, too.

In an age when books had to be copied out by hand, mistakes were bound to creep in, especially with lists of names. Anyone who has ever copied passages from his Bible into his notes knows how easy it is to make little errors in transcription. But no one should think that the scribes who transmitted the Scripture were careless and uncaring in their work. Quite the contrary. We know that the ancient scribes were professionals, highly trained and very meticulous in carrying out their work. We hold the evidence of that in our hands every time we open our Bibles.

> ⁶These were the descendants of Ehud, who were heads of families of those living in Geba and were deported to Manahath:
> ⁷Naaman, Ahijah, and Gera, who deported them and who was the father of Uzza and Ahihud.
> ⁸ Sons were born to Shaharaim in Moab after he had divorced his wives Hushim and Baara. ⁹By his wife Hodesh he had Jobab, Zibia, Mesha, Malcam, ¹⁰Jeuz, Sakia and Mirmah. These were his sons, heads of families. ¹¹By Hushim he had Abitub and Elpaal.
> ¹²The sons of Elpaal:
> Eber, Misham, Shemed (who built Ono and Lod with its surrounding villages), ¹³and Beriah and Shema,

who were heads of families of those living in Aijalon and who drove out the inhabitants of Gath. ¹⁴Ahio, Shashak, Jeremoth, ¹⁵Zebadiah, Arad, Eder, ¹⁶Michael, Ishpah and Joha were the sons of Beriah.

¹⁷Zebadiah, Meshullam, Hizki, Heber, ¹⁸Ishmerai, Izliah and Jobab were the sons of Elpaal.

¹⁹Jakim, Zicri, Zabdi, ²⁰Elienai, Zillethai, Eliel, ²¹Adaiah, Beraiah and Shimrath were the sons of Shimei.

²²Ishpan, Eber, Eliel, ²³Abdon, Zicri, Hanan, ²⁴Hananiah, Elam, Anthothijah, ²⁵Iphdeiah and Penuel were the sons of Shashak.

²⁶Shamsherai, Shehariah, Athaliah, ²⁷Jaareshiah, Elijah and Zicri were the sons of Jeroham.

²⁸All these were heads of families, chiefs as listed in their genealogy, and they lived in Jerusalem.

If there is a common theme that ties these genealogies together, it would be location. In the first section (verses 6-18), the names of Benjamites living outside Jerusalem are given. In the second section (verses 19-28), Benjamites living in Jerusalem are recorded.

In passing, we note the name of Ehud. This Benjamite (and patron saint of all left-handers) delivered God's people at the time of the judges when the king of Moab was oppressing them. For the full story, turn to Judges 3:12-30.

In verses 6 to 10 we have a list of what might be regarded as "displaced Benjamites," members of the tribe who, for various reasons, had moved from their ancestral inheritance. The descendants of Ehud, for example, are said to have been deported from Geba, a town in Benjamin some seven miles north of Jerusalem, to Manahath, a town in Judah lying southwest of Jerusalem. The details of their deportation and the reason why Gera saw fit to move the sons of Ehud are unknown. In verse 8 we are introduced to Shaharaim. He apparently moved to Moab after divorcing his first wives Hushim and Baara. There he had other sons by his new (or remaining) wife Hodesh. This is all the information we have on his move.

Shaharaim's descendants through one of his divorced wives remained on the west bank of the Jordan. Elpaal, Shararim's son by Hushim, was the father of a clan that inhabited the towns of Ono, Lod, Aijalon, and Gath. The Chronicler is establishing the connection between Benjamin as it was before the exile and Benjamin as it existed for his contemporaries after the exile. The towns of Lod and Ono are mentioned in several places as being inhabited by the Benjamites who returned from Babylon (see Ezra 2:33, Nehemiah 7:37, and 11:31,35).

Elpaal's listing concludes with verse 18. With verse 19 the Chronicler begins his record of those Benjamite clans who lived in Jerusalem prior to the exile: the sons of Shimei (verse 21), the sons of Shashak (verse 25), and the sons of Jeroham (verse 27). Again we note that the Chronicler is making connections here between the "Benjamin before" and the "Benjamin after" the exile. Many of the Benjamites who returned lived in Jerusalem (see 1 Chronicles 9:7-9).

These lists of names may at times seem endless, but as long as we keep in mind the Chronicler's original purpose for including them, we will recognize their value. The Jewish community after the exile was few in numbers and weak in hope. They wondered whether God's promises still applied to them and whether they could still claim any link with the past—so altered were the circumstances and conditions of their lives from the way things had been before! Through the device of genealogy the Chronicler could, by sheer preponderance of the evidence, establish those connections that God's people, in their weakness, had lost sight of. As Nehemiah built a physical wall to protect the inhabitants of Jerusalem, so the Chronicler is building a spiritual wall around the returnees to fortify their hope.

In a similar way, Scripture reminds us that the God with whom we have to do "gives life to the dead and calls things that are not as though they were" (Romans 4:17). As did the saints of old, so we must learn to judge, not by sight and sense, but by the Word of God alone. Only through the Word does God give us the new birth into "a living hope" (1 Peter 1:3). That hope will outlast kingdoms and empires, evil men and petty tyrants, chaos and death. Through that same Word God will preserve us as his eternal kingdom forever.

²⁹Jeiel the father of Gibeon lived in Gibeon.

His wife's name was Maacah, ³⁰and his firstborn son was Abdon, followed by Zur, Kish, Baal, Ner, Nadab, ³¹Gedor, Ahio, Zeker ³²and Mikloth, who was the father of Shimeah. They too lived near their relatives in Jerusalem.

³³Ner was the father of Kish, Kish the father of Saul, and Saul the father of Jonathan, Malki-Shua, Abinadab and Esh-Baal.

³⁴The son of Jonathan:

Merib-Baal, who was the father of Micah.

³⁵The sons of Micah:

Pithon, Melech, Tarea and Ahaz.

³⁶Ahaz was the father of Jehoaddah, Jehoaddah was the father of Alemeth, Azmaveth and Zimri, and Zimri was the father of Moza. ³⁷Moza was the father of Binea; Raphah was his son, Eleasah his son and Azel his son.

³⁸Azel had six sons, and these were their names:

Azrikam, Bokeru, Ishmael, Sheariah, Obadiah and Hanan. All these were the sons of Azel.

³⁹The sons of his brother Eshek:

**Ulam his firstborn, Jeush the second son and
Eliphelet the third. ⁴⁰The sons of Ulam were brave
warriors who could handle the bow. They had many
sons and grandsons—150 in all.**

All these were the descendants of Benjamin.

Having provided the setting for it, the Chronicler now
gives us the genealogy of Saul, Benjamite and first king of
Israel. Up through verse 38, it is substantially the same list as
is given to us in 1 Chronicles 9:35-44.

From a comparison of the Hebrew of the two genealogies
in Chronicles, we come across some problems that seem to
be the result of copying errors. Verse 30 is a case in point.
The NIV has the name "Ner" appearing between Baal and
Nadab. Yet as the text note points out, "Ner" is not found in
the Hebrew text, even though it appears in the parallel account of 1 Chronicles 9:36. Exactly the same thing is true of
the name "Jeiel" in verse 29. It seems clear enough that the
text was slightly damaged here. The translators were quite
right in reproducing the names found in chapter 9.

This may help us in harmonizing the genealogy of Saul
given in Chronicles with that given in 1 Samuel 9:1 and
14:49-51. The difficulty arises mainly from verse thirty-
three: "Ner was the father of Kish and Kish the father of
Saul." From the genealogies given in the book of Samuel, we
learn that Ner and Kish were related to each other as brothers, not as father and son. This also seems to be the natural
understanding of 1 Chronicles 9:36 (parallel to 8:30).

Now it is certainly possible that there was another "Ner" in
the family of Saul, one who could legitimately be called the
"father of" or ancestor of Kish. We would then understand
the reference in 1 Samuel 14 to be to a different "Ner" than
the one in verse 33, a "Ner" who is distinguished by being

brother to Kish and father to Abner, as the writer of Samuel informs us (1 Samuel 14:50). This explanation strikes a person as being a bit complicated. If we remember that we are dealing with a text that seems to have some errors in it, we may be more inclined to accept a simpler explanation some have put forward. They suggest that we read verse 33 as follows: "Ner was the father of Abner; Kish was the father of Saul." Somehow in copying, a scribe missed the word "Abner," and it ended up being lost from the text at this point.

The name "Jeiel" (verse 29) may just be an alternate spelling for the "Abiel" that the book of Samuel lists as a patriarch of Saul's family (1 Samuel 9:1 and 14:51).

Saul's ancestral home of Gibeon (verse 29) is well known for a number of reasons. Inhabitants of this town saved themselves from destruction by tricking Joshua into making a treaty with them at the time of the conquest. Chapter 9 of Joshua records the story. More importantly for us, Gibeon is the place where Israel's tabernacle was pitched prior to the building of the temple at Jerusalem (1 Chronicles 21:29). It was to Gibeon that Solomon went to make sacrifice and inquire of the Lord (2 Chronicles 1:3). Gibeon is also mentioned as being among the towns resettled at the time of the return from exile. The Chronicler is making connections for his readers again—connections between past and present.

Saul's sons are listed in verse 33. Sunday-school children still learn about Jonathan as a study in faith and loving friendship. Jonathan's loyalty to his friend David in the face of his father's unreasonable enmity is recorded for us in 1 Samuel 18, 19, and 20. The death of Jonathan along with two of his brothers, Malki-Shua and Abinadab, is described in 1 Chronicles 10 and 1 Samuel 31. The two sons who survived Saul were Esh-Baal and Merib-Baal. Other than referring to him by name, the Chronicler nowhere else mentions

105

the brief interim rule of Esh-Baal (also known as Ishvi and Ish-Bosheth). After the death of Saul, Abner, the commander of Saul's army, set Esh-Baal on the throne to rule over the northern tribes (see 2 Samuel 2-4), but he was unable to hold on to power.

Saul's grandson through Jonathan, Merib-Baal (verse 34), is more familiar to us as Mephibosheth. He was the one to whom David showed special kindness after he had ascended to the throne. For the details of David's dealings with Mephibosheth, read 2 Samuel 9, 16:1-4, and 19:24-30.

The names of Saul's son and grandson are fascinating studies in the history of how words develop in meaning. We are given their original names here: Esh-*Baal* and Merib-*Baal,* meaning "Man of Baal," and "Hero of Baal" respectively. Saul's descendants got these names in the days when the word "baal" could be used as a common noun in a generic reference to any deity. The word itself means "Owner" or "Master." Whatever else his faults may have been, Saul was someone who tried, at least, to pay homage to the true God of Israel. It is likely then that these names, when given to these particular individuals, were intended as a form of honor to the true God. At the time they meant no more than, "Man of the Master," or "Hero of the Master."

As the years rolled on, however, the word "baal" took on a more sinister meaning. Its usage as a reference to the Canaanite fertility god Baal began to supplant the original meaning in people's minds. And so it reached a point where an inhabitant of the land was unable to hear the word without thinking of that pagan god, the same one who caused Elijah so much grief. For that reason, the name became offensive to worshipers of the true God. At that point no one would want to use it in the name of a loyal son of Israel. It would appear to be giving honor to an idol. As a result, alternate spellings for these two names developed. Esh-Baal became "Ishvi" or "Ishbosheth," meaning, "Man of Jahweh" or "Man of Shame," depending on whether one wanted to honor the parents' original intent in giving the name or whether one wanted to heap contempt upon the heathen god. Similarly, Merib-Baal became "Mephibosheth," meaning "Hero of Shame." Since idols were so disgusting to worshipers of the true God, the word "shame" seemed to them to be an appropriate substitute for the hated name of Baal. These alternate spellings will be found mainly in the books of Samuel.

Our text reverts to the older and original spelling, probably because the time was long past when the worship of Baal posed a threat for the children of Israel. The Chronicler was thus free to use these spellings without fear of any reader getting the wrong idea. This biblical object lesson might be remembered if we are testing the "Christianity" of a particular custom. The custom itself may seem to be quite harmless. But if it conveys a heathen thought, it would be best to avoid it. On the other hand, a custom with roots in paganism may have lost all of its former meaning in peoples' minds. It is difficult to get too upset, for example, over throwing rice at Christian weddings or about Easter egg hunts for the kids at Easter breakfasts. Sometimes Christians object to these practices because in some dim, distant past they were fertility rites. But the time is long past when throwing a handful of rice in the direction of a white dress had any connection with the conferring of fertility. If he wishes, a Christian is free to throw rice without fear of sinning. He is advocating no heathen concept. He may, however, be making a big mess and causing great difficulties for those who have to clean up the carpet and parking lot afterwards. Maybe it would be better just to shake hands and call it a day.

From verse 34 to the end of the chapter, Saul's line is continued through Merib-Baal's son Micah (same name but different man than the prophet who wrote the book). What is of special interest is the lengths to which the Chronicler takes Saul's genealogy. Clearly Saul's family retained some prominence in the south, even after they had lost their position as the royal house. Including verses 39 and 40 there are nineteen generations given past the time of Saul. This would bring us to the time of the exile, possibly even further. These last verses serve as a bridge over into the next chapter, where the people who returned from exile to Jerusalem will be listed.

Saul was a tragic figure in Israel's history. He began his career as king with so much promise. Yet he was cut off because of faithlessness. Though his clan lost its former glory, under the grace of God it continued to exist down to the exile. We can look at the genealogy of Saul as a picture in miniature of the genealogies of all Israel. Israel itself started out as a people with so much promise. We think of the spiritual optimism of Joshua's time or the glory of the kingdom under David and Solomon. Yet tragically, Israel failed to fulfill its promise. It was uprooted because of its unfaithfulness to God. Though Israel lost its former glory, God in his grace still preserved it to the time of the exile. Now the faithful in Israel could read these words penned by the Chronicler after they had been replanted in the promised land. Surely, Israel should now realize that nothing is impossible for a people that relies upon the one true God.

In the last century, the Lutheran church in America began a new era with so much promise. We remember the glory days of Walther, the Pieper brothers, and the Synodical Conference. Much of that glory is gone now, gone because many Lutherans no longer want to be faithful to the Word by which we live. Yet God's grace has still preserved many who hold fast to that Word. Surely we should know that nothing is impossible for us when we rely upon our God.

The Remnant That Returned from Exile:

With the ninth chapter the Chronicler completes his overview of the history of the kingdom of God. He began with Adam, narrowed the focus to Abraham and his descendants through Israel, and highlighted the royal tribe of Judah and the priestly tribe of Levi. He traced each tribe, in turn, up to the Babylonian exile. Now he formally joins God's people, as they existed before the exile, to the people who came back after the exile to resettle Jerusalem.

9 **All Israel was listed in the genealogies recorded in the book of the kings of Israel.**

The people of Judah were taken captive to Babylon because of their unfaithfulness. ²Now the first to resettle on their own property in their own towns were some Israelites, priests, Levites and temple servants.

³Those from Judah, from Benjamin, and from Ephraim and Manasseh who lived in Jerusalem were:

The Chronicler's goal has been to recount the history of "all Israel." Those who returned from exile may have been only a pale shadow of the mighty people described in the genealogical overview. But though they were only a remnant, they were a remnant of "all Israel." Not only people from Judah and Benjamin, but also people from the two great northern tribes of Ephraim and Manasseh (verse 3) returned to the land God had promised to his people. Priests, Levites, even the temple servants (verse 2)—all were represented among those who resettled Jerusalem.

The people were uprooted "because of their unfaithfulness" (verse 1). Despite the many warnings issued through the prophets, Israel broke the covenant that God had made with them on Sinai and worshiped other gods. The curse of Deuteronomy then fell upon the faithless, "The LORD will drive you and the king you set over you to a nation unknown to you" (Deuteronomy 28:36). Faithless people—yet faithful God! Though they had forfeited all right to be his people, God preserved them while in exile and caused them to resettle in their homeland.

In joining Israel before the exile to Israel after the exile, the Chronicler is making a connection vital to the faith of his original readers. Only in this way could they be sure that they were heirs to all the promises made to Abraham. The link is no less vital to us. God promised to bless all nations through Abraham and his descendants. If those who returned from exile had no true connection to the past, then they had no real claim on God's promises. And if they had no claim on the promises—if they were not, in fact, "Israel"—then the promise of a Savior to be born for all through Israel fell to the ground along with that nation's extinction.

The return of Israel from exile assures us that God keeps his promises—all his promises—despite the faithlessness of men. The Savior born in David's town two thousand years ago was the same Savior God promised to send as the seed of Abraham. So we can be sure that "all Israel" (all true sons and daughters of Abraham by faith) "will be saved" for eternal life in heaven (Romans 11:26).

We might also dismiss here as romantic fantasies all the spurious connections made between the "lost ten tribes of Israel" and present day inhabitants of Great Britain, America, or even people tucked away in some yet to be revealed location in central Asia. The Holy Spirit has already made the connection for us here. All Israel was listed in the genealogies (verse 1), and the remnant chosen by grace

110

from all Israel returned and resettled the city of Jerusalem (verse 3).

The Inhabitants of Jerusalem:

In 539 B.C. a great power shift occurred in the Near East, bringing dramatic changes to that part of the world. Cyrus, the king of the Medo-Persians, conquered the city of Babylon. The empire of the Babylonians was replaced by the empire of the Persians. They would then go on to dominate affairs in Mesopotamia, Egypt, and the Holy Land for the next two centuries. Almost immediately after his conquest of Babylon, Cyrus issued an edict permitting the Jews in exile to return to their homeland and rebuild their temple. For more on this story read the book of Ezra, chapters one to six.

Even after the exiles returned, progress was slow. It was not until 516 B.C. that the temple was finally finished and dedicated. A person might have expected the dedication of the temple to have ushered in a time of great national and spiritual revival in Israel. Just the opposite took place, however. The restored community went into a period of decline for the next fifty years. It took the combined leadership of two gifted men to ensure the survival of God's people so that they were not absorbed by the nations around them. Their names were Ezra and Nehemiah, and the Biblical books named after them will give you more information on their ministries. Their times of service spanned the years from 458 to 415 B.C.

Nehemiah's chief concern was to rebuild the walls of Jerusalem. Without walls for protection, no city in those days could hope to be secure from its enemies. People were understandably reluctant to settle in a city with no security. Though the temple had been rebuilt, it could hardly thrive in a Jerusalem that had few inhabitants. To remedy this, Nehemiah saw to it that more people were settled in Jerusalem after its walls had been rebuilt. The list we have here dates from around Nehemiah's time and represents Jerusalem's inhabitants after his reforms. It shows many similarities to chapter 11 of Nehemiah.

4Uthai son of Ammihud, the son of Omri, the son of Imri, the son of Bani, a descendant of Perez son of Judah.
5Of the Shilonites:
Asaiah the firstborn and his sons.
6Of the Zerahites:
Jeuel.
The people from Judah numbered 690.
7Of the Benjamites:
Sallu son of Meshullam, the son of Hodaviah, the son of Hassenuah;
8Ibneiah son of Jeroham; Elah son of Uzzi, the son of Micri; and Meshullam son of Shephatiah, the son of Reuel, the son of Ibnijah.
9The people from Benjamin, as listed in their genealogy, numbered 956. All these men were heads of their families.
10Of the priests: Jedaiah; Jehoiarib; Jakin;
11Azariah son of Hilkiah, the son of Meshullam, the son of Zadok, the son of Meraioth, the son of Ahitub, the official in charge of the house of God;
12Adaiah son of Jeroham, the son of Pashhur, the son of Malkijah; and Maasai son of Adiel, the son of Jahzerah, the son of Meshullam, the son of Meshillemith, the son of Immer.
13The priests, who were heads of families, numbered 1,760. They were able men, responsible for ministering in the house of God.
14Of the Levites:
Shemaiah son of Hasshub, the son of Azrikam, the son of Hashabiah, a Merarite; 15Bakbakkar, Heresh,

> Galal and Mattaniah son of Mica, the son of Zicri, the
> son of Asaph; ¹⁶Obadiah son of Shemaiah, the son of
> Galal, the son of Jeduthun; and Berekiah son of Asa,
> the son of Elkanah, who lived in the villages of the Ne-
> tophathites.

Though the list is introduced in verse 3 as representing the tribes of Judah, Benjamin, Ephraim, and Manasseh, we discover that only clans from Judah and Benjamin are mentioned, along with the priests and Levites. No doubt Ephraim and Manasseh had lost their separate clan and tribal structures in the Assyrian invasion and were now only represented by individuals descended from those tribes.

Men of Judah (verses 3 through 6)

Israelites from the tribe of Judah who resettled Jerusalem could trace their lineage back to the three ancient clans of Perez, Zerah, and Shelah (see 1 Chronicles 2:3-6). "Shilonites" in verse 5 is best taken as a reference to descendants of Shelah, the son of Judah. The list has many features that distinguish it from a similar list in Nehemiah 11:4-6. Some are minor and involve merely the spelling of names. For example, the "Uthai" of 1 Chronicles 9:4 is the same man as the "Athaiah" of Nehemiah 11:4. Others are more striking. We notice, for example, that Uthai has different ancestors listed in Chronicles than the ones given in Nehemiah. The clan of Zerah is passed over completely in Nehemiah. 1 Chronicles 9:6 supplies us with the names of Zerah's descendant "Jeuel."

In addition to these differences, the numbers in 1 Chronicles 9 don't match up with the numbers in Nehemiah 11. One of these "mismatches" is easily explained: 1 Chronicles 9:6 gives us the total of all the people from Judah; Nehemiah 11:6 gives us the total of the *able men* from *Perez's* clan only. It is no wonder Nehemiah's number is considerably lower. While that solution came easily enough, the resolution of the differences between Chronicles and Nehemiah in the numbers of Benjamites and priests is not quite so easy to see. Nehemiah gives us 928 Benjamite inhabitants of Jerusalem (11:8), 1 Chronicles, 956 (verse 9). When we total up the priests in Nehemiah's account, we come up with the number 1192 (chapter 11:12-14). This does not jibe with the number of 1760 given in 1 Chronicles 9:13.

These differences lead us to make one overall observation. What we have here is not an exact parallel with the list of Jerusalem's inhabitants given by Nehemiah. It seems likely that we have in each case a snapshot of the same group of people taken at two different times. An intervening period of years would then account for the differences in numbers. No doubt the holy writers were working from the same basic document—perhaps a census document—which each edited, shaped, and updated to suit his own taste and individual purpose at his time of writing. In all probability, Nehemiah's is the earlier list, as seems plausible from his lower numbers.

Men of Benjamin (verses 7 to 9)

The Benjamite inhabitants are listed in Chronicles beginning with verse 7. Aside from the differences in totals already mentioned, the Chronicler adds the names of Ibneiah, Elah, and Meshullam to his "heads of family" list, and omits the names of Gabbai and Sallai, found in Nehemiah (11:8). Sallu's name appears in both 1 Chronicles and Nehemiah but with a slightly different genealogy in each case.

Priests (verses 10 to 13)

The roster of priestly inhabitants of Jerusalem is given in verses 10 to 13. Immediately we encounter a difficulty posed by the first four names. Are Jedaiah, Jehoiarib, Jakin, and Azariah contemporaries, or do we have here a compressed genealogy tracing Jedaiah's lineage back through Zadok to Ahitub, "the official in charge of the house of God?" As the text stands here, it would appear the four priests were from the same time period. But when we look at the parallel in Nehemiah, Jedaiah is listed as the "son of" Jehoiarib.

Might we then suppose that the words "son of" were in the original text between each of the four names and were somehow dropped when it was later transcribed? If so, we have Jedaiah's genealogy here. We could also hazard the guess that this priestly genealogy was so well known to the Chronicler's readers that he could list ascending generations in this telegraphic fashion without fear of being misunderstood. He does much the same thing with Adam's genealogy in chapter 1. It could also be that the present text of Nehemiah reflects the faulty reading and that the words "son of" somehow crept in between Jedaiah and Jehoiarib. Then we could simply view these men as being contemporaries. We don't know enough to say for sure which one of these possibilities is true. The reader will want to consult Professor Brug's thoughts on these points in the People's Bible Commentary on *Ezra, Nehemiah, Esther.*

Some of these technical difficulties in interpreting the text may remain, but the Chronicler's message is still clear. He wishes to link the great priests of Israel who served before the exile together with their successors who returned to inhabit the city of Jerusalem. The mention of Zadok in verse 11 is a good example. He was one of the high priests during David's time. He stood by David during Adonijah's rebellion and anointed David's rightful successor Solomon as king (1 Kings 1:39). For this act he became a model of priestly faithfulness in the book of Ezekiel (Ezekiel 44:15,16). His

115

descendants served as high priests from Solomon's time to 171 B.C.—a span of eight hundred years! Immer's name in verse 12 must be the priest of the same name who was head of one of the twenty-four divisions, or "courses," of priests. These were established by David to serve in rotation (see 1 Chronicles 24:3,14).

The Chronicler describes the priests who resettled Jerusalem as being "able men" (verse 13). The phrase in the original probably refers not only to their priestly prowess, but also to their financial status. These were men of means who took on temple service as a joyful and holy obligation, not because they had no other way to support themselves.

The Levite Musicians (verses 14 to 16)

In chapter 6 of Chronicles, we were introduced to the sons of Levi who served as musicians in the house of God. We learned that the three major clans of Levi (Kohath, Gershon, and Merari) were each represented in temple worship by its own guild of musicians, headed up by Heman, Asaph, and Ethan (also known as Jeduthun). Berekiah (verse 16) is connected to Elkanah, the ancestor of Heman the musician (see 1 Chronicles 6:33,34). Continuity with the past has been established. God remains faithful, his promises sure.

The Levite Gatekeepers

¹⁷The gatekeepers:
Shallum, Akkub, Talmon, Ahiman and their brothers, Shallum their chief ¹⁸being stationed at the King's Gate on the east, up to the present time. These were the gatekeepers belonging to the camp of the Levites. ¹⁹Shallum son of Kore, the son of Ebiasaph, the son of Korah, and his fellow gatekeepers from his family (the Korahites) were responsible for guarding the

thresholds of the Tent just as their fathers had been responsible for guarding the entrance to the dwelling of the LORD. [20]In earlier times Phinehas son of Eleazar was in charge of the gatekeepers, and the LORD was with him. [21]Zechariah son of Meshelemiah was the gatekeeper at the entrance to the Tent of Meeting.

[22]Altogether, those chosen to be gatekeepers at the thresholds numbered 212. They were registered by genealogy in their villages. The gatekeepers had been assigned to their positions of trust by David and Samuel the seer. [23]They and their descendants were in charge of guarding the gates of the house of the LORD—the house called the Tent. [24]The gatekeepers were on the four sides: east, west, north and south. [25]Their brothers in their villages had to come from time to time and share their duties for seven-day periods. [26]But the four principal gatekeepers, who were Levites, were entrusted with the responsibility for the rooms and treasuries in the house of God. [27]They would spend the night stationed around the house of God, because they had to guard it; and they had charge of the key for opening it each morning.

The Chronicler continues his account of the Levites who settled in Jerusalem after the exile. It might seem curious that he spends so much time on the Levites. After all, he gave the priests only a few verses. But when we remember that the Levites did not respond to the call to return to the holy land in as large numbers as did the priests, we can understand what the Chronicler is doing here. Perhaps the Levites were more reluctant to return because their work seemed less glorious, more humdrum, less central to worship than the work of the priests. We can almost hear their thoughts, "I'm only a Levite. Why should I go back? I have a comfortable life here." Or if they did return, we can imagine them casting envious eyes on the priests who occupied the worship "spotlight." The Chronicler patiently shows his brothers how vital

117

each member of the body of believers is by highlighting their own particular ministries in this way.

Since the Chronicler goes into more detail on the gate-keepers' organization, stations, and responsibilities in chapter 26, we will talk about those matters there. Here we want to notice the unique way he magnifies their ministry. He points out that their position goes back to the ancient past and is every bit as hallowed by time as the position of priest. They can trace their lineage back through Korah (verse 19), a member of Kohathites, the dominant clan in the tribe of Levi.

The Chronicler's use of language in verses 18 to 20 achieves the same purpose. In subtle ways it calls to mind the ancient past and the magnificent heritage of the gatekeepers, reminding them that they had carried out their duties even under Moses during the exodus. He does this by using allusive language, which would have reminded an Israelite of their march to the promised land at the time of Moses (see Numbers 2:17). The references he makes, for example to the "camp of the Levites" (verse 18), or his calling the temple that they guarded "the Tent" (verse 19), or the allusion to Phinehas (verse 20)—all of these point back to ancient Israel in the desert.

Phinehas deserves special mention by the Chronicler, since it was his decisive act of leadership which prevented all Israel from being further defiled by the Moabite women of Baal Peor. Consumed with a holy zeal for God's house and God's people, Phinehas killed an Israelite who was openly defying the God of Israel. The Chronicler's sub-text is not too hard to read. He is saying to the Levites of his day, "As he was zealous, so may you who still serve in his place be zealous for the honor of God's house! Prevent it from being defiled." For the full story, see Numbers 3:32 and Numbers 25:6-13.

Finally, the Chronicler gives the gatekeepers the glory due them under God by pointing to Zechariah (verse 21), the gatekeeper who served King David. He reminds them that not only David, but also "Samuel the seer" (verse 22) had considered their duties important enough to have a hand in organizing them. Theirs was a "position of trust."

Other Duties of Levites:

28Some of them were in charge of the articles used in the temple service; they counted them when they were brought in and when they were taken out. 29Others were assigned to take care of the furnishings and all the other articles of the sanctuary, as well as the flour and wine, and the oil, incense and spices. 30But some of the priests took care of mixing the spices. 31A Levite named Mattithiah, the firstborn son of Shallum the Korahite, was entrusted with the responsibility for baking the offering bread. 32Some of their Kohathite brothers were in charge of preparing for every Sabbath the bread set out on the table.

33Those who were musicians, heads of Levite families, stayed in the rooms of the temple and were exempt from other duties because they were responsible for the work day and night.

34All these were heads of Levite families, chiefs as listed in their genealogy, and they lived in Jerusalem.

By now we are familiar with the thought that Levites served as temple singers and guards. In this section the Chronicler lists some of the other Levitical duties. Besides giving us a valuable glimpse of what went on inside the temple at Nehemiah's time, this section also serves to remind us that, in the church of God, no job or activity is so small as to escape God's notice. Whatever is done to his glory, God values as a precious gift to him by one of his saints.

It is likely we have two kinds of temple artifacts referred to in verses 28 and 29. The ones in verse 28 would be the items made from precious metals: the gold and silver bowls, lampstands, forks, and pitchers mentioned in 1 Chronicles 28:14-16. Naturally it would be important to ensure that the same number of items that went into the temple for daily use would be returned at nightfall for storage. Some Levites were given this inventory duty. Their common sense told them that even priests were capable of stealing.

The articles mentioned in verse 29 were no less valuable—in the sense that they were also dedicated for use in God's temple—but they were probably not made of precious metals. The pans, pitchers, and bowls used in offering the gifts of the earth (flour, oil, incense, and wine) seem to be at least part of what the Chronicler had in mind. Some Levites were given charge over them.

To avoid possible misunderstanding, the Chronicler is quick to point out that the Levites did not mix the spices (verse 30). Apparently, mixing up the holy anointing oil and the sacred incense was a job reserved for priests alone. God's regulation of these matters included the exact recipe, as we learn from Exodus 30:22-38. Reading Old Testament texts like this certainly leads a person to appreciate the freedom a New Testament believer has in choosing our worship forms.

The last duties mentioned in this miscellaneous grouping have to do with the bread used in Israel's worship. First, there was the "offering bread" (verse 31). These were flat cakes of bread regularly offered in thanksgiving along with the animal sacrifices. Mattithiah, the son of Shallum the head gatekeeper, was given the job of baking it. Others from the clan of Kohath were responsible for baking "the bread set out on the table" (verse 32). Those familiar with the King James translation will remember this as the "shewbread," the twelve loaves of bread baked new every week and set before the Lord fresh each Sabbath day (see Leviticus 24:5-9). These twelve loaves symbolized the consecration of each tribe in its entirety to the Lord.

In rounding out his description of the Levites and their duties in the temple, the Chronicler points out a special honor given to the leading musicians. They were given permanent rooms in the temple and were also exempt from other duties. "All these . . . lived in Jerusalem" (verse 34) speaks to the Chronicler's purpose in this entire chapter. King Nebuchadnezzar had smashed temple worship to pieces by his invasions of Judah. But God's gracious and preserving hand rules over kings, mighty men, and those who think they make history. Once again, Levites have settled in Jerusalem and are busy at their posts.

The Genealogy of Saul

35Jeiel the father of Gibeon lived in Gibeon.

His wife's name was Maacah, 36and his firstborn son was Abdon, followed by Zur, Kish, Baal, Ner, Nadab, 37Gedor, Ahio, Zechariah and Mikloth. 38Mikloth was the father of Shimeam. They too lived near their relatives in Jerusalem.

39Ner was the father of Kish, Kish the father of Saul, and Saul the father of Jonathan, Malki-Shua, Abinadab and Esh-Baal.

40The son of Jonathan:

Merib-Baal, who was the father of Micah.

41The sons of Micah:

Pithon, Melech, Tahrea and Ahaz.

42Ahaz was the father of Jadah, Jadah was the father of Alemeth, Azmaveth and Zimri, and Zimri was the father of Moza. 43Moza was the father of Binea; Rephaiah was his son, Eleasah his son and Azel his son.

44Azel had six sons, and these were their names:

Azrikam, Bokeru, Ishmael, Sheariah, Obadiah and Hanan. These were the sons of Azel.

The genealogy of Saul we saw in the previous chapter is substantially the same as the one we have here. There it was included to put Saul in his proper place as a descendant of Benjamin. Here it is repeated to serve as a bridge to the summary of his reign described in 1 Chronicles 10.

Concluding Remarks on the Genealogies:

If you have kept at it all the way from chapter 1, I pray that, through your study, God has given you greater insight into the workings of his kingdom, not only as it was in Old Testament times, but also today. From this point on, our reading will get easier.

In a masterful way the Chronicler has summed up God's working in history up to his own time. He has introduced the major themes that will occupy him for the rest of his book: the exalted place the tribes of Israel hold in God's plan for saving the world, the key role David's royal house has to play in that plan, and the importance of the temple and its services. The Chronicler speaks to a people wondering about their identity as God's own and about the validity of their institutions. As a skillful lawyer might build a complex case piece by piece until the sheer weight of all the evidence points to one conclusion, so the Chronicler has built an airtight case from the genealogical evidence. He has reminded his people that God is still in charge and all Israel is present in them. Along the way he has issued warnings against apostasy and commendations for faithfulness.

In a similar way we study history—recent and remote—as the process of God at work bringing his children to glory. We see how God from age to age has always preserved his little flock. We consider each generation of saints in turn, their labors, their struggles, and their triumphs under the cross, and we are certain that God's kingdom continues to march along in measured steps from age to age. The gates of hell will not prevail against it. If we have this view of history, we owe it in large part to inspired writers like the Chronicler. He has helped us catch the vision, so that we see things from God's point of view. His message encourages us also to "run with perseverance the race marked out for us" (Hebrews 12:1). Surrounded by this cloud of witness to God's faithfulness in Christ, we are certain of victory.

PART II

GOD ESTABLISHES
HIS KINGDOM IN ISRAEL UNDER DAVID

1 CHRONICLES 10-29

The Chronicler now launches into the telling of David's story. It will be the story of "a man after the Lord's own heart" (1 Samuel 13:14). While his words reflect a familiarity with 1 and 2 Samuel, he has more in mind than to give a mere summary of events related more fully there. He assumes that his readers are acquainted with the facts of Saul's life and David's early career. It is the Chronicler's God-given task to select, shape, and present the same material to serve the needs of God's people of his own day.

What he omits from his account reveals his purpose to us. He passes over in silence most of Saul's reign. He says nothing about the jealousy Saul harbored in his heart against David or the years David spent on the run. He omits any reference to the seven-and-a-half years David ruled only over Judah while Saul's son Ishbosheth ruled over the northern tribes. He does not mention the way Abner was instrumental in bringing the northern tribes over to David's side. The Chronicler has one aim in mind and that is to paint a clear picture of God's kind of king. Details of David's life that do not help him achieve that goal are left out, not as unknown, but as irrelevant to his purpose.

In chapter ten, Saul is presented—by way of contrast to David—as a king gone wrong, a failed leader. The Chronicler brings that failure into focus by recounting the ultimate event of Saul's life: his defeat on Mt. Gilboa.

God Takes His Kingdom Away from Saul

10 Now the Philistines fought against Israel; the Israelites fled before them, and many fell slain on Mount Gilboa. [2]The Philistines pressed hard after Saul and his sons, and they killed his sons Jonathan, Abinadab and Malki-Shua. [3]The fighting grew fierce around Saul, and when the archers overtook him, they wounded him.

[4]Saul said to his armor-bearer, "Draw your sword and run me through, or these uncircumcised fellows will come and abuse me."

But his armor-bearer was terrified and would not do it; so Saul took his own sword and fell on it. [5]When the armor-bearer saw that Saul was dead, he too fell on his sword and died. [6]So Saul and his three sons died, and all his house died together.

[7]When all the Israelites in the valley saw that the army had fled and that Saul and his sons had died, they abandoned their towns and fled. And the Philistines came and occupied them.

[8]The next day, when the Philistines came to strip the dead, they found Saul and his sons fallen on Mount Gilboa. [9]They stripped him and took his head and his armor, and sent messengers throughout the land of the Philistines to proclaim the news among their idols and their people. [10]They put his armor in the temple of their gods and hung up his head in the temple of Dagon.

[11]When all the inhabitants of Jabesh Gilead heard of everything the Philistines had done to Saul, [12]all their valiant men went and took the bodies of Saul and his sons and brought them to Jabesh. Then they buried their bones under the great tree in Jabesh, and they fasted seven days.

The battle at Mt. Gilboa was a critical test of strength between the kingdom of Israel and the coastal cities of Philistia. At stake was the valley of Jezreel, which Mt. Gilboa overlooked from the south. Not only was the valley fertile farmland, it also connected the Israelite tribes living to the north with those living in the central regions of Palestine. In addition, a trade route linking Egypt with Mesopotamia passed through that same critical area.

The Chronicler's concern is not so much with the political and economic ramifications of the battle as with its spiritual outcome. He emphasizes the total defeat that comes upon God's people when they blindly follow a leader who is unfaithful to God's Word. Verse 1 in Hebrew is more pointed than the NIV's "the Israelites fled" would have us believe. "*Each man* of Israel fled," the Chronicler tells us. Again in verse seven he asserts, "*All* the Israelites in the valley . . . fled." When we put our trust in leaders more than in God and his Word, we will have no place to stand when those leaders fail us.

Saul's last moments in life only serve to underscore his bad qualities. Unnerved at the prospect of being captured by the Philistines and being abused as Samson was, he asked his armor-bearer to kill him. His concern was only for himself, not in how he might bring glory to God by living or dying. His own armor-bearer showed a keener sense of right and wrong by refusing to kill the Lord's anointed king. Unwilling or unable to recognize that his times were in God's hands (Psalm 31:15), Saul took his own life in a final act of unbelief.

In a summary statement the Chronicler says in verse six, "So Saul and his three sons died, and all his house died together." Gilboa marked the end, not only of Saul's personal rule, but also of any claim to rule that might be advanced by his descendants. Saul and his line would not form a royal dynasty in Israel. All this had been predicted by the Lord through the prophet Samuel (1 Samuel 13:14; 15:27,28). Now God's Word had been fulfilled in this horrifying way. The subsequent rule of Saul's son, Ishbosheth, as Abner's puppet king (see 2 Samuel, chapters 2-5) did not count as evidence to the contrary in the mind of the Chronicler. It was the mere settling of the wreckage of a house that had already collapsed on Mt. Gilboa.

The Chronicler describes the battle's aftermath in verses 7 to 12. The enemies of God's people had their little day of glory. They took over the valley of Jezreel, abandoned now by its Israelite inhabitants. After they had stripped Saul's body of his armor and cut off his head, they used these gruesome trophies to proclaim the good news of their victory "among their idols and their people" (verse 9). They gave glory for the defeat of Israel to their heathen god Dagon by hanging up Saul's head and armor in Dagon's temple. When a leader of God's people fails spiritually, it is not only a personal defeat for the individual, it is also a disaster for God's people as a whole. The heathen become bolder in their blasphemy. It appears to all the world as if Satan and false religion have triumphed.

The only thing left for a pious Israelite to do was to mourn the dead. The valiant men of Jabesh Gilead—who themselves had been rescued by Saul in the bright dawn of his early reign—came, not to praise him, but to bury what was left of him and his house. For a fuller account of this incident, read 1 Samuel 11 and 31:8-13.

There are times when it seems as if evil triumphs. Jesus himself refers to the "hour when darkness reigns" (Luke 22:53). But it is always a mere hour, a "little while" of mourning while the world rejoices (John 16:19,20). It never lasts beyond the time God has allotted for it. Out of the darkness God will make the light of his truth and goodness shine again. We will see that truth reflected in the next chapter as God raises up David to take Saul's place. By God's power he will restore more than was ever taken away from his people in this terrible defeat.

Yet before we move on to David, we take one last look at Saul to understand the nature of his failure. This "physical" defeat on Mt. Gilboa was only the outward evidence of Saul's prior spiritual collapse:

[13]Saul died because he was unfaithful to the LORD; he did not keep the word of the LORD and even consulted a medium for guidance, [14]and did not inquire of the LORD. So the LORD put him to death and turned the kingdom over to David son of Jesse.

In God's estimation any leader of God's people will be effective only so long as he is faithful to the Word. Another writer might have pointed out the good things Saul had accomplished—the battles he had won, for example—in order to balance out the account. But for the Chronicler, Saul's failure to heed the Word of God tipped the scales decisively against him. There was nothing more to say. He had been "unfaithful to the LORD."

A careful student of Scripture might wonder at the remark that Saul "did not inquire of the LORD." 1 Samuel 28:6 tells us that he tried, but that the Lord refused to answer. Heaven replied to his cries for guidance with a deafening silence. In desperation he took the utterly vile course of turning to a spirit-medium just to receive some communication from the spiritual realm before battle. He knew that such an act was contrary to God's will. In fact, he himself had seen to it that spiritists, witches, and wizards were expelled from the land of Israel. But when people let go of the Word, they will grasp at any straw. The fact that he so quickly turned to a medium for answers demonstrates the superstitious nature of his initial quest for information from the Lord.

Saul did not seek the Lord when he could be found. On two occasions he spurned the message of the prophet Samuel and trusted his own judgment over the revealed Word (see 1 Samuel 13:11-14; 15:3-10). This final act of seeking answers from God in superstitious desperation did not qualify as true "seeking of the LORD." We may learn from this passage the sobering truth that if people continue to despise the Word of God, there could come a point, even in their earthly lifetimes, when God gives them up to the terrifying clamor of their own futile thoughts.

The concluding words give the final verdict. "So the LORD put him to death and turned the kingdom over to David" (verse 14). An archer's arrow had struck him. He fell on his own sword. Yet, in the final analysis, it was the Lord who put Saul to death. Sin always pays the same wage to its slaves.

What comfort we may glean from this passage is found in the name of God that is used. The NIV translates it in English as *the LORD*". Whenever we see the word *LORD* in full capital letters, the NIV editors are telling us that the great covenant name of God is found here in the original. It was probably pronounced *Yahweh,* though we are not certain of this. The King James Version sometimes rendered it in English with the word *Jehovah.*

Many Hebrew names are descriptive, and so it is with this name of God. Derived from the Hebrew verb *to be,* it points to him as the Ever Living One, the eternal "I AM" God (see Exodus 3:14,15). He does not remain aloof and unknown to sinful humanity. He is the one who invades our space and time, revealing himself to men. He was the God who made an everlasting covenant with Abraham to bless all nations "through his offspring" (Genesis 22:18). To him he demonstrated his power as Almighty God, promising whole nations of children to Abraham—a man who had none—and promising the inheritance of a large and fruitful land to the same Abraham—a man who lived in a tent to the end of his days. Through

Moses, he showed himself to be our Savior-God, willing to redeem his people from all their enemies "with an outstretched arm and with mighty acts of judgment" (Exodus 6:6). Since he is totally free in his actions and utterly independent in his nature, we can be assured that this God will remain faithful to the promises he graciously makes to his people.

The use of God's covenant name in this context assures us that the God who freely bound himself to his people by a promise to save is at work here in the demise of Saul. The end of Saul did not mark the end of God's saving plan. The Lord raised up David in his place, entrusting his kingdom to a man who would gather again the scattered sheep of God's flock. Even God's judgments serve the interests of his mercy!

God Turns His Kingdom over to David

All Israel Anoints David King

11 **All Israel came together to David at Hebron and said, "We are your own flesh and blood. [2]In the past, even while Saul was king, you were the one who led Israel on their military campaigns. And the LORD your God said to you, 'You will shepherd my people Israel, and you will become their ruler.'"**

[3]When all the elders of Israel had come to King David at Hebron, he made a compact with them at Hebron before the LORD, and they anointed David king over Israel, as the LORD had promised through Samuel.

In presenting David to us as God's kind of king, the Chronicler contrasts him with Saul in almost every conceivable way. "All Israel" (verse 1) gathered before him at Hebron to acclaim him as their ruler. The people were united in their allegiance to David. They recognized him as their brother, their own flesh and blood (verse 1). He was preeminent in Israel as the army's battle leader even before he ascended the throne. His elevation now was seen as the fulfillment of prophecy, "You will shepherd my people Israel" (verse 2). Thus he ruled according to the will and Word of God. The people were referring, no doubt, to Samuel's anointing of David as king while he was still a youth, shepherd of his father's flocks (see 1 Samuel 16:11-13).

The term "shepherd" is particularly expressive of God's ideal for leadership. It connotes a leadership exercised in tender care of the flock placed into its charge. Who can look at the Chronicler's picture here and not see Christ? David was a "shadow of things to come," a type of our Lord Jesus. Jesus is the Good Shepherd (John 10) who lays down his life for the sheep. He leads us beside the still waters of his Word (Psalm 23). True man, born of the virgin Mary, he is not ashamed to call us brothers (Hebrews 2:11). He bears our burdens for us and with us as one of us. May all the Savior's people be willing to acclaim him King and serve him wholeheartedly all their days!

David is also demonstrated to be God's ideal king in the way he "made a compact" with the elders of his people to serve them. No king of Israel was ever to be an absolute monarch whose sovereign will was law. Rather, kings were meant to serve under God in keeping with his Word. The "law of the king," which defined and limited his powers, was laid down by God already in the time of Moses (see Deuteronomy 17:14-20). David showed his desire to be faithful to the Word of God by freely making such a compact with his people.

The Newly-Anointed King Captures Jerusalem

⁴David and all the Israelites marched to Jerusalem (that is, Jebus). The Jebusites who lived there ⁵said to David, "You will

not get in here." Nevertheless, David captured the fortress of Zion, the City of David.

⁶David had said, "Whoever leads the attack on the Jebusites will become commander-in-chief." Joab son of Zeruiah went up first, and so he received the command.

⁷David then took up residence in the fortress, and so it was called the City of David. ⁸He built up the city around it, from the supporting terraces to the surrounding wall, while Joab restored the rest of the city. ⁹And David became more and more powerful, because the LORD Almighty was with him.

United under God's king, God's people marched triumphantly to Jerusalem and captured it. Jerusalem or Jebus was an enclave of heathen power left over from the conquest of the land of Canaan under Joshua. It was listed in the book of Joshua as one of those portions of land that remained for Joshua's successors to conquer (Joshua 15:63). This heathen city was a stronghold perched near the center of the mountainous spine of the Holy Land, standing between Judah and the tribes of the north. The conquest of the city would unite north and south, not only by removing this heathen wedge, but also by providing a central location where the tribes could gather. Captured by a united army, it was a city, not of Judah, nor of Ephraim, but of David (verse 7), belonging at once to both north and south.

The Jebusites proudly asserted, "You will not get in here" (verse 5). They imagined they were secure in their mountain fortress. But they were no match for the united army that marched under the banner of God's king. Joab took the initiative in the attack and received the promised post of commander-in-chief under David. After the Jebusites had been thrust out, David took up residence in the city to which he gave his name. Immediately he set to work beautifying and building it up. Joab, too, is given credit for extensive restoration projects.

This was a dramatic turning of the tide. After Gilboa, God's people lay prostrate. Now they ruled in triumph over the heathen. God's kind of king made the difference, and he made the difference because he was faithful to the one true God. "David became more and more powerful," not because of his brilliance in combat or his sagacity in statecraft, but "because the LORD Almighty was with him" (verse 9).

"If God is for us, who can be against us?" (Romans 8:31). United under Christ our King, we "demolish strongholds . . . arguments and every pretension that sets itself up against the knowledge of God, and we take captive every thought to make it obedient to Christ" (2 Corinthians 10:4,5). No matter how weak the church may seem or how strong the proud enemies of God's people may appear, the sword of the Spirit with which we are equipped is more than sufficient to win the victory for us. By God's Word and promise we will storm even the citadel of death itself and convert it into the place through which we enter the quiet rest of eternal life.

All Israel Fully United Under One King

The Chronicler continues by giving us a list of the great leaders and fighters of David's army. It is closely parallel to a similar list in 2 Samuel 23. There it serves as a postscript to David's illustrious career. Here it is intended to underscore the truth that David became king because he had won the *full* support of *all* Israel.

¹⁰**These were the chiefs of David's mighty men—they, together with all Israel, gave his kingship strong support to extend it over the whole land, as the LORD had promised—¹¹this is the list of David's mighty men:**

Jashobeam, a Hacmonite, was chief of the officers; he raised his spear against three hundred men, whom he killed in one encounter.

¹²Next to him was Eleazar son of Dodai the Ahohite, one of the three mighty men. ¹³He was with David at Pas Dammim when the Philistines gathered there for battle. At a place where there was a field full of barley, the troops fled from the Philistines. ¹⁴But they took their stand in the middle of the field. They defended it and struck the Philistines down, and the LORD brought about a great victory.

¹⁵Three of the thirty chiefs came down to David to the rock at the cave of Adullam, while a band of Philistines was encamped in the Valley of Rephaim. ¹⁶At that time David was in the stronghold, and the Philistine garrison was at Bethlehem. ¹⁷David longed for water and said, "Oh, that someone would get me a drink of water from the well near the gate of Bethlehem!" ¹⁸So the Three broke through the Philistine lines, drew water from the well near the gate of Bethlehem and carried it back to David. But he refused to drink it; instead, he poured it out before the LORD. ¹⁹"God forbid that I should do this!" he said. "Should I drink the blood of these men who went at the risk of their lives?" Because they risked their lives to bring it back, David would not drink it.

Such were the exploits of the three mighty men.

²⁰Abishai the brother of Joab was chief of the Three. He raised his spear against three hundred men, whom he killed, and so he became as famous as the Three. ²¹He was doubly honored above the Three and became their commander, even though he was not included among them.

²²Benaiah son of Jehoiada was a valiant fighter from Kabzeel, who performed great exploits. He struck down two of Moab's best men. He also went down into a pit on a snowy day and killed a lion. ²³And he struck down an Egyptian who was seven and a half feet tall. Although the Egyptian had a spear like a weaver's rod in his hand, Benaiah went against him with a club. He snatched the spear from the Egyptian's hand and killed him with his own spear. ²⁴Such were the exploits of Benaiah son of Jehoiada; he too was as famous as the three mighty

men. ²⁵He was held in greater honor than any of the Thirty, but he was not included among the Three. And David put him in charge of his bodyguard.

²⁶The mighty men were:

    Asahel the brother of Joab,

    Elhanan son of Dodo from Bethlehem,

²⁷Shammoth the Harorite,

    Helez the Pelonite,

²⁸Ira son of Ikkesh from Tekoa,

    Abiezer from Anathoth,

²⁹Sibbecai the Hushathite,

    Ilai the Ahohite,

³⁰Maharai the Netophathite,

    Heled son of Baanah the Netophathite,

³¹Ithai son of Ribai from Gibeah in Benjamin,

    Benaiah the Pirathonite,

³²Hurai from the ravines of Gaash,

    Abiel the Arbathite,

³³Azmaveth the Baharumite,

    Eliahba the Shaalbonite,

³⁴the sons of Hashem the Gizonite,

    Jonathan son of Shagee the Hararite,

³⁵Ahiam son of Sacar the Hararite,

    Eliphal son of Ur,

³⁶Hepher the Mekerathite,

    Ahijah the Pelonite,

³⁷Hezro the Carmelite,

    Naarai son of Ezbai,

³⁸Joel the brother of Nathan,

    Mibhar son of Hagri,

³⁹Zelek the Ammonite,

    Naharai the Berothite, the armor-bearer of Joab son of Zeruiah,

⁴⁰Ira the Ithrite,

    Gareb the Ithrite,

⁴¹Uriah the Hittite,
   Zabad son of Ahlai,
⁴²Adina son of Shiza the Reubenite, who was chief of
   the Reubenites, and the thirty with him,
⁴³Hanan son of Maacah,
   Joshaphat the Mithnite,
⁴⁴Uzzia the Ashterathite,
   Shama and Jeiel the sons of Hotham the Aroerite,
⁴⁵Jediael son of Shimri,
   his brother Joha the Tizite,
⁴⁶Eliel the Mahavite,
   Jeribai and Joshaviah the sons of Elnaam,
   Ithmah the Moabite,
⁴⁷Eliel, Obed and Jaasiel the Mezobaite.

Various difficulties confront us in coming to a full understanding of all the details of these verses. But we have no problems whatever in determining the Chronicler's chief point. Verse 10 sums it up: "David's mighty men . . . gave his kingship strong support to extend it over the whole land, as the LORD had promised." In throwing their lot in with David, these leaders were confessing their faith in the Word of God. In supporting him, they were aligning themselves with the Lord's anointed. Through their support he became king over the whole land.

Our chief problem consists in harmonizing this list of names with the one found in 2 Samuel 23:8-39. Clearly they are parallel. Yet there are slight differences that perplex us. Most of these seem due to variations in the spelling of names. We have met these before in similar situations, and it does not surprise us. Whether he is called "Shammah the Harodite" (2 Samuel 23:25) or "Shammoth the Harorite" (1 Chronicles 11:27) makes little difference. Others seem simply to be different names for the same person, e.g.,

Jashobeam (1 Chronicles 11:11) versus Josheb-Bashebeth (2 Samuel 23:8).

Still other differences may be chalked up to mistakes that were made as these ancient manuscripts were copied and re-copied. For example, there seems to be a gap in the Chronicler's text at verse 13, from which the account of Shammah's stand against the Philistines (see 2 Samuel 23:12) dropped out. It is not hard to see how this might have happened, since the accounts of Eleazar's and Shammah's mighty deeds are so similar. The copyist's eye must have drifted in glancing back and forth from the manuscript he was copying to the new copy he was making. For a discussion of the problem of copying mistakes and the inspiration of Scripture, the reader may wish to refer back to chapter 8, verses 1-3 and the comments made there.

We run into still another difficulty in connection with the interpretation of the words "chief of the *officers*" (verse 11), "chief of *the Three*" (verse 20), and "chief of *the Thirty*" (verse 25 and 1 Chronicles 12:18). In organizing the command structure within his army, David must have had different groupings of officers. One group was called *the Three;* another, *the Thirty;* and (perhaps) still another, *the officers.* There may have been more than one group called *the Three* and more than one group known as *the Thirty.* The relationship of these groups to one another is not clear. What made matters worse for the ancient copyist was the fact that, in Hebrew, the spelling and sound of *officers, three,* and *thirty* are very similar. Apparently, there were times the copyists got confused. This would explain why Jashobeam is called "chief of the officers" in 1 Chronicles and "chief of the Three" in 2 Samuel.

We mention these things, not to compound confusion—nor to shake anyone's faith in inspiration—but simply to shed a little light on the reasons for some of the differences between these two parallel accounts in Scripture. Due to our own present lack of knowledge, we may not be able to resolve each apparent discrepancy. But it matters little, because these issues have relatively little to do with the thrust of the passage taken as a whole. We confidently place such matters in the hands of God, trust his faithful Word, and wait for our Lord's coming to dispel all the clouds that get in the way of us comprehending him fully.

The main point of the passage is this. The Chronicler wants to teach his people some things about the *caliber* of men who flocked to David's banner and also about the *character* of the man they served. Confident in the Lord and his anointed king, Eleazar is willing to face the enemy alone if need be. Through such faith, "the LORD brought about a great victory" (verse 14). He does the same today through men of God who display the same faith. In verses 15-19 we hear of a daring exploit carried out by three of David's mighty men. In it the holy writer opens up for us a window of understanding into David's character. The incident dates from David's outlaw days. At a low moment, when he felt the loneliness of his exile, he expressed a longing for a taste of the water of home. Three of his men crossed enemy lines to get it for him. We can applaud their zeal to serve, if not their judgment. Heartsick at the way these men risked their lives over such a trivial matter, David poured out the water as an offering to the Lord. He would not drink it. Life is precious and must not heedlessly be thrown away in any cause.

In verses 20 and 22 the Chronicler supplies us with the names of two men who achieved special prominence in David's army: Abishai and Benaiah. David promoted men to positions of leadership, not because of who they were or where they came from, but because of their zeal and skill in combat, as this section demonstrates. Abishai was distinguished by his ability to take on all comers, no matter what their quantity (even three hundred at a time!). Benaiah had the gift of defeating great adversaries, no matter what their quality. An interesting wordplay contained in verse 22 remains hidden to the reader of the English. The "best men" of Moab are literally called "mighty lions" in the Hebrew. Benaiah is given the credit for defeating three "lions"—two human and one animal! Not only that, but he was able, with only a club, to take on an Egyptian who was a true "Goliath" of a man (compare verse 23 with 1 Samuel 17:7).

The listing of mighty men from 26 to the end of the chapter is comprised of men who came mostly from the tribal areas belonging to Judah and Simeon. Since David was from the tribe of Judah, this is not unusual. What is surprising is the inclusion of two men who hailed from the tribe of Ephraim (Benaiah and Hurai, verses 31 and 32) and one who even came from Benjamin, the tribe of Saul (Azmaveth in verse 33). More surprising still is the inclusion of a number of foreigners: Zelek the Ammonite (verse 39), Uriah the Hittite (verse 41), and Ithmah the Moabite (verse 46). The Chronicler rounds off the list with a contingent of mighty men who came from the tribe of Reuben. Not only did David have the support of men from all over Israel—even Gentiles were attracted to the power of Israel's king and entered his service.

When we think of what these men were willing to dare for the sake of the Lord's anointed king (even though he was a sinful human being like themselves), how much more shall we, in the full boldness of faith, be willing to (as Luther put it) "do and endure all things, and live and die fully confident of God's mercy." We serve no mere man, but the Lord Jesus Christ!

12 These were the men who came to David at Ziklag, while he was banished from the presence of Saul son of Kish (they were among the warriors who helped him in battle; ²they were armed with bows and were able to shoot arrows or to sling stones right-handed or left-handed; they were kinsmen of Saul from the tribe of Benjamin):

³Ahiezer their chief and Joash the sons of Shemaah the Gibeathite; Jeziel and Pelet the sons of Azmaveth; Beracah, Jehu the Anathothite, ⁴and Ishmaiah the Gibeonite, a mighty man among the Thirty, who was a leader of the Thirty; Jeremiah, Jahaziel, Johanan, Jozabad the Gederathite, ⁵Eluzai, Jerimoth, Bealiah, Shemariah and Shephatiah the Haruphite; ⁶Elkanah, Isshiah, Azarel, Joezer and Jashobeam the Korahites; ⁷and Joelah and Zebadiah the sons of Jeroham from Gedor.

⁸Some Gadites defected to David at his stronghold in the desert. They were brave warriors, ready for battle and able to handle the shield and spear. Their faces were the faces of lions, and they were as swift as gazelles in the mountains.

⁹Ezer was the chief,
  Obadiah the second in command, Eliab the third,
¹⁰Mishmannah the fourth, Jeremiah the fifth,
¹¹Attai the sixth, Eliel the seventh,
¹²Johanan the eighth, Elzabad the ninth,
¹³Jeremiah the tenth and Macbannai the eleventh.

¹⁴These Gadites were army commanders; the least was a match for a hundred, and the greatest for a thousand. ¹⁵It was they who crossed the Jordan in the first month when it was overflowing all its banks, and they put to flight everyone living in the valleys, to the east and to the west.

¹⁶Other Benjamites and some men from Judah also came to David in his stronghold. ¹⁷David went out to meet them and said to them, "If you have come to me in peace, to help me, I am ready to have you unite with me. But if you have come to betray me to my enemies when my hands are free from violence, may the God of our fathers see it and judge you."

141

¹⁸Then the Spirit came upon Amasai, chief of the Thirty, and he said:

> "We are yours, O David!
>   We are with you, O son of Jesse!
> Success, success to you,
>   and success to those who help you,
>   for your God will help you."

So David received them and made them leaders of his raiding bands.

¹⁹Some of the men of Manasseh defected to David when he went with the Philistines to fight against Saul. (He and his men did not help the Philistines because, after consultation, their rulers sent him away. They said, "It will cost us our heads if he deserts to his master Saul.") ²⁰When David went to Ziklag, these were the men of Manasseh who defected to him: Adnah, Jozabad, Jediael, Michael, Jozabad, Elihu and Zillethai, leaders of units of a thousand in Manasseh. ²¹They helped David against raiding bands, for all of them were brave warriors, and they were commanders in his army. ²²Day after day men came to help David, until he had a great army, like the army of God.

Chapter 12 of 1 Chronicles might be entitled, "How God Helped David Attain His Royal Power." It shows how—over a period of time ranging from his outlaw days to his coronation—the hearts of all Israel's warriors were moved to acknowledge him as king. This first section deals with defectors from the tribes who rallied to David's cause while he was still under Saul's ban. Here we notice another feature about the Chronicler's writing style. He is not afraid to depart from the strict chronology of history if it serves its purpose. The defections mentioned here occurred before the coronation of David that was described at the beginning of 1 Chronicles 11. In his desire to give us a complete picture of the newly anointed king, the holy writer decided to follow a topical approach, rather than locking himself into describing events in a strict time sequence.

Ziklag (verse 1), a town in the south of Judah, was David's base of operations when he was in the service of the Philistine ruler Achish of Gath. This period in David's life came towards the end of his "outlaw" phase, just before Saul's defeat by the Philistines at Gilboa. At that time, some men from the tribe of Benjamin—Saul's own tribe—threw in their lot with David. Their specialty was fighting with bow or sling. Their skill of being able to use either hand to hurl projectiles is considered worthy of special mention. Their names are given in verses 3 through 7. Even natives of Gibeah, Saul's hometown, are listed among the refugees from that king's regime (verse 3)! Thus, Saul's fall and David's rise are also demonstrated by the fact that Saul's own kinsmen preferred an outlaw chosen by God to a king rejected by him.

Abandoning Saul's cause for David's was no easy matter. The men of Gad mentioned next (verses 8 through 14) serve to bring this out. They came over to David (the Hebrew in verse 8 reads literally "they separated themselves unto") when he was living in his desert stronghold. This period preceded his Ziklag phase and is described for us more fully in 1 Samuel 23:14 to 26:25. The Gadites lived east of the Jordan, an area particularly loyal to Saul. It was in the Transjordan that Ishbosheth, the son of Saul, set up his abortive rule over Israel after Saul's death. In order to defect to David, these men not only had to overcome the natural obstacle of the Jordan in flood, they also had to fight their way through their fellow-tribesmen who apparently tried to prevent their escape (verse 15). This tells us a great deal about the courage of those who came over to David and about their commitment to the one they saw as the Lord's truly anointed king.

When the Lord Jesus came—great David's greater Son—
not all in Israel had the faith to see him as "the Christ, the
Son of the living God" (Matthew 16:16). He offended their
sense of what the glorious King of Israel should do and say
(see John 6:60,66), and so they abandoned him. It is the
same way today for anyone who wants to follow the true
King. We can expect to endure the hostility of the world, the
hatred of the devil, and the unending harassment of our own
sinful flesh. Courage and commitment are called for, the
courage and commitment born of faith in him who "[has]
the words of eternal life" (John 6:68).

Another batch of defections to David during his "stronghold period" is presented in verses 16 through 18. The conversation between David and Amasai contains the chief
thought the Chronicler wants to put across in this chapter. At
this point in his career, David was still somewhat suspicious
of those who wanted to come over to his side. It was no wonder, since he had experienced hostility and betrayal by those
from whom he had every right to expect friendship. Nevertheless, he went to meet this latest contingent of men and was
willing to receive them. Characteristic of David was the way
he meekly placed his cause in God's hands, should they have
come only to betray him (verse 17). Around this same time,
he was inspired to sing, "Surely God is my help; the LORD is
the one who sustains me" (Psalm 54:4).

The Holy Spirit used this occasion to speak through Amasai, inspiring in him a wonderful confession of faith: "We
are yours, O David! We are with you, O son of Jesse! Success, success to you, and success to those who help you, for
your God will help you" (verse 18). These men had come to
believe that God's Word and promise were with David.
They were convinced that God was his helper, and so they
were also convinced that those who helped David would

win the ultimate victory. These defections of warriors from various parts of Israel were not the assembling of a group of malcontents around some bandit chief. They were evidence of God's gracious help and blessing upon David. They demonstrated that God was at work, bringing his chosen one to royal power over all Israel. *Help* is such a feeble word in English; in Hebrew it carries a much greater impact. It denotes that God is exercising his almighty power in David's behalf.

So, too, the word translated *success* in verse 18 requires some comment. Many readers may be familiar with the Hebrew word *shalom,* which the word *success* in our text is intended to reflect. A more literal translation might be *peace,* which was a very rich concept for the ancient Israelite. It meant not simply the absence of war, but the positive state of well-being that results when all things stand in harmony with God's will. It included material as well as spiritual well-being. We have no quarrel with the translation *success,* so far as it goes. We just wish to make the point that Amasai was expressing an expectation for David which went beyond mere *success,* as we usually think of it. He was expressing his confidence that God, through his chosen king, would give Israel the state of tranquility and well-being he had promised under Moses: "[The LORD your God] will give you rest from all your enemies . . . so that you will live in safety" (Deuteronomy 12:10).

We remind ourselves here that one of the Chronicler's goals in writing was to hold before his discouraged people the enduring hope of the Righteous King, still to come from David's house in fulfillment of all God's promises (see Introduction, pages 9 and 10). The holy writer shows his readers how, even during the dark period of David's outlaw days, God wanted his man to be sure that he would help him and give him suc-

145

cess over his enemies. Those words came true. So also the promises of the Righteous King would come true. The Chronicler's people could be certain of this. God was working in history, preparing things for his Son's rise to power. He would come to "rescue [them] from the hand of [their] enemies, and enable [them] to serve him without fear in holiness and righteousness all [their] days" (Luke 1:74,75). If we feel ourselves besieged by fightings without and by fears within, we can yet find comfort in God's promise. True peace is God's gift to us through Christ our Lord.

This portion of the chapter concludes with a list of defectors who came over to David at the eleventh hour when the battle between Saul and the Philistines was about to begin (verses 19 through 22). At the time David was in an extremely difficult position. He was still in the service of Achish, the Philistine ruler; yet he could hardly have wanted to join forces with the enemies of Israel in a pitched battle against his own people. As it turned out, God spared him the ordeal (verse 19). The other Philistine princes were leery of going to war with someone who might betray them at a critical moment. So Achish sent David back to Ziklag. It was there the Manassites mentioned in these verses joined him.

Verse 22 is significant for the way it repeats once more the chief point the Chronicler wishes to make, "Day after day men came to help David, until he had a great army, like the army of God." David's support in Israel grew by leaps and bounds, since God and the angel hosts were with him.

²³These are the numbers of the men armed for battle who came to David at Hebron to turn Saul's kingdom over to him, as the LORD had said:

²⁴men of Judah, carrying shield and spear—6,800 armed for battle;

²⁵men of Simeon, warriors ready for battle—7,100;

26 men of Levi—4,600, 27 including Jehoiada, leader of the
family of Aaron, with 3,700 men, 28 and Zadok, a brave
young warrior, with 22 officers from his family;

29 men of Benjamin, Saul's kinsmen—3,000, most of whom
had remained loyal to Saul's house until then;

30 men of Ephraim, brave warriors, famous in their own
clans—20,800;

31 men of half the tribe of Manasseh, designated by name
to come and make David king—18,000;

32 men of Issachar, who understood the times and knew
what Israel should do—200 chiefs, with all their relatives under their command;

33 men of Zebulun, experienced soldiers prepared for battle with every type of weapon, to help David with undivided loyalty—50,000;

34 men of Naphtali—1,000 officers, together with 37,000
men carrying shields and spears;

35 men of Dan, ready for battle—28,600;

36 men of Asher, experienced soldiers prepared for battle—
40,000;

37 and from east of the Jordan, men of Reuben, Gad and
the half-tribe of Manasseh, armed with every type of
weapon—120,000.

38 All these were fighting men who volunteered to serve in the
ranks. They came to Hebron fully determined to make David
king over all Israel. All the rest of the Israelites were also of
one mind to make David king. 39 The men spent three days
there with David, eating and drinking, for their families had
supplied provisions for them. 40 Also, their neighbors from as
far away as Issachar, Zebulun and Naphtali came bringing
food on donkeys, camels, mules and oxen. There were plentiful
supplies of flour, fig cakes, raisin cakes, wine, oil, cattle and
sheep, for there was joy in Israel.

The Chronicler brings us back again to Hebron where the
armies of Israel acclaimed David as their king. They came

"armed for battle" to turn the kingdom over to David "as the LORD had said" (verse 23). In truth, it was the Lord who had made David king; these troops were simply gathering to demonstrate their faith in the Word of God.

Several things are noteworthy about this list. First, *all* the tribes are represented, even the priestly tribe of Levi (normally not included in troop musters), and "Saul's kinsmen," the tribe of Benjamin. Next, the large numbers of those who came demonstrate that this was no grudging show of support performed out of a sense of fear or obligation. Around 340,000 assembled for the coronation, over two-thirds of whom came from the most distant tribes in the north and east of Israel. This spontaneous outpouring of love for David is so amazing that some have been led to question the size of the numbers. But all attempts to reduce them to a "more reasonable" size must be recognized as a venture of unbelief that always balks at clear statements of Scripture. There is something more curious in the account than the fact that so many came from the further reaches of Israel. It is the comparatively poor showing on the part of Judah and Simeon, who list 6,800 and 7,100 respectively. Perhaps it is true, as one commentator has suggested, that since these tribes had already enjoyed David's rule for eight years, they felt it sufficient to send only a representative number to show their continued support.

In addition to this, a person cannot fail to miss the Chronicler's emphasis on the *battle-readiness* of those who came: "Armed for battle" (verses 23 and 24), "ready for battle" (verses 25 and 35), "prepared for battle" (verses 33 and 36), "carrying shields and spears" (verses 24 and 34), "armed with every type of weapon" (verse 37). This display of military might on behalf of God's king must have rivaled even that awesome show of force we used to see parading around Red

Square in Moscow. Coupled with the outward readiness went their inner readiness. These troops came to help "with undivided loyalty" (verse 33), "fully determined" to make David king (verse 38).

It could well have been a sight like this that inspired David to utter the prophetic words of Psalm 110:3: "Your troops will be willing on your day of battle. Arrayed in holy majesty, from the womb of the dawn you will receive the dew of your youth." With hearts set free by the gospel, the Savior's troops, too, are completely willing to serve him! We cannot fail to win the victory over every evil force that stands against us. Our Lord and King rules in triumph over all.

Finally, the joyful feast of good things in plenty that is described in the final verses (39,40) must be seen as a foreshadowing of that great feast to come. Our King has promised, "People will come from east and west and north and south, and will take their places at the feast in the kingdom of God" (Luke 13:29). Then there truly will be "joy in Israel" (verse 40). It will be an eternal joy, a joy which no one will ever take away from us. We will be united, of one heart and mind with our King. In the words of a beautiful paraphrase of a passage in Revelation, our state will be that of those who "need no light, nor lamp, nor sun; for Christ will be their all!"

All Israel Fully United Under One God

a) Preparing to Restore the Ark—
David's Confidence Shattered

After telling us about the uniting of Israel under David, the Chronicler immediately proceeds to give the account of David's first attempt to move the ark, even though David must have done this *after* dealing with the Philistine threat described in 1 Chronicles 14. The holy writer has given it pride of place in order to emphasize the truth that Israel's king was above all meant to be a spiritual leader of God's people. David was far more than a great warrior who ushered in an era of material peace and prosperity. *As God's kind of king,* he gave spiritual matters top priority. He was the king who, more than any other, devoted himself to reverent worship of the true God. David reinvigorated the worship life of his people and put God back into the center of the Israelite kingdom.

13 **David conferred with each of his officers, the commanders of thousands and commanders of hundreds. ²He then said to the whole assembly of Israel, "If it seems good to you and if it is the will of the LORD our God, let us send word far and wide to the rest of our brothers throughout the territories of Israel, and also to the priests and Levites who are with them in their towns and pasturelands, to come and join us. ³Let us bring the ark of our God back to us, for we did not inquire of it during the reign of Saul." ⁴The whole assembly agreed to do this, because it seemed right to all the people.**

⁵So David assembled all the Israelites, from the Shihor River in Egypt to Lebo Hamath, to bring the ark of God from Kiriath Jearim.

More than seventy years had gone by since the ark of the covenant had occupied its rightful place at the center of Israelite worship. We do not need to trace its wanderings since that time when Israel lost it in battle to the Philistines. It is enough to say that the Philistines captured the ark, held onto it for a while, and then sent it back because it had proved to them to be more trouble than it was worth. It came to rest in the house of Abinadab, in Kiriath Jearim, a village about ten miles west of Jerusalem. For the complete story the reader will want to consult 1 Samuel, chapters 4 to 6. While the ark rested in obscurity in Abinadab's house, it was unable to serve its purpose as the focal point around which Israel could gather to worship God. Since God had given the ark to his people as the visible sign of his gracious presence among them, this was a very great loss indeed. For all those years something sacred had been missing in the heart of Israel.

Small wonder, then, that David took the first opportunity he could to restore the ark to the worship life of his people. All the tribes had united around him as their king; now let them unite in the true and complete worship of their God. The task was too important for David to attempt on his own. Only after consultation with the leaders of Israel did David think it right to proceed with his plan. Even then the goal was set under God—"if it is the will of the LORD" (1 Chronicles 13:2). David had no intention of proceeding rashly or in haste. After finding out that Israel's leaders agreed with his idea, he went on to assemble "all the Israelites" (verse 5) so that they could unite with him in this joyful task. "From the Shihor River in Egypt to Lebo Hamath" is a geographical way of emphasizing David's desire to have all his people participate. It means much the same thing as when we say, "All Americans, from Key West to Maine!"

Worship was never meant to be a one-man show, with the worship leader entertaining a chancel full of "pew potatoes." God's people worship as a body, each serving the others with his gifts. The presence of each person gives strength to the whole. David understood that. It is good to remind ourselves of this truth, too.

⁶David and all the Israelites with him went to Baalah of Judah (Kiriath Jearim) to bring up from there the ark of God the LORD, who is enthroned between the cherubim—the ark that is called by the Name.

It may be hard for us who live in the light of Jesus fully to understand what the ark of the covenant meant to Israel.

Even the language of this verse might strike us as difficult to understand. Yet the Chronicler uses words that would have been very easy for his original readers to grasp. It will be worth our while to unlock their meaning.

The believers in the Old Testament knew that God was an infinite Spirit whom "the heavens, even the highest heavens" (2 Chronicles 6:18) could not contain. They knew that no sinful human being could bear the sight if God should reveal himself in his full glory as the Almighty God. "You cannot see my face," God said to Moses, "for no one may see me and live" (Exodus 33:20). They were well aware of the fact that this Almighty Being was present everywhere—ruling, controlling, and sustaining the world that he had made. "'Can anyone hide in secret places so that I cannot see him?' declares the LORD. 'Do not I fill heaven and earth?' declares the LORD" (Jeremiah 23:24).

Yet as Luther once said, "It is one thing to know that God is there, quite another to know that he is there for you." Any person who has ever thought seriously about God has asked himself the question, "Where can I find God in a way I can grasp? He is a vast ocean; I am a tiny cup. How can I be sure this infinite being loves me, concerns himself with me, and has my interests in mind? Where can I meet God?"

For the Israelite, the answer to those questions was, "At the tabernacle," and later, "at the temple." The reason why the Old Testament believer could be so confident of this was that he knew that in tabernacle and temple he would find the ark of the covenant. And God had told Moses, "Before the ark of the Testimony—before the atonement cover that is over the Testimony—[there] I will meet with you" (Exodus 30:6). According to God's own word and promise, then, the believer knew that the infinite God had condescended to live among his people Israel, taking up "residence" in the sanctuary where the ark was placed. There they could find him in a way they could grasp. There God would show himself to them as the God of grace, "forgiving wickedness, rebellion and sin" (Exodus 34:7).

We who bask in the light of the New Testament know that this Old Testament shadow pointed ahead to God's coming down to us in human form in the person of Jesus. We look at the man Jesus, and we see God. The sight of God in his infinite majesty would crush us, since sinners cannot bear the weight of such glory. But the sight of Jesus, as the sacred text shows him to us, consoles and comforts us. There is nothing to be afraid of in the presence of the one who died for love of us.

7They moved the ark of God from Abinadab's house on a new cart, with Uzzah and Ahio guiding it. 8David and all the Israelites were celebrating with all their might before God, with songs and with harps, lyres, tambourines, cymbals and trumpets.

9When they came to the threshing floor of Kidon, Uzzah reached out his hand to steady the ark, because the oxen stumbled. 10The LORD's anger burned against Uzzah, and he struck him down because he had put his hand on the ark. So he died there before God.

11Then David was angry because the LORD's wrath had broken out against Uzzah, and to this day that place is called Perez Uzzah.

12David was afraid of God that day and asked, "How can I ever bring the ark of God to me?" 13He did not take the ark to be with him in the City of David. Instead, he took it aside to the house of Obed-Edom the Gittite. 14The ark of God remained with the family of Obed-Edom in his house for three months, and the LORD blessed his household and everything he had.

How quickly triumph turned into tragedy that day! The infraction for which the Lord held Uzzah accountable seems to us to be a relatively minor one, given the pious intent of those present. Yet, when we keep in mind what the ark of the covenant was and consider this incident in its Old Testament context, we will see that it was not a minor misstep at all.

Apparently taking his cue from the way the pagan Philistines had transported the ark many years before, David had it placed on a new cart drawn by two oxen. This method, however, was not the way in which God had commanded the ark to be moved. "Make poles of acacia wood and overlay them with gold," God had instructed his people through Moses. "Insert the poles into the rings on the sides of the chest to carry it" (Exodus 25:13,14). Why David did not carry out that command, we do not know. Was it simply ignorance on his part? Did he know of it but not think it important enough to bother with? The first possibility seems the more likely, but it does not excuse David's failure. He still had shown a disregard for the holy things of God and for God's holy Word. He had consulted with his princes and his people, but he had not consulted God nor listened to his Word on this matter.

As a result, the procession to Jerusalem became a disaster looking for a place to happen. There is a strong flavor of dramatic irony in the account. King and people are dancing and celebrating "with all their might" in the presence of the Lord, yet all the while storm clouds of wrath are gathering. At the threshing floor of Kidon (or, possibly, Nacon as 2 Samuel 6 has it), God's wrath "breaks out" with the devastating force of lightning against Uzzah. The cattle stumble, the cart shakes, the ark looks as if it might tumble out. Acting on a natural impulse to protect the holy cargo, Uzzah touches the ark to hold it steady and immediately pays for that act with his life. God had strictly forbidden anyone to touch the holy furnishings of the tabernacle (Numbers 4:15). He had also prescribed the penalty of death for those who disregarded his command. In that moment of truth on Kidon's threshing floor, Uzzah and all Israel learned to their sorrow that God meant exactly what he said.

We no longer have God-prescribed "holy furnishings" to reverence as did God's Old Testament people. Living in the times of fulfillment, we no longer see God acting in judgment at all times with quite the same immediacy when the line of his will is crossed. (Although as the account of Ananias and Sapphira makes clear, God certainly hasn't tied his hands behind his back!) The Apostle Paul says that God is pleased to treat us as "grown-ups," no longer as children in elementary school who need a stricter discipline (see Galatians 3:4 to 4:6). Led by the Spirit of Christ, we have great freedom in the outward, ceremonial aspects of worship.

Yet in speaking of another Old Testament account in which God intervened to punish sin, Paul also wrote, "Now these things occurred as examples to keep us from setting our hearts on evil things as they did" (1 Corinthians 10:6). Across the ages, the Chronicler speaks to believers in the New Testament with great clarity. He tells us, "Don't kid yourselves. God is serious about his law. He expects it to be obeyed. And he expects it to be obeyed completely, with outward actions and inward motivations both conforming exactly to his stated will. God looks at the heart, to be sure, but he also looks at the act." It is an empty hope to believe—as so many do nowadays—that as long as we feel good about what we're doing, it is a good thing to do. If we pray about it, ask for God's guidance, and if it feels right, then it is right, even if there may be some troublesome Bible passages in which God may say it is not right. Against those thoughts we must firmly say, "However good the intentions may be, they cannot purify an action that is in itself wrong."

David responded to God's "outburst" of anger against Uzzah with an anger of his own. The text does not say he was angry with God. He may have been initially, as his personal triumph turned into a terrible tragedy for which he could not evade responsibility. His plans had been frustrated. His will had been broken. Yet even if he was momentarily angry with the Lord, his believing self must quickly have reasserted control over his emotions, transforming the anger into repentant grieving for his sin and a holy fear of God. Certainly we know that he came to understand what his guilt was, since the next time the ark was transported, he would give explicit instructions to "do it right" (see 1 Chronicles 15:3 and 15:12-15).

"David was afraid of God that day," might just as well be translated, "David stood in awe of God that day." This entire affair had renewed in him a sense of what a holy God Israel had, how he stood apart from sinners, and how he would not let the guilty go unpunished. David had learned to be suspicious of his own will and less inclined to follow his own thoughts and desires, however pious they might have seemed to himself and to others. David had also learned that God's will was to be eagerly sought out and then conscientiously carried out in every matter. These are good things for every Christian to learn. As we pray, "Thy will be done," we need to ask God that his will be formed in us, rather than that he conform to our will. We need to ask God to give us patience as he breaks our will and shows us the more excellent way. We need to beg the God and Father of our Lord Jesus, not only to give us the grace to seek out what he wants for us in any given matter, but also to want what he wants with a holy and ardent desire.

It was a considerably chastened David who, as the day was drawing to a close, accepted the change in plans that God had imposed on him and took the ark to the house of Obed-Edom the Gittite instead of to Jerusalem. There it remained for three months as David waited for God to make clear what he wanted Israel to do with his ark. By way of reply we read that, "The LORD blessed [Obed-Edom's] household and everything he had" (1 Chronicles 13:14). Israel's God was a God of grace as well as a God of wrath. By blessing Obed-Edom, God made it clear to Israel that he had not abandoned them in his anger. He was still the God who loved them. He intended to keep his promise to save them.

b) Preparing to Restore the Ark—
David's Confidence Regained

God had given David good reason to remain confident in his help, even though it may have seemed for a time as if he had turned his back on his anointed king. The Chronicler continues by listing some of the ways God showed his love to David. As we noted before, this chapter does not maintain a strict chronological order with either the chapter preceding or the one following. Chronology is not the Chronicler's concern here. Instead, he wants to point out to us that David had enjoyed God's help and blessing in many ways. There was no reason for him to suppose that God would not continue to help him now, even after Perez Uzzah. For that reason—and to encourage us to lay hold of the same truth by faith—the holy writer arranges his material the way he does.

14 Now Hiram king of Tyre sent messengers to David, along with cedar logs, stonemasons and carpenters to build a palace for him. ²And David knew that the LORD had established him as king over Israel and that his kingdom had been highly exalted for the sake of his people Israel.

³In Jerusalem David took more wives and became the father of more sons and daughters. ⁴These are the names of the children born to him there: Shammua, Shobab, Nathan, Solomon,

⁵Ibhar, Elishua, Elpelet, ⁶Nogah, Nepheg, Japhia, ⁷Elishama, Beeliada and Eliphelet.

Shortly after David came to power in Jerusalem, Hiram, king of Tyre, concluded an alliance with him. Hiram was one of the first to recognize that there had been a shift in the balance of power among the nearby nations. David was now a man he needed to reckon with. The kingdom of Israel was a crossroads, through which many important trade routes of the ancient world passed. With David's rise to power, the Israelites now controlled those vital trade links. Tyre was a port city to the north of Israel along the Mediterranean coast. The Tyrians were great sea-traders, people who depended for their very existence upon the free flow of goods between nations. As their king, Hiram could not afford to ignore David. We, of course, see the handiwork of God in placing his Old Testament people where he did in the world.

There were other practical reasons why an alliance between the city of Tyre and the kingdom of Israel was "a marriage made in heaven." Perched on a rocky coast with mountains reaching right up to the sea, Tyre was not located in the world's most ideal spot for agriculture. Their food had to be imported. Israel was a farming country. They could supply what Tyre lacked. On the other hand, Israel did not have a ready supply of the massive timbers for which Tyre was famous, the so-called "cedars of Lebanon." While this dearth may not have caused Israel any great sense of deprivation in the past, as the kingdom became more organized and centralized under David and Solomon, she would need to find both the materials and the skilled craftsmen to erect her public buildings. Tyre could supply what Israel lacked.

David saw the hand of God behind his rise to prominence. Unlike a later empire builder by the name of Nebuchadnezzar, David did not say, "Is not this the great [kingdom] I have built . . . by my mighty power and for the glory of my majesty?" (Daniel 4:30). For David, Hiram's emissaries were evidence that God had blessed him "for the sake of his people Israel" (verse 2). This was not the exaltation of a person, but of a people, and not an exaltation of a people for their own sake, but as the bearers of the promise that through them "all nations on earth [would] be blessed" (Genesis 22:18).

There are times in our lives as individuals and in our corporate lives as members of a church that we may enjoy the blessings of God, not only in an inward way by faith, but also in an outward way by sight. We attain some personal goals, achieve some personal success, and receive recognition from those around us. Our church is growing, the statistics look good, and people start asking about our "methods." "You must be doing something right," they say. It is at times like these when it is especially important to remember that God blesses us, not because we have personally earned or deserved it for all our good "doing," but for the sake of our Lord Jesus Christ—because of his "doing" and dying on the cross. With David, we ought to boast not in ourselves, but in the Lord.

As another sign that God's favor rested on king David, the Chronicler gives us the names of the sons born to him while he was living in Jerusalem. We note Solomon's name listed among the thirteen who are mentioned. Serious students of Scripture have long been troubled by the references to "wives" in connection with several of the great men of faith in the Old Testament. It is troubling because we recognize that God's will for marriage—ordained in the beginning in Genesis 2 and reasserted by Christ in Matthew 19—is that one man ought to marry one woman and remain with her until parted by death. Passages like the one before us increase our difficulty, because there can be no question that David's polygamous marriages are mentioned in a context where the holy writer is describing how God blessed David with many sons. How can God bless that which he abhors?

To begin with, it needs to be said that however one resolves this difficulty, Christians are bound by the will of God as it is expressed in the clear passages of Scripture that talk about marriage. To argue anything else from this passage would be to use something uncertain to throw into confusion that which is clear. In addition, we should observe that what God allows or even commands in particular cases cannot be made into universal truths. If we would permit that method of interpretation to stand, it would be easy for anyone to turn Scripture inside-out. For example, God commanded Abraham to sacrifice his firstborn son Isaac. We have no such command. Let no one dare to justify the sacrifice of their children on the basis of what God told Abraham to do.

Finally, the cases of plural marriage described in the Old Testament are hardly examples of wedded bliss and harmony. No matter what reference you may look up—Abraham, Jacob, David, or Solomon—you will see a great deal of heartache and family strife burdening the lives of everyone involved. After reading those accounts, who would be so bold to say that God wants us to pattern our family life after theirs? Rather, their unhappiness encourages us all the more to seek our marital happiness in conforming our lives to the pattern laid down in Eden. Let one man be joined to one woman, and let both rest assured that their spouses are God's gift to them.

⁸When the Philistines heard that David had been anointed king over all Israel, they went up in full force to search for him, but David heard about it and went out to meet them. ⁹Now the Philistines had come and raided the Valley of Rephaim; ¹⁰so David inquired of God: "Shall I go and attack the Philistines? Will you hand them over to me?"

The LORD answered him, "Go, I will hand them over to you."

¹¹So David and his men went up to Baal Perazim, and there he defeated them. He said, "As waters break out, God has broken out against my enemies by my hand." So that place was called Baal Perazim. ¹²The Philistines had abandoned their gods there, and David gave orders to burn them in the fire.

¹³Once more the Philistines raided the valley; ¹⁴so David inquired of God again, and God answered him, "Do not go straight up, but circle around them and attack them in front of the balsam trees. ¹⁵As soon as you hear the sound of marching in the tops of the balsam trees, move out to battle, because that will mean God has gone out in front of you to strike the Philistine army." ¹⁶So David did as God commanded him, and they struck down the Philistine army, all the way from Gibeon to Gezer.

¹⁷So David's fame spread throughout every land, and the LORD made all the nations fear him.

To complete the chapter, the Chronicler cites a third example of how God's favor rested on David. This section describes his victories over the Philistines, the enemies of Israel whom Saul had been unable to overcome.

It must have caused no little consternation among the five cities of Philistia when they suddenly realized that this little pet dog had slipped his leash and turned into a lion! Until David had been anointed king over all Israel, Philistia had had no reason to fear him or to suppose he was anything more than one of their vassals. After all, hadn't he served under their own prince Achish, ruler of Gath? Achish had not found anything to complain about concerning him (see 1 Samuel 29:3). But once the tribes had rallied to David's banner and made him king over all, the Philistines knew they had a problem on their hands. David's conquest of Jerusalem was proof of it. This was not the act of a king who intended to stay quietly in the background. There was no time to waste. The full weight of Philistine armed power was brought to bear upon the problem.

Leaving their homeland on the coastal plain, the Philistines invaded the hill-country of Israel, thrusting deep into David's new kingdom. They overran the valley of Rephaim, located just to the south and east of Jerusalem. The Hebrew word used to describe the Philistine activity in the valley conjures up images of marauding bands of soldiers stripping the land and terrorizing farming hamlets. Clearly the Philistines were issuing a challenge to their former vassal: "If you want to keep your kingdom, you will have to fight us for it!"

David calmly took the time to "inquire of God" (verse 10). Though the crisis was upon him and though it seemed as if there could be no real question as to what his response should be, David knew that "There is . . . no plan that can succeed against the LORD" (Proverbs 21:30). What a tremendous promise he received by way of reply! The God of Israel assured him that he would hand the Philistines over to him. Armed by the word of God, David walked by faith into battle and received the promised blessing.

David then worshiped God by word and by deed. He carried out the Lord's command, given through Moses, to "burn the images" of the powerless heathen gods. They were detestable to the true God (Deuteronomy 7:25). He also gave glory to the Lord in a poetic exclamation, "As waters break out, God has broken out against my enemies by my hand" (verse 11). With the unstoppable power of floodwaters bursting through a retaining wall or surging over the banks of a river, God burst out in judgment against the enemies of his people and used David's hand to defeat them. To commemorate the victory, the battlefield was named Baal Perazim, literally, "the Lord who bursts forth."

It is this section that helps us to see how chapters 13 and 14 are connected in the Chronicler's mind. In chapter 13 we had an *outburst* of God's wrath against his people for failing to seek his will and comply with his commands. The result? Plans to move the ark had to be temporarily shelved. Here in chapter 14 David seeks the Lord's will, carries out his commands, and there is an *outburst* of judgment on Israel's enemies. The Chronicler is telling his people that the one whose mercies never fail will not abandon them. One outburst of wrath should not cause them to give up. Let them remember the way he also burst forth against those that threatened them. "His anger lasts only a moment, but his favor lasts a lifetime; weeping may remain for a night, but rejoicing comes in the morning" (Psalm 30:5). The stage has been set for the description of the second attempt to move the ark.

Before launching into that description, however, the Chronicler gives one more example of the Lord's steadfast love in helping David. Bloodied, but not completely beaten, the Philistines returned again to challenge the rule of God's anointed king. Again David consulted the Lord, only this time he received more explicit instructions as to how the battle was to be fought. He was not to meet the Philistines head-on. Rather, he was to go around the side to a forest of balsam trees. When he heard the sound of marching in the treetops, he would know that the Lord was giving him the signal to move out and attack the enemy.

An Israelite familiar with the account of Joshua's conquest of the promised land would have understood something here that might not be readily apparent to us. God was going to give an audible demonstration to his people that the "commander of the LORD's army" of angelic warriors would fight this battle alongside the armies of Israel (see Joshua 5:13-15). David would hear more than the rustle of the leaves in the balsam trees. He would actually hear the sound of God's angelic armies going forth to fight his battles!

We are not to think that the Lord inspired David with a brilliant battle plan so that he was able to win the victory over the Philistines. This instruction to move over to the balsam trees did not necessarily have to have a strategic motivation behind it. There are many cases in the Old Testament when God's instructions to the leaders of the Israelite armies seem to fly in the face of good military common sense. Joshua's marching around the walls of Jericho is just one such example. The whole point of God giving such explicit instructions is simply to make clear that God is in charge and that this is his battle. Victory is assured because the Lord commands Israel and fights alongside them with his angelic armies.

David obeyed the Lord and so became his instrument in crushing the Philistines. He not only defeated them on the battlefield, but he also was able to secure a complete victory by pursuing them from the heights of Gibeon down to the coastal plain. He broke off his "hot pursuit" only when he reached the town of Gezer, situated near the border of the enemy homeland. The shame of Gilboa (10:8,9) was erased. The period when the Philistines dominated Israel had come to end. What faithless Saul could not do, faithful David did do. God gave Israel success through his anointed one.

As a result David's fame spread far and wide. The heathen nations sat up and took notice. God himself was at work in this process the Chronicler notes. The expression for the fear that God put in the hearts of the nations surrounding Israel calls to mind a promise God had made to his people during Moses' era (see Deuteronomy 2:25; 11:25). He had pledged to inflict an incapacitating dread and horror of Israel in the hearts of the heathen. This supernatural dread would unman them in battle, rendering them unable to fight against God's people. It would move them to leave Israel alone. During the time of Joshua, this fear proved to be Israel's secret weapon (see Joshua 2:9). With the rise of faithful David, that weapon was restored to Israel's arsenal.

God is fearsome in his judgments and fierce in his zeal to fight for his people through his anointed king. This was true not only for ancient Israel; it is true also for God's people today. In all things Jesus, our anointed King, sought to do the will of the Father. This was especially true of the last great battle of his earthly ministry. After he had placed his life into the hands of the Father, he followed his will to the cross for our sakes. As the "commander of the army of the LORD" came in human form, he succeeded in doing what no mere human king could ever have done. He stormed the gates of hell, destroyed the devil's power over us, and set us free from our miserable slavery to death and sin. All praise be to God alone!

Having secured that victory for us, the Lord's Anointed now rules at God's right hand, subduing all our enemies and working in all things for our good. Those who submit in faith to his rule become part of his family. Those who oppose him will only be crushed in the end. For us who know him, it is particularly comforting to remember that the one who fights for us has all God's resources at his disposal, since he himself is God. When we are overcome with a sense of our own weakness, we need to remember that his power has no limit. There are times when we all feel the anxieties of life press hard on us, and the dread of death overshadowing us. Often we feel the shame of realizing how easily our enemy, the devil, can get the better of us. Then it is good to know that we have a powerful Lord on our side to fight and win our battles for us. In him we cannot fail.

All Israel Fully United Under One God

c) Success! The Ark Comes to David's City

"Well begun is half done." Had David believed in that proverb, he might have left the ark where it lay at Obed-Edom's house. His first attempt to move it had not gone well at all. Yet with heart refreshed in the knowledge of God's steadfast love, David resolved once more to venture out in faith and bring the ark up to Jerusalem.

15 After David had constructed buildings for himself in the City of David, he prepared a place for the ark of God and pitched a tent for it. ²Then David said, "No one but the Levites may carry the ark of God, because the LORD chose them to carry the ark of the LORD and to minister before him forever."

³David assembled all Israel in Jerusalem to bring up the ark of the LORD to the place he had prepared for it. ⁴He called together the descendants of Aaron and the Levites:

⁵From the descendants of Kohath,
Uriel the leader and 120 relatives;
⁶from the descendants of Merari,
Asaiah the leader and 220 relatives;
⁷from the descendants of Gershon,
Joel the leader and 130 relatives;
⁸from the descendants of Elizaphan,
Shemaiah the leader and 200 relatives;
⁹from the descendants of Hebron,
Eliel the leader and 80 relatives;
¹⁰from the descendants of Uzziel,
Amminadab the leader and 112 relatives.

¹¹Then David summoned Zadok and Abiathar the priests, and Uriel, Asaiah, Joel, Shemaiah, Eliel and Amminadab the Levites. ¹²He said to them, "You are the heads of the Levitical families; you and your fellow Levites are to consecrate your-

selves and bring up the ark of the LORD, the God of Israel, to the place I have prepared for it. [13]It was because you, the Levites, did not bring it up the first time that the LORD our God broke out in anger against us. We did not inquire of him about how to do it in the prescribed way." [14]So the priests and Levites consecrated themselves in order to bring up the ark of the LORD, the God of Israel. [15]And the Levites carried the ark of God with the poles on their shoulders, as Moses had commanded in accordance with the word of the LORD.

A sense of God's grace and mercy does not make someone soft on sin or careless in the way he serves his God. David made careful preparations before moving the ark the second time. He pitched a tent for it on prepared ground. He gave an explicit command, "Levites alone are to have charge of carrying it." This time God's Word would be his guide from beginning to end. He assembled "all Israel" once more and took special care in mustering the Levites according to their clans and clan leaders. He held a meeting with the two chief priests and the Levitical clan-heads to plan out and prepare for the move.

We note in passing the presence of three major sub-clans besides the expected grouping of the house of Levi under his sons Kohath, Merari, and Gershon. At this time the houses of Elizaphan, Hebron, and Uzziel had also become clans in their own right. All of them traced their descent from Kohath, son of Levi.

If we compare this account with its parallel in 2 Samuel 6, we observe that, in 2 Samuel, more of David's personality as a worshiper comes out. The picture there is of a man who has given himself over completely to the events of the day, so much so that his ecstatic dancing strikes his wife Michal as being a bit much. In 1 Chronicles, David's role as king, leader, and organizer is brought to the fore. The careful preparations he makes here for the moving of the ark serve to give us a foretaste of the tremendous work he later put into organizing the ongoing worship of God at Jerusalem and his careful preparations for the building of the temple.

Sometimes we act as if there is a great gulf fixed between formal worship and personal worship, between careful organization and the spirit of spontaneity. These parallel accounts lead us to conclude that it doesn't have to be a matter of either/or. David's conduct demonstrates we can be spontaneous and personally involved in worship that has been carefully organized.

Before we take a closer look at the meeting held with the religious leaders of Israel, perhaps a word needs to be said about the words in verse one, "He prepared a place for the ark of God and pitched a *tent* for it." The reader should not confuse this temporary tent, used to house the ark, with the tabernacle fashioned by Moses according to God's design. The tabernacle was located at that time in Gibeon, where offerings and sacrifices were still regularly being made (see 1 Chronicles 16:39). This tent in Jerusalem was intended to serve only to house the ark in the interim, until a permanent temple for it could be built. That temple, once built, would replace both tent and tabernacle. Until then, there would be two focal points for Israel's worship: the ark of the covenant in Jerusalem and the tabernacle at Gibeon.

In the meeting with the religious leaders, the first item on David's agenda was the matter of ritual preparation. He commanded the priests and Levites to "consecrate themselves" for the task of bringing the ark up to Jerusalem (verse 12). From other passages in Scripture (notably Exodus 19:10-15, Exodus 29:1-9, and Exodus 30:19,20) we understand David to be telling these men to prepare themselves and those under them by ritual washings, by abstaining from sexual relations for a time, and by the wearing of special garments. Those who would participate in this holy procession were to set themselves completely apart to the Lord and to prepare themselves in body and mind to serve him only.

We, too, needed a special washing before we were fit to worship the Lord with our lives. We needed the bath of Holy Baptism, by which Christ cleansed us and presented us to himself as a radiant people, "without stain or wrinkle or any other blemish, but holy and blameless" (Ephesians 5:27). In that same water, Christ met us and clothed us with the holiest of garments: his irreproachable righteousness. All who have been baptized have been "clothed . . . with Christ," as Paul says (Galatians 3:27). No one can stand in God's presence without this garment (see Matthew 22:11-13). While we are free from the ritual requirements of the Old Testament, no sinner dare think he can come before God without preparation or handle holy things with careless unconcern. Paul says in another place, "Whoever eats the bread or drinks the cup of the Lord in an unworthy manner will be guilty of sinning against the body and blood of the Lord. A man ought to examine himself before he eats of the bread and drinks of the cup" (1 Corinthians 11:27,28). That preparation is complete when the penitent sinner holds fast in faith to Jesus, the friend of sinners.

David showed that he was a penitent sinner by confessing his sin publicly before the leaders of the people in verse 13, "It was because you, the Levites, did not bring it up the first time that the LORD our God broke out in anger against us. We did not inquire of him about how to do it in the prescribed way." David is not blaming the Levites, as if the failure had been solely theirs. He says "*We* did not inquire of the LORD." To paraphrase David's thoughts here, he is saying, "In ignorance, you Levites failed to bring up the ark according to

169

God's law given by Moses. Yet ignorance does not excuse our sin. We did not know, but we didn't try to find out either! We simply blundered ahead thinking any old way would do. That is why the Lord broke out in anger against us." A literal translation of the last phrase of the verse reads, "We did not inquire of him . . . *according to judgment."* With this phrase David refers to a specific command or judgment that had been laid down in the law of Moses. In this case, it would be the command we referred to in the last chapter, found in Exodus 25:13,14, concerning the prescribed method for carrying the ark. David is saying that he had failed to read his Bible carefully before going ahead with his plan. If he had, he would have known what the Lord wanted him and the Levites to do.

We can learn from David's example here about the nature of leadership in the church. To be a leader of God's people does not mean a person always has to be right. Neither does true leadership mean one has to pretend, for the sake of saving face, that all past decisions were good decisions. Rather, it means to confess the wrong when wrong has been done and to acknowledge in a forthright way the sins of the past. We do this, not so as to wallow in guilt, but to demonstrate God's grace in forgiving us. It also clears the way for making right in the future what has been wrong in the past. Finally, David's example teaches us that one who leads in the church needs to let his plans flow out of and be shaped by the Word of God, not his own personal desires.

¹⁶David told the leaders of the Levites to appoint their brothers as singers to sing joyful songs, accompanied by musical instruments: lyres, harps and cymbals.

¹⁷So the Levites appointed Heman son of Joel; from his brothers, Asaph son of Berekiah; and from their brothers the Merarites, Ethan son of Kushaiah; ¹⁸and with them their

brothers next in rank: Zechariah, Jaaziel, Shemiramoth, Jehiel, Unni, Eliab, Benaiah, Maaseiah, Mattithiah, Eliphelehu, Mikneiah, Obed-Edom and Jeiel, the gatekeepers.

[19]The musicians Heman, Asaph and Ethan were to sound the bronze cymbals; [20]Zechariah, Aziel, Shemiramoth, Jehiel, Unni, Eliab, Maaseiah and Benaiah were to play the lyres according to *alamoth*, [21]and Mattithiah, Eliphelehu, Mikneiah, Obed-Edom, Jeiel and Azaziah were to play the harps, directing according to *sheminith*. [22]Kenaniah the head Levite was in charge of the singing; that was his responsibility because he was skillful at it.

[23]Berekiah and Elkanah were to be doorkeepers for the ark. [24]Shebaniah, Joshaphat, Nethanel, Amasai, Zechariah, Benaiah and Eliezer the priests were to blow trumpets before the ark of God. Obed-Edom and Jehiah were also to be doorkeepers for the ark.

David wanted the ministry of music to be featured prominently on the day he moved the ark. To achieve his goal he asked the Levitical leaders to appoint people to serve in that capacity. A list of all the appointments according to rank follows in verses 17 and 18. Their individual responsibilities are described in verses 19 through 21.

In the first rank we see the names Heman, Asaph, and Ethan—names familiar to us already from 1 Chronicles 6. In the second rank of musicians, we notice the name of Obed-Edom. It seems likely that he is the same man in whose household the ark found a temporary resting-place.

While it is impossible for us to reproduce the exact sound of the music performed by these musicians of ancient Israel, a closer look at their instruments gives us some idea of what it might have been like. Heman, Asaph, and Ethan were given the assignment of playing *the bronze cymbals*. It seems likely that these were two large disks of bronze, held one in each hand. No doubt they were played by bringing the hands together at rhythmic intervals. Next came the people who were appointed *to play the lyres according to alamoth* (verse 20). No one is quite sure about the meaning of the phrase *according to alamoth*. It probably is some kind of musical direction (see also Psalm 46:1). Some have suggested that it means "playing on a higher octave." The lyre was a large stringed instrument played by plucking the strings with the hand or with a pick. The last rank of instrumentalists mentioned in verse 21 was skillful in playing the *harps according to sheminith*. Again, no one is quite sure what *sheminith* means. All we can say is that it appears to be some kind of technical musical term (see Psalm 6:1; 12:1). If the world lasts another 2,000 years, it may one day be difficult for our descendants to know what we meant with the word *andante* on top of a piece of music. Similar to, but smaller than the the lyres mentioned in verse 20, were the harps played by Obed-Edom and the others.

This list of instruments is by no means a complete catalogue of the musical resources available to the ancient Israelites. They were just the ones used the day the ark was moved. We note also that the instrumental musicians were appointed to give beauty and emphasis to the psalms sung by Kenaniah and the choirs. Kenaniah himself was chosen, because of his skill, to train and lead others in choral singing.

In addition to the Levitical singers and musicians, David arranged for the priests to participate as well. They were to blow the trumpets at the head of the procession. The king had learned his lesson. He was careful to observe God's command given by Moses, "The sons of Aaron, the priests, are to blow the trumpets" (Numbers 10:8). The priests selected for this honor are mentioned by name. Their trumpets were made out of beaten silver and had a long, straight stem that fanned out at the end. As such we can make a distinction between them and the rams' horns mentioned below in verse 28. Through Moses, God had directed the priests to use the trumpets to call on him whenever the Israelites marched into battle against their enemies. They were also to use them to mark special days of celebration, such as this occasion. God then promised to hear and answer with his help (see Numbers 10:9,10).

The mention of "doorkeepers for the ark" in verse 24 seems somewhat unusual in a listing of musical participants in the march to bring the ark up to Jerusalem. It is possible they had some special function within the procession, perhaps to provide security around the ark itself. In any case, after reading this whole description, a person has no doubt that David did everything within his power to prepare for the day when this visible sign of the invisible God would once again take its rightful place at the heart of Israelite worship. It was bound to be a beautiful and soul-stirring event.

²⁵So David and the elders of Israel and the commanders of units of a thousand went to bring up the ark of the covenant of the LORD from the house of Obed-Edom, with rejoicing. ²⁶Because God had helped the Levites who were carrying the ark of the covenant of the LORD, seven bulls and seven rams were sacrificed. ²⁷Now David was clothed in a robe of fine linen, as were all the Levites who were carrying the ark, and as were the singers, and Kenaniah, who was in charge of the singing of the choirs. David also wore a linen ephod. ²⁸So all Israel brought up the ark of the covenant of the LORD with shouts, with the sounding of rams' horns and trumpets, and of cymbals, and the playing of lyres and harps.

²⁹As the ark of the covenant of the LORD was entering the City of David, Michal daughter of Saul watched from a win-

dow. And when she saw King David dancing and celebrating, she despised him in her heart.

16 They brought the ark of God and set it inside the tent that David had pitched for it, and they presented burnt offerings and fellowship offerings before God. ²After David had finished sacrificing the burnt offerings and fellowship offerings, he blessed the people in the name of the LORD. ³Then he gave a loaf of bread, a cake of dates and a cake of raisins to each Israelite man and woman.

While it is parallel to the account in 2 Samuel 6, the Chronicler's description of the moving of the ark adds many details that round out the picture for us. The procession was led by David, the elders of Israel, and the commanders of Israel's army. This was a national day of celebration! In 2 Samuel we are told that, once the Levites had successfully walked six steps with their holy burden, David sacrificed a bull and a fattened calf in thanksgiving. The Chronicler adds that David sacrificed another seven bulls and seven rams besides—possibly when the Levites had completed their task—"because God had helped [them]" (verse 26). We take this to mean that David was moved to thank God for having enabled the Levites to carry the ark safely to its destination. Through the disaster of Perez Uzzah God had made David doubly aware that all is by grace—all we are, all we have, all we do. His sacrifices were a heartfelt acknowledgment of that fact. In a similar way we are moved "in view of God's mercy, to offer [our] bodies as living sacrifices" (Romans 12:1). This is our spiritual act of worship. We owe God our thanks for every breath we take. Without his merciful help, we cannot take a step in any direction.

The last two verses of chapter 15 form an interesting contrast. "All Israel" brought the ark up to Jerusalem with music and shouts of joy. The mouth will speak what the heart is full of. And yet not quite all were able to take pleasure in the day. There was one who saw the celebration and found something to despise. Michal, Saul's daughter, apparently had inherited her father's lack of spiritual insight. She looked down on David's joyful dancing and found it contemptible. So, too, others today may observe the joy God's people have in their Savior and despise it. This is no great wonder, since such people do not understand the reason for such joy. True worship is not always and immediately accessible to everyone. Some may never "get" what's going on.

Of far greater interest to us in these verses is the Chronicler's description of David. He makes it clear that on that happy day David served not only as a king, but also as a priest. For example, in verse 27 we are told that he wore "a robe of fine linen," a costly type of garment most often associated in Scripture with the high priest (see Exodus 28:4 and Leviticus 8:7). Underneath the robe he wore a "linen ephod." An ephod was a close-fitting garment without sleeves, reaching down to the knees. Only priests could wear such a garment. In chapter 16 we also notice that David offered sacrifices and blessed the people. These were actions that were the sole prerogative of the priests serving in their role as mediators between God and man (see Numbers 6:22-27 and Numbers 18:1,7).

These details would have been obvious to an Israelite reading this account. He would have concluded that David was truly an extraordinary individual, since he combined in himself the offices of both priest and king and was both a mediator for and a protector of God's people. When we recall that part of the Chronicler's purpose is to foreshadow the coming of the Lord's Anointed, we can readily see what his goal is here. Through his description of David as a priest-king, the holy writer is reminding his people of the King who would come to offer a better sacrifice, so that all people might be set free from sin to "serve the living God" (Hebrews 9:14). David's life formed a definite pattern in history, and the pattern of his life served to delineate the kind of individual the Messiah was going to be. We see the fulfillment of all these patterns in Jesus. He truly was a priestly king and a royal priest. Through passages like these, the Holy Spirit means to strengthen our faith in the God who works out all things in the vast sweep of history to save.

With royal generosity David portioned out gifts to each one of the assembled worshipers. He supplied not only the necessities ("a loaf of bread"), but also luxuries ("a cake of dates and a cake of raisins"). It is likely that these gifts were distributed as the worshiper's portion of the fellowship offerings mentioned in verse two. Fellowship offerings, as their name suggests, were intended to express the fellowship and harmony that existed among the Israelite, his God, and all who participated in the sacrificial worship. The worshipers consumed the sacrifices in a communal meal, eating and drinking in the presence of God and the priest.

We, too, have received a meal from our Priest and King. In the Lord's Supper he comes to us with royal generosity and gives us more than we could ever ask or imagine. "Forgiveness of sins, life and salvation" are the blessings he delivers when he gives us his body and blood along with bread and wine. The ultimate fulfillment of all these meals will occur when we will receive a place at the heavenly table of our King, "where [we] shall eat of the eternal manna and drink of the river of [his] pleasure forevermore."

⁴He appointed some of the Levites to minister before the ark of the LORD, to make petition, to give thanks, and to praise the LORD, the God of Israel: ⁵Asaph was the chief, Zechariah sec-

ond, then Jeiel, Shemiramoth, Jehiel, Mattithiah, Eliab, Benaiah, Obed-Edom and Jeiel. They were to play the lyres and
harps, Asaph was to sound the cymbals, 'and Benaiah and Jahaziel the priests were to blow the trumpets regularly before
the ark of the covenant of God.

David here makes permanent the temporary arrangements
he had made for musicians to sing and celebrate before the
ark of God on the day when it was moved (chapter 15:16).
Later in the chapter we will see David also making provisions for the altar services to continue at the high place in
Gibeon, where the tabernacle was located. David did not
want public worship in God's kingdom to consist merely of
one extraordinary day upon which they had pulled out all the
stops. Under his leadership worship became a regular and
continuous offering of praise and thanksgiving to the God
whose "love endures forever" (1 Chronicles 16:41).

⁷That day David first committed to Asaph and his associates
this psalm of thanks to the LORD:

⁸Give thanks to the LORD, call on his name;
   make known among the nations what he has done.
⁹Sing to him, sing praise to him;
   tell of all his wonderful acts.
¹⁰Glory in his holy name;
   let the hearts of those who seek the LORD rejoice.
¹¹Look to the LORD and his strength;
   seek his face always.
¹²Remember the wonders he has done,
   his miracles, and the judgments he pronounced,
¹³O descendants of Israel his servant,
   O sons of Jacob, his chosen ones.
¹⁴He is the LORD our God;
   his judgments are in all the earth.

177

¹⁵He remembers his covenant forever,
  the word he commanded, for a thousand generations,
¹⁶the covenant he made with Abraham,
  the oath he swore to Isaac.
¹⁷He confirmed it to Jacob as a decree,
  to Israel as an everlasting covenant:
¹⁸"To you I will give the land of Canaan
  as the portion you will inherit."

¹⁹When they were but few in number,
  few indeed, and strangers in it,
²⁰they wandered from nation to nation,
  from one kingdom to another.
²¹He allowed no man to oppress them;
  for their sake he rebuked kings:
²²"Do not touch my anointed ones;
  do my prophets no harm."

²³Sing to the LORD, all the earth;
  proclaim his salvation day after day.
²⁴Declare his glory among the nations,
  his marvelous deeds among all peoples.
²⁵For great is the LORD and most worthy of praise;
  he is to be feared above all gods.
²⁶For all the gods of the nations are idols,
  but the LORD made the heavens.
²⁷Splendor and majesty are before him;
  strength and joy in his dwelling place.
²⁸Ascribe to the LORD, O families of nations,
  ascribe to the LORD glory and strength,
²⁹ ascribe to the LORD the glory due his name.
  Bring an offering and come before him;
    worship the LORD in the splendor of his holiness.
³⁰Tremble before him, all the earth!
  The world is firmly established; it cannot be moved.
³¹Let the heavens rejoice, let the earth be glad;
  let them say among the nations, "The LORD reigns!"

³²Let the sea resound, and all that is in it;
    let the fields be jubilant, and everything in them!
³³Then the trees of the forest will sing,
    they will sing for joy before the LORD,
    for he comes to judge the earth.
³⁴Give thanks to the LORD, for he is good;
    his love endures forever.
³⁵Cry out, "Save us, O God our Savior;
    gather us and deliver us from the nations,
  that we may give thanks to your holy name,
    that we may glory in your praise."
³⁶Praise be to the LORD, the God of Israel,
    from everlasting to everlasting.

Then all the people said "Amen" and "Praise the LORD."

The king provided for Israel's worship by composing songs for them to sing. From his youth David had been known for his musical skill (see 1 Samuel 16:18). Now God led him to use his talents in service of the Word. The psalm that follows is also found in the book of Psalms. There it appears as portions within three different psalms (Psalm 105, 96, and 106), rather than as the single work we find here. Sections like these in Scripture give us helpful insights on the way individual psalms were composed, gathered, and used in early Israel. Here we see a psalm of thanksgiving being composed and sung on the occasion of the ark's being moved to Jerusalem.

We also observe how, from early on in the monarchy, psalms played a significant role in Israel's worship. We see the key part David and the leaders of the Levitical musical guilds played in their collection and preservation. Finally we notice how psalm verses might be detached from their original settings and used in other psalms, as the Spirit and the need might dictate.

The psalm itself falls into four major sections: the call to worship (verses 8-11), the basis for Israel's worship (verses 12-22), a celebration of God's royal rule and its consummation (verses 23-33), and a concluding prayer asking God to gather his people from all the nations (verses 34-36). We now look at each section in more detail.

The Call to Worship (verses 8-11)

Hebrew is rich in terms to describe the worship of God in all its aspects: "Give thanks . . . call on his name . . . sing . . . glory in . . . look to the LORD. . . seek his face." Worship is a verb that describes the urgent desire that exists in a believer's heart to honor God once he has come to know him as the one who has planned his eternal good. The longing is continuous, wholehearted, urgent, and joyful. It must express itself by celebrating in song all that God has done to save. And since the mouth speaks what the heart is full of, a believer will also tell others what God has done. Finally, as this section also suggests, believers encourage one another to worship the Lord, just as one flame will kindle another.

A person can worship God in this way only when he is certain that all he is and all he does is acceptable to God. With this thought we advance into the next section of the psalm.

The Basis for Israel's Worship (Verses 12-22)

David states the reason for Israel's confidence before God: "He remembers his covenant forever, the word he commanded, for a thousand generations" (verse 15). Out of all the nations of the world, God had chosen the children of Israel to be his very own. God's intent was to display his saving power and purpose through them. The covenant that God had made with Abraham and his descendants was one of pure grace. It depended on God's merciful promise, not on Abraham's personal worthiness. An integral part of that covenantal promise was God's declaration to Abraham, "All peoples on earth will be blessed through you" (Genesis 12:3). Through the descendants of Abraham God intended to bless all nations by sending them a Savior.

The bequest of Canaan as the cradle of the Savior was also part of that same promise, forming one important facet of it. As we have seen, God intended to save the world through the people of Israel. Their homeland was Canaan. David in his psalm celebrates the entire covenant by zeroing in on God's gift of the land. We can readily see why. At every point of its history, Israel remained surrounded by heathen and hostile nations. The sons of Jacob needed to have their inspired poet reassure them that the land was theirs because Almighty God had willed it so. This would also serve to comfort the Chronicler's original readers. They had returned to the land after seventy years of exile in Babylon. God had kept his promise! They could see this in connection with the land to which God had restored them. God would also fulfill the rest of his promises to save and to bless. The grace of God was a firm basis for worship.

That is why the word "remember" is so important in the vocabulary of worship. Because God is faithful, we know that he cannot "forget," as mortal men do. He will always "remember"—and act upon—his promises of love to us. It is vital for us, then, to remember God's promises in our worship. To remember them, of course, means more than to call them to mind. It also means to repeat and proclaim them, to celebrate the specific ways God has fulfilled them in the past. "Remember the wonders he has done," David urges God's people here (verse 12). In all of Jacob's wanderings, and the

181

subsequent migrations of his descendants, God was with his chosen people. He delivered them from every enemy that oppressed them. For their sake he even put to shame proud kings like Pharaoh. "Remember this," David says, "remember what God has done for us!"

The word *remember* is no less a part of the New Testament believer's worship vocabulary. The high point of our worship comes when we remember and proclaim Christ crucified in our sermons. "Do this in remembrance of me" our Lord said, in giving us his holy Supper (Luke 22:19). This aspect of our worship led one Christian writer to remark, "There is no event in history so remembered as Christ's sacrifice for us on Calvary." This is as it should be, since the grace of our Lord Jesus Christ is the basis of our worship.

Remembering God and his acts of love is so much different from remembering a person or a happy time in our past. The person we remember has changed over the years, and the happy time we recall is gone forever. But God remains the same, and he is living and active in our present circumstances to do us good. To remember God's help in the past is to call on his aid in the present. To sing God's praises for what he has done in the past is to remind ourselves that he will always be giving us fresh songs to sing in the future.

A Celebration of God's Royal Rule and its Consummation (verses 23-33)

"It is interesting to note that people outside Israel are also called upon no less than 175 times in the book of Psalms to worship God and to glorify his name." So wrote Professor E. H. Wendland in his book *Missiological Emphases in the Old Testament* (page 38). We have a perfect example of that here in these verses: "all the earth" is invited to sing to the Lord, the God of Israel (verse 23). God's royal rule of grace is over all and for all, even though it is exercised through Israel and its anointed king. To paraphrase David here, we might say, "This God whom we worship—the God who saved us from Egypt and bound himself to us in an enduring covenant of love—he is not just *my* God, nor even simply *our* God. He is the *only* God of *all* the earth. Declare his glory to all that all may turn from their useless idols to the Lord who made the heavens, the only God who can save mankind."

The gracious rule of God is so all-encompassing that even the sea, the fields, and the trees of the forest will one day be brought under its sway. This will happen on that happy day when the Lord comes to "judge the earth" (verse 33). Then "creation itself will be liberated from its bondage to decay and brought into the glorious freedom of the children of God" (Romans 8:21). If we could stretch the limits of language, we could say that we not only "remember" God's past acts of mercy done according to his promise, but we also remember the future actions God will carry out in establishing his kingdom. They are as good as done, since God has promised to do them. Therefore, we can remember them in thanksgiving already before the fact.

Concluding Prayer:
"God, Gather Us From All the Nations!" (verses 34-36)

It may seem unusual that David should conclude this great hymn with a request for God to gather his people from the nations. After all, this day marked a high point in the unity of God's Old Testament people. They were gathered in one place, united under one king, for the purpose of worshiping one God. Yet David saw clearly that this gathering of God's people in Jerusalem had not brought God's promise to its ultimate fulfillment. In this time of shadows and types, David recognized that God had not yet brought his kingdom to its final consummation, nor had he completed the gathering of his people into one. Another King would do that.

For the Chronicler's first readers this prayer would have been clothed with a new urgency, as they considered their small numbers and how few had responded to the call to return to the land of promise. God's work of gathering his people was not complete. We, too, can pray these words with the same urgency. We have been gathered into Christ's church, a "people that are his very own" (Titus 2:14). Yet as long as this world stands, there will still be more of God's elect to be gathered from the unbelieving nations of this world. Jesus has given us the mandate to gather them by proclaiming the gospel. Pray that God would accomplish this through us and bless us with both the eagerness and the means to do his work. And pray for the day when all God's people "from every nation, tribe, people and language" (Revelation 7:9) will be united in singing praises to the one "who sits on the throne, and to the Lamb" (Revelation 7:10).

37David left Asaph and his associates before the ark of the covenant of the LORD to minister there regularly, according to each day's requirements. 38He also left Obed-Edom and his sixty-eight associates to minister with them. Obed-Edom son of Jeduthun, and also Hosah, were gatekeepers.

39David left Zadok the priest and his fellow priests before the tabernacle of the LORD at the high place in Gibeon 40to present burnt offerings to the LORD on the altar of burnt offering regularly, morning and evening, in accordance with everything written in the Law of the LORD, which he had given Israel. 41With them were Heman and Jeduthun and the rest of those chosen and designated by name to give thanks to the LORD, "for his love endures forever." 42Heman and Jeduthun were responsible for the sounding of the trumpets and cymbals and

for the playing of the other instruments for sacred song. The sons of Jeduthun were stationed at the gate.

As mentioned earlier, David saw to it that the musicians and priests gathered to move the ark were given permanent appointments to lead God's people in their worship. Previously the Chronicler had mentioned only the appointments of Asaph and his associates to serve in Jerusalem. Here he repeats the assignments mentioned earlier (with some additional details). Then he goes on to mention the stationing of Zadok as priest at Gibeon, along with Heman and Jeduthun, who were put in charge of the music. United in bringing the ark to Jerusalem, the priests and Levites now would be divided between the ark at Jerusalem and the tabernacle at Gibeon. In this simple way the Chronicler points out that there was still work to be done in bringing all the elements of God's worship together at one place. Presumably, God was worshiped before his ark in Jerusalem through sacrifices of prayer and praise, while the regular animal sacrifices, as prescribed by Moses, continued to be made on the altar of burnt offering at Gibeon (1 Chronicles 16:40). The Chronicler has set the stage for the declaration of David's desire to build a temple, a matter the holy writer will take up in the next chapter.

Before we leave our study of Chapter 16, however, it is worth looking at the concluding words, "David returned home to bless his family" (verse 43). The worship of our daily lives follows naturally from the worship gathering. There is a sense in which our worship of God never ends. We gather together to be revived and restored in our relationship to the Savior God. This empowers and strengthens our love in all our earthly relationships. Christ's love shapes the love of a husband for his wife. Christ's willing obedience enables the wife to yield her life to her husband (Ephesians 5:21-28).

The hearts of the fathers are turned back to their children (Luke 1:17). A true love of God leads into a true love for our neighbor. There is no need, except in the most extreme cases, to divide our loyalties or to act as if service of God renders service to our families optional. The same love that moves us to worship God also compels us to offer our lives as a blessing to those with whom we live.

God Establishes His Kingdom Under David

God Promises to Build a House for David

While every word of the Holy Scripture is precious, there are some portions of the Bible so important that, unless a person is familiar with them, he can hardly have a good understanding of the rest of Scripture. We have a chapter like that before us now. Here the Lord reveals to David the role he and his descendants will play in the kingdom of God. This promise served to keep Israel's hope alive during the many years in which they waited for the Messiah to come. We find an account parallel to this one in 2 Samuel 7. There are only a few minor differences that are easily explained by taking into account the different purposes of the two inspired authors.

17 **After David was settled in his palace, he said to Nathan the prophet, "Here I am, living in a palace of cedar, while the ark of the covenant of the LORD is under a tent."**

²Nathan replied to David, "Whatever you have in mind, do it, for God is with you."

We can hardly fault David for his pious desire here. He was troubled by the fact that he lived in a fine house built out of cedar, while the Lord's ark rested behind the curtains of a tent. Clearly, he wanted to do something to remedy that incongruous situation. It could be that the Chronicler is contrasting David's good intentions with the attitude displayed by the exiles who returned from Babylon—that attitude is described for us by the prophet Haggai, "Is it a time for you yourselves to be living in your paneled houses, while [the] house [of God] remains a ruin?" (Haggai 1:4).

In any case, David shared his mind with Nathan the prophet, who, incidentally, is mentioned here for the first time. Nathan had no direct revelation from God to speak by way of reply, but he gave his best opinion, "Whatever you have in mind, do it" (1 Chronicles 17:2). He recognized that the kind of success David had enjoyed could only have come about if God was with him. Nathan had no reason to suppose that God would not be with David on this new plan of his.

But pious desires and godly opinions do not revelation make. Nathan had spoken out too soon.

³That night the word of God came to Nathan, saying:

⁴"Go and tell my servant David, 'This is what the LORD says: You are not the one to build me a house to dwell in. ⁵I have not dwelt in a house from the day I brought Israel up out of Egypt to this day. I have moved from one tent site to another, from one dwelling place to another. ⁶Wherever I have moved with all the Israelites, did I ever say to any of their leaders whom I commanded to shepherd my people, "Why have you not built me a house of cedar?"'

⁷"Now then, tell my servant David, 'This is what the LORD Almighty says: I took you from the pasture and from following the flock, to be ruler over my people Israel. ⁸I have been with you wherever you have gone, and I have cut off all your enemies from before you. Now I will make your name like the names of the greatest men of the earth. ⁹And I will provide a place for my people Israel and will plant them so that they can have a home of their own and no longer be disturbed. Wicked people will not

oppress them anymore, as they did at the beginning ¹⁰and have done ever since the time I appointed leaders over my people Israel. I will also subdue all your enemies.

" 'I declare to you that the LORD will build a house for you:

"You are not the one to build me a house" (verse 4). How keen David's initial disappointment must have been when he heard those words! David was a man with blood on his hands (see 1 Chronicles 22:8). True, it had been shed for the honor of God and for the sake of God's people. Nevertheless, his life as a warrior rendered him unfit in God's sight to build that peaceful house of prayer where God would dwell among his people.

Another reason why God did not want David to build him a house is that he wanted David (and us) to understand who is God and who isn't. He wanted to remind David how important it is to let God be God. That means, among other things, that we need God's help. God does not require our help. We need God to serve us *first* (John 13:1-8). God does not need us to serve *him* (Psalm 50:10-12). God is the one who exalted and showed his favor to David. He did not *need* David to show favor to him. God had experienced no sense of privation in having his ark—a visible symbol of his presence on earth—dwelling in a tent. He did not feel his eternal changelessness threatened by the fact that the ark had been moved over the years "from one tent site to another, from one dwelling place to another" (verse 5).

On the contrary, God had been the one who had made David "out of nothing." "I took you from the pasture and from following the flock, to be ruler over my people Israel" (verse 7). There is some wonderful irony here as God contrasts his and David's situations. It's as if God is saying,

"Even though I was always on the move, going from one en-campment to another, I still managed to bring you up from camping out in the fields with sheep to living in a cedar palace as king over my people." In addition, God had granted David victory over his enemies (verse 8). And he had far more in mind to do for David and for his people.

While David would not receive the recognition as the temple builder, God promised, "I will make your name like the names of the greatest men of the earth" (verse 8). Whenever people sat down to praise famous men, the name of David would come up as one of the greatest of them all. God also reminded David of the important work he intended to accomplish through him. Back in the days of Moses, God had predicted a time when his people would enjoy rest from all their enemies (Deuteronomy 12:9). Then, and only then, would it be possible for his people to gather at the place the Lord would choose "as a dwelling for his Name" (Deuteronomy 12:11). God gave David the task of subduing the enemies of Israel, so that they could live in their homeland undisturbed by their enemies (verses 9,10). In other words, David was to lay the groundwork so that a temple could be built later. In Chapters 18 through 20, the Chronicler demonstrates how David fulfilled the role God had in mind for him.

Luther once remarked, "It is the nature of God to create out of nothing; therefore, God cannot make anything out of him who has not yet become nothing" (WA 1 183). If you think that you are something, there is not much God can do with you. God makes righteous only those who see their sin. He opens the eyes only of those who know they are blind. He heals only those who recognize that they are sick (see Luke 5:31,32). Before we become so busy about our doing, we need God to be busy about his doing for us! We need to guard ourselves against that sense of self-exaltation that comes from all our good deeds. How easy it is to let our perception of ourselves as being "heroes for Christ" slip into the center of our spiritual lives! There it replaces the love and forgiveness Christ has for us, from which alone true spiritual life comes. In the end, such self-exaltation leads only to weariness and the despair that comes from carrying an unmanageable burden of guilt. Far better to let God be God. He exalts us in Christ and in him gives us a new identity that cannot be touched by sin or failure or sorrow!

After exalting us in Christ, God also gives us work to do. It may not always be the work we would have chosen—just as David did not in the end accomplish what he had in his heart to do. But it is the work God has chosen for us. Each one has his own role to play in the kingdom of God. "To each one the manifestation of the Spirit is given for the common good" (1 Corinthians 12:7). One may plant, another may water. One may lead God's people up to the promised land, another may bring them all the way in (see Numbers 27:12-21). One may have the gift of encouraging others, another may be gifted in speaking, and still another may have the ability to provide leadership (see Romans 12:4-8). No gift is unimportant. The church needs them all, and for each to use his own particular gift "for the common good." In the end, building the kingdom is not about securing our own position, but about living for the glory of God.

"'I declare to you that the LORD will build a house for you: "When your days are over and you go to be with your fathers, I will raise up your offspring to succeed you, one of your own sons, and I will establish his kingdom. ¹²He is the one who will build a house for me, and I will establish his throne forever. ¹³I will be his father, and he will be my son. I will never take my love away from him, as I took it away from your predecessor. ¹⁴I will set him

over my house and my kingdom forever; his throne will be established forever.'"

[15]Nathan reported to David all the words of this entire revelation.

God was far from finished in telling David about the plans he had for him. Though the Lord would not let David build him a house, God would build a house for David. The Lord communicated his will to David by means of a pun, a divine play on words. As in English, the Hebrew word for house can be taken in more than one sense. It can mean a dwelling place, or it can refer to the family that lives within the dwelling. Its second meaning can also be extended to refer to an entire genealogy, a succession of people coming from a common ancestor. God used the second meaning in his promise to David. God would not permit David to build him a dwelling place, but God would build a dynasty for David.

We now turn to a study of the prophecy in detail. God declared to David that, after he passed from the scene, one of his sons would build the temple (verse 12). What was more, God said, "I will establish his throne *forever*," in such a way that one of his descendants would always be ruling over God's kingdom (verses 12,13). This son of David would also enjoy a father-son relationship with the God of Israel (verse 13). The enduring nature of that intimate relationship is further described in God's promise, "I will never take my love away from him" (verse 13). What had happened to Saul and his family would not be repeated in David's case. As God's house and kingdom would endure, so would the rule of David's son over it (verse 14).

In the first instance, these words referred to Solomon. This was David's own understanding of them (see 1 Chronicles 22:9,10). Solomon would succeed David and rule over God's

191

people, as also would his sons after him. The dynasty of David would endure, unlike Saul's. And Solomon would build the temple as the dwelling place for God. Yet Solomon could hardly exhaust the full scope of God's intent here or complete what God had in mind for the house of David. David knew that much. The Chronicler wanted to remind his contemporaries of it as well.

At the time of the return from exile, Solomon's temple was a ruin and the house of David had lost its authority over the land of Israel. The great kingdom of David and Solomon was a mere memory for that small band of settlers who had come back to the land of their forefathers. The Chronicler repeated the promise made to David, not to remind his people of glories forever gone, but to restore their hope in the majestic future God had in mind for them. God had said that one of David's descendants would rule over the kingdom of God forever. God had promised that one of David's descendants would build him a house. God had said that this house and kingdom would endure forever. Finally God had said that this son of David would also be his son. The Chronicler's point to his people, "Wait for the Lord, therefore, and in his words and promises put your hope!"

By now it should be clear to any student of Scripture what God was telling David, "One of your descendants will be the Messiah, the Savior of the human race." Jesus was the true "Son of David," while remaining the eternal Son of God (Romans 1:3,4, John 1:14,18). The intimate and enduring relationship between the Father and our Lord Jesus was reaffirmed several times during his earthly ministry (e.g., Matthew 3:17,17:5). The decisive demonstration of it came when God raised Jesus from the dead (Romans 1:4). By sending his Son into the world, God intended to establish his eternal kingdom and build through him his everlasting house.

As the angel Gabriel said to Mary, "[Your son] will be great and will be called the Son of the Most High. The Lord God will give him the throne of his father David, and he will reign over the house of Jacob forever; his kingdom will never end" (Luke 1:32,33).

The house that Jesus built for God is, of course, the holy Christian church. The church is God's temple, "a dwelling in which God lives by his Spirit" (Ephesians 2:22). Jesus puts it together by bringing people to faith in him as their Savior from sin. Faith in Christ transforms us children of Adam—mere dust from dust—into "living stones . . . built into a spiritual house" (1 Peter 2:5).

Just like the Chronicler's people, however, we do not see this temple and this kingdom as realities visible to our physical eyes. The church, as we see it, is covered over with weakness, divisions, and sin. At times, we may even esteem it stricken, smitten by God, and afflicted! When we look at the visible state of the church, the tempter often comes to fill us with discouragement and doubt. We are not the first whom the devil has assaulted in this way. As we have seen, it was no different for that small band of Jews come home from exile. What the Chronicler said to them remains God's message to us, "Wait for the Lord, and in his word put your hope!"

The final fulfillment of these words is yet to come. God's ultimate intention will be revealed at the creation of the new universe. At that time the voice from heaven will declare, "Now the dwelling of God is with men" (Revelation 21:3). God and man will live together openly, and not in the hidden way he does now with his church. Today he is *seen* only by those whose eyes the Spirit has opened by faith. On that happy day God's people will bask in the light of his presence forever. Then we will all enjoy the intimate and enduring fellowship with God presaged by the words, "I will be his God and he will be my son" (Revelation 21:7). How our hearts long for that day!

The Chronicler continues by giving us David's response to this gracious revelation:

¹⁶Then King David went in and sat before the LORD, and he said:

"Who am I, O LORD God, and what is my family, that you have brought me this far? ¹⁷And as if this were not enough in your sight, O God, you have spoken about the future of the house of your servant. You have looked on me as though I were the most exalted of men, O LORD God.

¹⁸"What more can David say to you for honoring your servant? For you know your servant, ¹⁹O LORD. For the sake of your servant and according to your will, you have done this great thing and made known all these great promises."

David was stunned. What God had said to him had exceeded the grasp of his imagination. God's answers to our prayers always do. David went before the Lord's ark in the tent he had pitched for it, and there sat down to speak what was in his heart. The first part of his prayer breathes a sense of grace received, "Who am I that you should have honored me by making me king over your people? You chose me and you chose my family out of pure grace and grace alone. As if that were not enough, you have also told me about the far-off future. You intend to found your eternal kingdom upon my house through one of my offspring. What is still more, you have taken me into your confidence and have revealed to me what you intend to do. What more can I say, for you already know me better than I know myself!"

This was David's defining moment. Not that he had defined himself by his own great accomplishments or by anything he had done. God had defined him by telling David what he would do for him. David simply received that promise and trusted that what God had said to him would most certainly be done. In that moment David realized that he was more than a king, more even than a king of God's people. God had so raised him up that now he and his offspring were to be inextricably woven into the substantial fabric of God's eternal will to save a world gone wrong. From now on all God's people would find comfort and strength from "the sure mercies of David" (Isaiah 55:3, Acts 13:34).

Throughout his book the Chronicler has been preparing us for this revelation. By tracing the genealogies in chapters one to three, he led us step by step through the history of God's promise. From Adam to Shem, from Abraham to Israel, in ever tightening circles God marked out the ones from whom the world was to expect its Savior. Among Israel's sons, Judah was selected as the one to bear the promise. From Judah to Perez, Hezron to Ram, and then to the house of Jesse. Inexorably, inevitably, the circles were drawn more tightly until they came to a point in David. Inexorably, inevitably, the line of David continued through the four and a half centuries of the monarchy and the seventy years of exile, until at last governor Zerubbabel, David's descendant, led a group of people back to the land of Judah. Inexorably the Savior God is carrying out his loving purpose for his elect. Inevitably his words of promise come true.

The magnitude of God's promise to David can hardly be exaggerated, since it leads us right into the heart of God, sweeps us along all the generations of history, and stretches into the future where it comes to perfect fulfillment in the consummation of the kingdom of God. David's defining moment becomes our defining moment when we realize in faith that the Son of David, our Savior, is pleased to be identified with us and permits us to be called by his name: I am now God's child, God's heir, God's son (John 1:12, Romans 8:16,17, Galatians 3:26,27). In Baptism, God graciously grafted us into our Savior's genealogy. In stunned wonder we can only echo David's words and praise the God who has such love for sinful people and such great plans for us!

> **[20]"There is no one like you, O LORD, and there is no God but you, as we have heard with our own ears. [21]And who is like your people Israel—the one nation on earth whose God went out to redeem a people for himself, and to make a name for yourself, and to perform great and awesome wonders by driving out nations from before your people, whom you redeemed from Egypt? [22]You made your people Israel your very own forever, and you, O LORD, have become their God.**

What was true for David as an individual was also true for God's people, Israel, as a group. God had chosen David by grace; God had chosen his people Israel by grace. As Moses had expressed this truth many years earlier, "The LORD did not set his affection on you and choose you because you were more numerous than other peoples, for you were the fewest of all peoples. But it was because the LORD loved you and kept the oath he swore to your forefathers that he brought you out with a mighty hand and redeemed you from the land of slavery, from the power of Pharaoh king of Egypt" (Deuteronomy 7:7,8). This is what makes God unique. He alone can save. He alone can rescue the powerless, the sinful, the enslaved. He graciously calls by his name those who had no name, and makes into his people what before was not a people (1 Peter 2:10, Titus 2:14). He breaks into history and intervenes on behalf of those he loves. He did it for Israel in Egypt. He did it for us on Calvary. Who is like God? What earthly nation can be compared to God's people?

The true glory of the church will never be found in our own strength of numbers, the great men and women among us, or the mighty things we can do. The true glory of the church will always be found in this that we have been graciously chosen by God to bear his name and to be his very own. It is all by grace, and it must remain by grace so that in the end, all glory will go to the true God, to whom it truly belongs.

> [23]"And now, LORD, let the promise you have made concerning your servant and his house be established forever. Do as you promised, [24]so that it will be established and that your name will be great forever. Then men will say, 'The LORD Almighty, the God over Israel, is Israel's God!' And the house of your servant David will be established before you.
>
> [25]"You, my God, have revealed to your servant that you will build a house for him. So your servant has found courage to pray to you. [26]O LORD, you are God! You have promised these good things to your servant. [27]Now you have been pleased to bless the house of your servant, that it may continue forever in your sight; for you, O LORD, have blessed it, and it will be blessed forever."

David now draws his prayer to a close. In the first part he had expressed his awe and wonder at the great promise God had made to him. To praise God is to rehearse, recount, and rejoice in his promises, as David has done here. Now he concludes by asking God to fulfill his word to him and to establish his house. For what reason? "That your name will be great forever" (verse 24). There is no better way for Christians to pray than to take God's words and promises, repeat them before God, and then say, "Do as you [have] promised!" (verse 23). There is no greater courage or confidence we can have in prayer than that we are using God's own words. We are building on the same firm foundation David did, "You, my God, have revealed to your servant that you will build a house for him. So your servant has found courage to pray to you" (verse 25).

How can we doubt that God hears our prayers if (as Luther once suggested in a striking figure of speech) we "rub his own words under his nose"? Prayer is always at its best when it is an earnest seeking of the will of God. And we can never be more certain that we are truly seeking God's will than when we deal with God on the basis of his own promise to us. When David expressed his own desire, he heard the prophet say, "Do whatever you have in mind." But that plan came to nothing. How much better it is when we listen to God's desire. Then we can say to God, "Do whatever you have in mind!" And everything will be certain. Then God remains God—the giver. We remain his people—those who receive from him by faith. And his name remains great forever, glorified in us as our Savior God!

That is also why David can close his prayer on the same note of absolute certainty, "You, O LORD, have blessed [my house], and it will be blessed forever" (verse 27). God never uttered an idle word. His promise, therefore, is "an everlasting covenant, arranged and secured in every part" (2 Samuel 23:5). Nothing is left for God's people to do but to speak the glad, "Amen! Praise and glory and wisdom and thanks and honor and power and strength be to our God for ever and ever. Amen!" (Revelation 7:12).

The difficult thing for us, at times, is to close our prayers with that firm, "Amen!" This is because we are not entirely willing to let God be God nor let his will be done in our lives. We trust him, but because of our sinful nature, not completely. We take our worries to God in prayer, lay them in his lap, and then we take them back again, as if we could manage them better. We say to God, "Thy will be done," and yet secretly breathe another petition along with it, "O may your desires and my will coincide!" These sinful thoughts are part of what we must put off when we pray to God. Let them be buried along with Christ, so that Christ may rise in our hearts and teach us to say, "Lord, let my will be shaped by your desire, and let me find myself in your gracious gift of forgiveness by which I know that I am your child and you are my God." All of God's promises are "yes" to us in Christ. When our spirit finds rest in the love of Christ, then and only then do we find the power to speak a firm "Amen" to all his will (see 2 Corinthians 1:20).

David Prepares for the Building of God's House Under Solomon

A. David's Victories over Israel's Enemies

The rest of 1 Chronicles deals with the preparations David made to enable Solomon, his son, to build a house for the Lord. The next three chapters summarize David's victories in battle. While other kings and empire-builders have their stories told so that they might win lasting glory for themselves or for their people, David's victories are discussed by the Chronicler within the context of building a house for the Lord. As we noted previously, one of the divine prerequisites for the building of the temple was that the holy land of Israel would be at rest from her enemies (Deuteronomy 12:8-11). The Chronicler describes these battles to show how God provided that rest through David. North and south, east and west, "The LORD gave David victory everywhere he went" (1 Chronicles 18:6,13).

Since he is far more interested in developing his main themes of king and temple, the holy writer does not follow a strict chronology in the arrangement of his material. Many of these battles, for example, may have occurred after the capture of Jerusalem and before the ark was brought up to the city. The Chronicler also seems to be following a common biblical pattern of writing, giving first of all a summary account, following it with some additional details, and then rounding off the entire discourse with some suitable conclusion. If this is true here, then we could take 1 Chronicles 18 as giving us the summary of David's victories, 1 Chronicles 19:1—20:3 as giving us further information about David's wars with the Arameans and how they developed out of a dispute with the king of Ammon. Finally, in 1 Chronicles 20:4-8, all the accounts of David's battles are rounded off in the same place where they began, with his struggles against the Philistines (see 1 Chronicles 14:8-17; 18:1).

We also notice in what he passes over that the Chronicler is still intent upon telling the story of David in such a way that the pattern of the Righteous King continues to emerge from David's life. A simple comparison of these chapters with their parallels in 2 Samuel shows that the Chronicler has dropped any material that does not fit the mold of David as a righteous king. David's dalliance with Bathsheba and murder of Uriah is not discussed (see 2 Samuel 11, 12), nor are David's family problems (2 Samuel 13, 14), nor the rebellions against his rule (2 Samuel 15-20). Various other smaller incidents in which David might not appear in the best light are also omitted. Again it is worth noting that the Chronicler is writing with the full knowledge that his readers are aware of all these things, but he does not mention them because his purpose is different from that of the writer of 2 Samuel. The Chronicler's God-given task is to portray David as a type of the coming Messiah.

18 In the course of time, David defeated the Philistines and subdued them, and he took Gath and its surrounding villages from the control of the Philistines.

²David also defeated the Moabites, and they became subject to him and brought tribute.

³Moreover, David fought Hadadezer king of Zobah, as far as Hamath, when he went to establish his control along the Euphrates River. ⁴David captured a thousand of his chariots, seven thousand charioteers and twenty thousand foot soldiers. He hamstrung all but a hundred of the chariot horses.

⁵When the Arameans of Damascus came to help Hadadezer king of Zobah, David struck down twenty-two thousand of them. ⁶He put garrisons in the Aramean kingdom of Damascus, and the Arameans became subject to him and brought tribute. The LORD gave David victory everywhere he went.

⁷David took the gold shields carried by the officers of Hadadezer and brought them to Jerusalem. ⁸From Tebah and Cun, towns that belonged to Hadadezer, David took a great quantity of bronze, which Solomon used to make the bronze Sea, the pillars and various bronze articles.

⁹When Tou king of Hamath heard that David had defeated the entire army of Hadadezer king of Zobah, ¹⁰he sent his son Hadoram to King David to greet him and congratulate him on his victory in battle over Hadadezer, who had been at war with Tou. Hadoram brought all kinds of articles of gold and silver and bronze.

¹¹King David dedicated these articles to the LORD, as he had done with the silver and gold he had taken from all these nations: Edom and Moab, the Ammonites and the Philistines, and Amalek.

¹²Abishai son of Zeruiah struck down eighteen thousand Edomites in the Valley of Salt. ¹³He put garrisons in Edom, and all the Edomites became subject to David. The LORD gave David victory everywhere he went.

Some are quick to take offense at the scenes of warfare depicted in the Old Testament. They are particularly troubled with the thought of the God of heaven sending his people out to win victories for his kingdom on bloody battlefields. We must remember that, even in Old Testament times, Israel's struggles with the surrounding nations were not only battles "against flesh and blood, . . . but against the spiritual forces of evil in the heavenly realms" (Ephesians 6:12). Through these nations—the kingdoms of this world—the devil bared his fangs in mindless rage against the kingdom of God. When he was not mounting a frontal assault through military confrontation, he was attempting to seduce Israel into forbidden alliances with the worldly nations and the worship of their false gods that inevitably followed.

Chief among the enemies David faced was *Philistia* (verse 1). As we learned from 1 Chronicles 15, the Philistines had been the first to try to unseat the Lord's anointed early in his rule. The other neighbors of Israel generally were content with raiding and plundering God's people, but the Philistines wanted to control the holy land and the valuable trade routes that crossed it. In his first bout with them David had repelled their attacks and defeated their attempts to remove him from the throne. In this account we see David on the offensive, defeating Philistia in her own homeland and even capturing Gath, one of her five major cities. Even though the Philistines remained to trouble Israelites of future generations, never again would they pose the kind of serious threat to God's people that they had in the past.

The wars with *Moab* (verse 2) and *Edom* (verse 12) were more in the nature of a family conflict. At the time when Israel was preparing to enter the promised land, God had given his people strict instructions not to disturb those nations in any way (Deuteronomy 2:5,9). Part of the reason that God gave for this was that the Edomites were descended from Esau—this made them Israel's cousins. The Moabites were off-limits for a similar reason—they were descended from Lot, Abraham's nephew.

In spite of this instruction—and Israel's willingness to follow it—the Edomites and the Moabites viewed Israel's migration to the promised land with deep suspicion. In a thoroughly unbrotherly way, the Edomites had refused Israel permission to pass through their country, thereby forcing their own relatives to cross some of the most rugged and hostile terrain on earth (see Numbers 20:14-21). Moab, for its part, had brought shame upon Israel (and God's retribution) by seducing her into adultery and idolatry. They did this only after a first attempt to bring Israel down had failed. Their king Balak had hired a sorcerer named Balaam to curse God's people. But Balak discovered to his chagrin that God's Spirit can turn a soothsayer's curse into the sweetest blessing. The Moabite king then realized that the only way he could hurt Israel was by turning Israel's God against her. So with Balaam's help, he hit upon the plan of leading Israel into the worship of Baal through sexual enticements. For the whole story, read Numbers 22—25.

Even though the nation of *Ammon* is mentioned here only in passing (verse 11), it also needs to be included among that group of nations who could claim close blood ties with Israel. They, too, had descended from Lot, Abraham's nephew (Genesis 19:36-38). Sad to say, we must also include them among those nations whose hostility to God's people led them to seduce Israel into idolatry (Deuteronomy 23:3-6). The Chronicler passes over this nation quickly here because he intends to describe their enmity against David and their conquest by him more fully in the next chapter.

The scriptural record is clear enough that throughout the time of Joshua and the Judges Israel had remained faithful to God's command to leave her relatives alone in the lands God had provided for them. But though Israel was willing to live in peace, Moab, Ammon, and Edom were not. They became enemies of the sort described by David in Psalm 35, hating without reason (Psalm 35:19, see also John 15:25). In raising up David, the warrior king, God was now pronouncing his judgment on that unreasoning enmity. Moab, Ammon, and Edom were defeated by the Lord's anointed and were forced to submit to his righteous rule (verses 2,11,13; see also 1 Chronicles 20:2,3).

By this whole account, the Chronicler wished to remind his people that "friendship with the world is hatred toward God" (James 4:4). No agreement was possible with the nations of Edom, Moab, and Ammon, who were still present to trouble the Jews who had returned from exile. Nor should God's people be surprised at the irrational hatred these nations displayed against them. This was nothing new; it had ever been so. They could find courage and comfort in the thought that the Lord's Anointed was coming to set Israel free from all her enemies. They would all, in the end, submit to his righteous rule. In the meantime, they were not to compromise with those who might seem to be friends, but who truly wanted nothing good for the kingdom of God.

In a similar way, there is no compromise possible between us and the unbelieving world. Christians have an entirely different mindset from those whose heart is set upon the things of this life. Because this is true, a by-product of the gospel is the sword of division. This sword cuts so deep that it may even make enemies out of one's own family members. Jesus, our Anointed One, clearly wants us to understand this (see Matthew 10:34-36). This fact ought not surprise us and dare not unnerve us. After all, we follow the one of whom it is most absolutely true to say, "They hated me without reason" (John 15:25). We also take comfort from his words, "I have overcome the world" (John 16:33). Our victory is assured. In the meantime, we cannot be in collusion with any person who is living in a state unreconciled to God. We can only win them over by preaching repentance and remission of sins in the name of our victorious Messiah.

The majority of these verses discuss David's wars with the Arameans. These people formed a very loose confederation of states to the north and northeast of Israel, extending up to and beyond the Euphrates River. They were known individually as *Aram Zobah* (verse 3), *Aram Damascus* (verse 5), *Aram Maacah* (see 1 Chronicles 19:6), and *Aram Naharaim* (see 1 Chronicles 19:6). There were other petty Aramean states involved in this conflict, too, as we learn from 2 Samuel 10:6, but the Chronicler doesn't deem them worthy of mention in his account. It is very likely that these wars grew out of the Ammonite campaign described in 1 Chronicles 19. Here the Arameans under Hadadezer are given their own place in the spotlight. In 1 Chronicles 19 they only get the supporting role.

Hadadezer was apparently the paramount chief of all the lesser Aramean chieftains at the time. His name incorporates the name of his false god and means "Hadad is my help" (verse 3). It is with no little irony that the Chronicler points out that one who claimed Hadad as his help was forced to seek the help of his brothers from Damascus (verse 5). But their help was of no use against the one whose help "[came] from the LORD, the Maker of heaven and earth" (Psalm 121:2). "The LORD gave David victory everywhere he went" (verse 6). It was an expression of his confidence in the Lord that David felt no particular need to hang on to the horses and chariots he had captured from Hadadezer. Even though they represented the high-tech weaponry of his day, he kept but a fraction of them and destroyed the rest, so they could no longer be used against Israel (verse 4).

It was also an expression of his righteousness as a king (verse 14) that David did not use the booty from battle to swell his own personal bank account. Freely he had received from the Lord, freely he gave. God had granted him the victories; David returned the spoils of war to him. The great quantities of bronze captured from two of Hadadezer's cities were dedicated to the Lord and later used by Solomon to build the bronze sea and the two pillars flanking the entrance to the Lord's temple. The bronze sea referred to here was the great basin standing in the temple court, used to hold water. From there the water was transferred to smaller, moveable basins and used to wash the sacrifices in the way prescribed by Moses (Leviticus 1:13). David also won a considerable amount of silver and gold in his various campaigns. He turned it over to the Lord (verses 7,11). As we shall see later, this amassing of wealth made it possible for God's house to be built and furnished in the glorious way it was by Solomon.

Not all of this wealth came by way of conquest. Some of it was freely given by nations who wished to honor the Lord's anointed for his victories in battle. The Chronicler mentions the name of Hadoram, king of Tou, in this connection. Hadoram was grateful to David, since David's victory over their common enemy Hadadezer had also given him a respite from war (verse 10). It is probably not too far from the facts of the case here to see the Chronicler making an oblique reference to the prophecy found in Isaiah 60, in which the prophet sees the wealth of the nations flowing to Zion. In this, too, David prefigured the Ideal King and Kingdom to come.

In Psalm 60 David gives credit for all these victories where the credit is due. He was not like other ancient conquerors who used up tons of marble to etch in stone their own marvelous achievements. With David, it is *soli deo gloria,* to God alone be glory!

God has spoken from his sanctuary:
"In triumph I will parcel out Shechem
and measure off the Valley of Succoth.
Gilead is mine, and Manasseh is mine;
Ephraim is my helmet,
Judah my scepter.
Moab is my washbasin,
upon Edom I toss my sandal;
over Philistia I shout in triumph."

(verses 6-8)

In a similar way, the Lord Jesus dedicated the benefits won by his victory over our three great enemies—sin, death and hell—to the purpose of building his temple, the Holy Christian church. All this he did for the glory of God!

[14]David reigned over all Israel, doing what was just and right for all his people. [15]Joab son of Zeruiah was over the army; Jehoshaphat son of Ahilud was recorder; [16]Zadok son of Ahitub and Ahimelech son of Abiathar were priests; Shavsha was secretary; [17]Benaiah son of Jehoiada was over the Kerethites and Pelethites; and David's sons were chief officials at the king's side.

After summarizing David's conquests, the Chronicler characterizes David's entire reign as just and righteous. David was not a perfect king— but he was a forgiven king. God chose to regard David's life through the prism of his pardoning grace. The love of God had also produced such good fruit in David that he was able to serve as an example of what a "man after God's own heart" will do as a king.

We have talked about this in many places before. People could find in David's life a foreshadowing of the way God's perfect King would behave when he came. When that King came, he would need no forgiveness; his life would be the embodiment of all that was just and right. Because of Christ's righteousness, we Christians have the comfort of knowing that God regards our lives—so marred and sinful in our own estimation—as perfect and perfectly acceptable to him. May we live from that grace in such a way that people "see our good deeds and praise our Father in heaven" (Matthew 5:16).

Success brings its own challenges, as the list of David's officials indicates. As Israel's empire had grown, so also had the need for a more permanent, centralized, and formal system of government. If there were now tributary states, someone had to be there to receive the tribute. If there were conquests of land, these new lands had to be administered. If there were now two sanctuaries at which to worship God, there had to be two priests in charge of administering those sanctuaries. If there was now a standing army instead of a rough-and-ready militia, someone had to serve as the military commander. If there were new laws that needed to be made, someone had to make the official copies of those laws. Since there was now an empire to administer instead of a confederation of tribal states, one presumes that there would be more petitioners, each seeking a piece of the king's precious time. Someone had to serve to sort the important cases from the trivial so that each would receive appropriate attention.

Joab, David's nephew, was the field commander of David's army. Whenever the king and commander-in-chief could not be there, Joab would be in charge. Under him served his brother Abishai (see verse 12). Jehoshaphat was David's *recorder,* a word that probably indicates that he served in David's court as his chief of staff. Zadok and Ahimelech were the priests in charge of the two sanctuaries:

Zadok at the tabernacle in Gibeon and Ahimelech at the ark of the covenant in Jerusalem. Shavsha served as the secretary. He was probably involved in making the official copies of the laws expressing the king's will for his lands. Benaiah was in charge of the Kerethites and Pelethites, a group of professional fighting men who served as David's royal bodyguard (compare 1 Chronicles 11:22-25). The terms *Kerethite* and *Pelethite* indicate that they were foreigners, some of them possibly being Philistines. It was not unknown in the ancient world to hire warriors of your enemies as soldiers for your army. We remember David himself once served the Philistine ruler Achish of Gath (1 Samuel 27:5-12). Finally, the Chronicler also mentions that David's sons were prominent in the king's court.

Many scholarly commentators see a similarity between the organization of David's court and the organization of the court of the Egyptians at the time. If true, this would tell us that David borrowed some of his organizational ideas from the Egyptians. Sometimes people today complain about the church being run "like a business," as if it were thoroughly unchristian ever to incorporate good ideas from the business world into the administration of the external affairs of the church. Sometimes, too, people decry the growing "bureaucracy" of the church visible and speak with righteous passion about the good old days of smaller budgets, fewer meetings, and simpler organizational charts. One cannot defend organization for organization's sake or the addition of layer upon layer of officialdom in the mistaken idea that more is always better. Yet David's example of leadership here does speak a gentle "no" to those who would never change with the times, nor learn from those outside their own circles. Doesn't even Jesus have a word to say in praise of the shrewd manager when he tells his disciples, "For the people of this world are more shrewd in dealing with their own kind than are the people of the light" (Luke 16:8)?

19 In the course of time, Nahash king of the Ammonites died, and his son succeeded him as king. ²David thought, "I will show kindness to Hanun son of Nahash, because his father showed kindness to me." So David sent a delegation to express his sympathy to Hanun concerning his father.

When David's men came to Hanun in the land of the Ammonites to express sympathy to him, ³the Ammonite nobles said to Hanun, "Do you think David is honoring your father by sending men to you to express sympathy? Haven't his men come to you to explore and spy out the country and overthrow it?" ⁴So Hanun seized David's men, shaved them, cut off their garments in the middle at the buttocks, and sent them away.

⁵When someone came and told David about the men, he sent messengers to meet them, for they were greatly humiliated. The king said, "Stay at Jericho till your beards have grown, and then come back."

In describing the Ammonite campaign, the Chronicler gives us further details of events he has dealt with in more summary fashion in the previous chapter. He has chosen the subject matter for his special focus with care. Conquests of the Philistines had left the homeland of Israel secure from external threat. At the end of the Ammonite campaign, David was left alone on the battlefield of Palestine as master of all he surveyed. There were no challengers left who had sufficient strength to take him on.

Curiously enough, it all began in an innocuous fashion. David wanted to extend his sympathy to Hanun, the king of Ammon, after the death of his father. The expression David used ("show kindness") most likely indicates that it was his intention to renew with Hanun a treaty of friendship he had enjoyed with the deceased king (verses 1,2). At any rate,

David sent a delegation worthy of representing him to this foreign state funeral—even as Americans send their vice presidents on such occasions. Though the Israelite dignitaries came to express sympathy, they were greeted with suspicion.

There are a number of cases in the book of Chronicles where bad advice is given to a king, who then acts upon it. The bad advice results in disaster for both king and people. It was no different in this case. After impugning the motives of David's delegates, Hanun's counselors went on to suggest to him that these men were the spying vanguard of a secret campaign David intended to wage against the Ammonites (verse 3). Inflamed by these lies, the young king not only refused to receive the delegation, but he also sent them packing with the most degrading and insulting of actions he could have committed on their persons—short of carving his initials in their faces. In an age when beards were a sign of worthy manhood, Hanun shaved the beards of David's men (in half—as we learn from 2 Samuel 8:4). And in an age far more modest than our own, the king of Ammon exposed David's men to public ridicule by having them walk back home with their underwear flapping in the breeze (verse 4).

When David heard what happened, he showed true princely tact by interrupting their journey back to his court. Wishing to spare them further embarrassment, he suggested that his men stay in the deserted mound of rubble that had been Jericho, at least until their beards (and with them their dignity) came back (verse 5; see also Joshua 6:26). Noteworthy, too, is the royal restraint David displayed in making no immediate plans to retaliate.

The biggest mistake Hanun and his advisors had made was to suppose that God's kind of king was just like themselves. If their power had grown to the extent David's had, they more than likely would have cast envious eyes on

Israel. So they simply assumed that David was casting envious eyes on them. The perversity and irrationality of evil is so obvious at times that we wonder how anyone could ever be so foolish. Yet it is just when we feel this way that we need to remind ourselves that the same irrationality and perversity exists in us, in our own sinful natures. With Paul, we, too, must always confess, "I do not understand what I do" (Romans 7:15). Otherwise our sinful natures will overcome us unaware and lead us into the same kind of self-destructive and irrational behavior.

⁶When the Ammonites realized that they had become a stench in David's nostrils, Hanun and the Ammonites sent a thousand talents of silver to hire chariots and charioteers from Aram Naharaim, Aram Maacah and Zobah. ⁷They hired thirty-two thousand chariots and charioteers, as well as the king of Maacah with his troops, who came and camped near Medeba, while the Ammonites were mustered from their towns and moved out for battle.

⁸On hearing this, David sent Joab out with the entire army of fighting men. ⁹The Ammonites came out and drew up in battle formation at the entrance to their city, while the kings who had come were by themselves in the open country.

Ruled by their perverse thoughts, the Ammonites realized that the time for laughing at their little joke had passed; the time to prepare for war with David had come. They simply could not believe that David would let such an insult pass by unchallenged. Perhaps he would not have. But in any case, it is clear that the Ammonites provoked the war. And so they would have no one to blame for the coming disaster but themselves. David wrote in Psalm 18, "With the crooked, you show yourself shrewd, O LORD" (verse 26). God let the Ammonites go on pursuing their perverse thoughts. They mobilized for war. They made themselves ripe for their own destruction.

First the Ammonites "internationalized" the conflict by hiring the Aramean nations to fight on their side in the war. A thousand talents of silver (about 37 tons as the NIV note tells us) was no mean sum to pay for their services (verse 6). By way of comparison, King Omri of Israel later paid two talents of silver to buy the hill of Samaria (1 Kings 16:24); King Hezekiah of Judah bought peace from the king of Assyria at the price of three hundred talents of silver and thirty of gold (2 Kings 18:14). No doubt the Arameans were already alarmed at the rising power of Jerusalem; the money was just an added incentive to stop David. From the previous chapter we may deduce that Hadadezer himself, the king of Zobah, was the leader of the Arameans during this phase of the conflict (see comments above under 1 Chronicles 18:1-13).

The Ammonites could not complain that they did not get value for their money. The armies of four nations and enough chariotry to raise a mighty cloud of dust assembled to do battle on behalf of those who had become "a stench in David's nostrils" (verse 6). In addition the Ammonites themselves mobilized their own forces (verse 7). It was only then that David finally responded to these blatantly hostile actions by sending out the Lord's army under Joab's command.

¹⁰Joab saw that there were battle lines in front of him and behind him; so he selected some of the best troops in Israel and deployed them against the Arameans. ¹¹He put the rest of the men under the command of Abishai his brother, and they were deployed against the Ammonites. ¹²Joab said, "If the Arameans are too strong for me, then you are to rescue me; but if the Ammonites too strong for you, then I will rescue you. ¹³Be strong and let us fight bravely for our people and the cities of our God. The Lord will do what is good in his sight."

¹⁴**Then Joab and the troops with him advanced to fight the Arameans, and they fled before him. ¹⁵When the Ammonites saw that the Arameans were fleeing, they too fled before his brother Abishai and went inside the city. So Joab went back to Jerusalem.**

Humanly speaking, what the Israelites faced was an impossible situation: a two-front war. The Ammonite army was drawn up on one side of the Israelite forces, the Aramean armies on the other. The Ammonites had their capital city of Rabbah close at hand, their home and their fortress to give them an extra sense of security. The Arameans had thirty-two thousand chariots and the right kind of open country in which to operate (see verse 9). Israel had none of these advantages. Most generals in Joab's position would have been filled with a powerful longing to go home.

Capable strategist that he was, Joab quickly assessed the situation and made the best of it. He took the finest troops under his own command and turned them to face the Arameans because they posed the greater threat. He put the rest of his army under brother Abishai's command to take on the Ammonites. His plan? "If the Arameans are too strong for me, then you are to rescue me; but if the Ammonites are too strong for you, then I will rescue you" (verse 10). Hardly the most confident of pre-battle pep-talks! There is no whiff here of military braggadocio. No pre-game locker room crowing: "C'mon Abishai ol' buddy, we'll cream 'em!" Joab expected trouble and made plans for it. He did not dare to presume that he could control the outcome. Yet even though the Israelites had no control over the results of the battle, they could be strong and fight bravely for "the cities of our God" (verse 13). The battle itself was in the Lord's hands, and he "would do what is good in his sight."

Israel had a secret weapon in their fight. True, they did not have the best of high-tech chariotry, but they did have the Lord and the armies of heavenly angels fighting on their side. They did not have a fortress city at their backs to which they could flee, but they did have God as their mighty fortress and as an ever-present help in trouble. None of Joab's fears were realized. He advanced. The Arameans fled. The Ammonites saw their costly allies routed, and they suffered a greater and more public humiliation than they had ever inflicted on Israel. They turned tail and ran back to Rabbah. There was nothing left for Joab to do but to go home.

In our struggles with our great spiritual enemies, we often talk about our weaknesses. Certainly it is not right for us to put any "confidence in the flesh" (Philippians 3:3). Yet as C. F. W. Walther said, "Der Christ ist ein Optimist—Christians are optimists!" We have every reason to be so, since we can do "everything through him who gives me strength" (Philippians 4:13). While not presuming to dictate to God how he should order all the lesser outcomes in the skirmishes of our lives, we have his promise that every outcome of every battle leads inevitably to that great victory Christ will grace us with when he returns for us at last (1 Corinthians 15:57). Thanks be to God!

¹⁶After the Arameans saw that they had been routed by Israel, they sent messengers and had Arameans brought from beyond the River, with Shophach the commander of Hadadezer's army leading them.

¹⁷When David was told of this, he gathered all Israel and crossed the Jordan; he advanced against them and formed his battle lines opposite them. David formed his lines to meet the Arameans in battle, and they fought against him. ¹⁸But they fled before Israel, and David killed seven thousand of their

charioteers and forty thousand of their foot soldiers. He also killed Shophach the commander of their army.

¹⁹When the vassals of Hadadezer saw that they had been defeated by Israel, they made peace with David and became subject to him.

So the Arameans were not willing to help the Ammonites anymore.

20 In the spring, at the time when kings go off to war, Joab led out the armed forces. He laid waste the land of the Ammonites and went to Rabbah and besieged it, but David remained in Jerusalem. Joab attacked Rabbah and left it in ruins. ²David took the crown from the head of their king—its weight was found to be a talent of gold, and it was set with precious stones—and it was placed on David's head. He took a great quantity of plunder from the city ³and brought out the people who were there, consigning them to labor with saws and with iron picks and axes. David did this to all the Ammonite towns. Then David and his entire army returned to Jerusalem.

Apparently the Arameans had not yet learned the lesson that seems so clear to us already. They could not win this battle. After sending for more help from their brothers beyond the river Euphrates, they renewed the conflict. This time they weren't in it for Ammonite money. This time they were trying to save their own skins and to preserve their control over the rich trade routes leading north from Palestine through their lands (see 1 Chronicles 18:3 above). It is hard to know exactly how to sort out the temporal sequence of the battles described in 1 Chronicles 18 and 19. It seems that David's wars with the Arameans consisted of three major campaigns: (a) the one described in connection with the Ammonite insult (1 Chronicles 19:6-15), (b) the Arameans desperate bid to stem the rising tide of David's power (1 Chronicles 19:16-19) followed by (c) David's final offensive against the Arameans to bring them into his sphere of influence (1 Chronicles 18:3-6 and 19:19). We have already mentioned the Chronicler's preference for writing topically rather than chronologically.

When David heard about the renewed threat, he personally led out the armies of Israel. Unlike the previous campaign, Israel this time was able to engage Aram in pitched battle. The Arameans suffered a shattering defeat that included the death of General Shophach, one of Hadadezer's appointees. After this, the Aramean confederation lost the stomach to lend their support to the Ammonites.

Following the conclusion of his successful offensive against the Arameans, David sent Joab to administer the *coup de grace* to the Ammonites holed up in Rabbah. After reducing the chief fortress in Rabbah to rubble, Joab summoned David from Jerusalem to lead the final assault against the now helpless city (see also 2 Samuel 12:26-30). In triumph David marched into the capital of the Ammonites, where his envoys had been shamed. He took the crown from the head of the man who had acted so rashly. The king who had degraded David's men was now himself degraded, and, since he was the leader of an entire people, he became responsible for their ruin as well as his own. He could have received friendship from the Lord's anointed, and all his people would have been blessed. But since he had opposed David, he lost his right to rule, and his people lost their freedom. They became slaves assigned to menial and degrading work.

Every knee will bow and every tongue confess that Jesus is Lord (Philippians 2:10,11). This is true also of everyone who, in rash unbelief, now opposes him and insults his envoys by refusing to accept his Word. We are those envoys, ambassadors for Christ, no less! Christ has sent us to reach out in friendship to a world unwilling by nature to be reconciled to God (2 Corinthians 5:18-21). Some will have a change of heart, listen to the message of reconciliation, and receive the blessing of being united with those who are graciously ruled by the Lord's Anointed. Some will refuse to listen and receive in their bodies the penalty for their sin. The Chronicler's message to his own people and to us is clear. It makes no sense to oppose the Anointed One. Either serve him in joyful faith, or be enslaved forever by your unbelief. In either case, Christ will be Lord of all.

⁴In the course of time, war broke out with the Philistines, at Gezer. At that time Sibbecai the Hushathite killed Sippai, one of the descendants of the Rephaites, and the Philistines were subjugated.
⁵In another battle with the Philistines, Elhanan son of Jair killed Lahmi the brother of Goliath the Gittite, who had a spear with a shaft like a weaver's rod.
⁶In still another battle, which took place at Gath, there was a huge man with six fingers on each hand and six toes on each foot—twenty-four in all. He also was descended from Rapha.
⁷When he taunted Israel, Jonathan son of Shimea, David's brother, killed him.
⁸These were descendants of Rapha in Gath, and they fell at the hands of David and his men.

The Chronicler closes out the account of David's wars by going back to the place where he began. He returns to have one more look at David's battles with the Philistines (compare 1 Chronicles 18:1). The common thread uniting these incidents is that all of them describe the death of a Philistine giant at the hands of one of David's men.

One of the fears that had unmanned ten of the spies who had reconnoitered the promised land for Moses was that some of the people who inhabited the land were "strong and tall" and quite beyond the Israelites' ability to conquer on their own power (Numbers 13:28, 33; Deuteronomy 1:28;

Deuteronomy 9:2). These ancient inhabitants of the land were known variously as Rephaites (see Genesis 15:19,20) or Anakites (Deuteronomy 9:2). While the identification of Rephaites with Anakites is not absolutely certain, it seems likely that the first name designates them as a people of great size—"the Giants"—and the second name refers to the founding ancestor of their race—"the sons of Anak." In one of his farewell sermons to the Israelites, Moses relayed this promise to them from their God, "Be assured today that the LORD your God is the one who goes across ahead of you like a devouring fire. He will destroy (the Anakites), he will subdue them before you. And you will drive them out and annihilate them quickly, as the LORD has promised you" (Deuteronomy 9:3).

What the Lord had promised had been partially fulfilled in Joshua's conquest of the land and Caleb's destruction of the Anakites living in Hebron (Joshua 14:12-15). David had continued the process by his singlehanded defeat of the Philistine Goliath, while Saul and the rest of Israel's army still cowered in fear (1 Samuel 17). Now the army of Israel had finally found its courage and had discovered the strength to do the impossible. The Lord's anointed turns his people into giant-killers!

Christians are locked in deadly combat with an enemy who is not mere flesh and blood, but the prince of this world. Peter compares him to a "roaring lion" hungry for food (1 Peter 5:8). Anyone who has seen a lion in action against one of his intended victims knows that the object of the lion's desire has no chance by itself. At the end of each contest between a lion and an antelope, the score will read LION 1: ANTELOPE: 0! We could only cower in fear or mourn our inevitable defeat if our great champion Jesus had not gone "forth to war" and decisively defeated him for us (see Luke

4:1-14). The power and the promise in Jesus' victory is simply this: we will find strength in the Lord's mighty power. After we have put on his full armor, the day of evil need not frighten us. We will be able to "stand our ground." Our spiritual enemy will not defeat us (Ephesians 6:10-18). The Lord's Anointed makes giant-killers out of each one of us.

With the defeat of the Philistine giants, the Chronicler winds up his description of David's wars. He has achieved his purpose in retelling the story. God would not let the man with blood on his hands build him a house. But God did provide through him "a place for my people Israel . . . so that they (could) have a home of their own and no longer be disturbed" (1 Chronicles 17:9). A fundamental prerequisite for the building of God's temple has been secured. Now that God's people have "rest from their enemies," the stage is set for Solomon, the man of peace, to build God's house (Deuteronomy 12:10,11; 1 Chronicles 22:9,10).

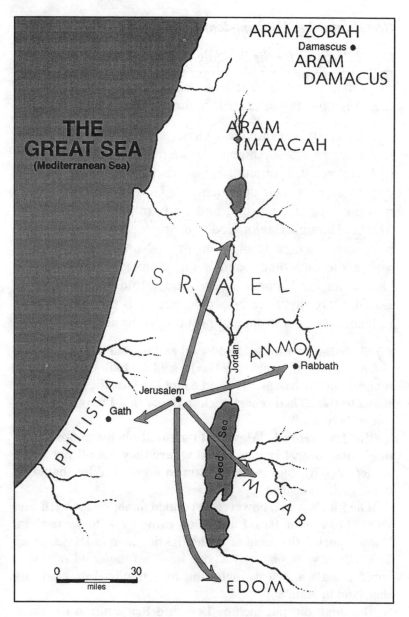

David Wins Rest for the Land

God Establishes His Kingdom Under David

David Prepares for the Building of God's House Under Solomon

B. The Lord Provides a Place for His House

"The LORD will provide" (Genesis 22:14). Ever since the LORD saw to it that Abraham had a ram to sacrifice in place of Isaac on Mt. Moriah, these words have given believers a way to express their confidence in God's gracious care. "I nothing lack if I am his, and he is mine forever!" (CW 375:1). Through David, God had provided rest for his people—a land secure from its enemies. Now God would provide a site on which David's son, Solomon, could build a "house for his Name." Again, God would do this through David. Only this time he would not do it through David's righteousness, but in spite of his unrighteousness!

21 Satan rose up against Israel and incited David to take a census of Israel. ²So David said to Joab and the commanders of the troops, "Go and count the Israelites from Beersheba to Dan. Then report back to me so that I may know how many there are."

³But Joab replied, "May the LORD multiply his troops a hundred times over. My lord the king, are they not all my lord's subjects? Why does my lord want to do this? Why should he bring guilt on Israel?"

⁴The king's word, however, overruled Joab; so Joab left and went throughout Israel and then came back to Jerusalem. ⁵Joab reported the number of the fighting men to David: In all Israel there were one million one hundred thousand men who could handle a sword, including four hundred and seventy thousand in Judah.

⁶But Joab did not include Levi and Benjamin in the numbering, because the king's command was repulsive to him.

⁷This command was also evil in the sight of God; so he punished Israel.

⁸Then David said to God, "I have sinned greatly by doing this. Now, I beg you, take away the guilt of your servant. I have done a very foolish thing."

Without warning, Satan, the great enemy of God's people, makes a personal appearance—as rare in the Old Testament as it is sudden. Clearly, he perceived David and Israel as a threat against the kingdom of chaos and darkness over which he presides. Since God's people lived in safety, free from the danger posed by the kingdoms of this world, they could be brought down now only from within. In the parallel account of 2 Samuel 24, we read that "The anger of the LORD burned against Israel, and he incited David against them, saying, "Go and take a census of Israel and Judah" (2 Samuel 24:1). We wonder how God and the devil can both be involved in the same act of moving David to number his people. We point ourselves in the right direction by using the compass of James 1:13, "God doesn't tempt anyone (for evil)." After that, we can only say that God had his good reasons and Satan had his evil reasons. God's overall good intent and purpose is affirmed by what we read later. For some loving reason known to God (even if hidden to us), the Lord gave the devil room to maneuver in this matter. In spite of the devil's malice, the Savior God overruled the evil to make it "work for good" (Romans 8:28).

If we wonder why the taking of the census itself constituted such a grave offense in God's sight, we find the answer in David's reasons for taking it. As such, the taking of a census was not a sinful act. God even laid down the proper procedures for taking one in Exodus (see 30:11-16). The trouble with bean counting does not lie in the counting of beans, but in the swelling of the head that either leads to or results from it. Even though each one of his victories had been the Lord's gift, David began to glory in the gift more than the giver. When David was still a "nothing," he knew enough not to find his security in armaments or fighting men but "in the name of the LORD" (1 Samuel 17:45). Now that God had made him something and filled his hands with success, David thought he had something to lose. That is why he stopped finding security in the Lord and began instead to seek it in "how many (Israelites) there are" (verse 2).

Sensing something wrong at work in Israel's head of state, Joab tried to warn David, telling him that his action would only "bring guilt on Israel." His king ought to have had no doubts that the Lord would "multiply his troops a hundred times over"(verse 3). After all he had promised to make Abraham's offspring as numerous as the stars in the sky (see Genesis 15:5,6 and 1 Chronicles 27:23). In the previous chapter Hanun the king of Ammon heeded bad advice. Here we see David paying no mind to Joab's good advice. Either way spells disaster. David wanted his will to be done; "the king's word overruled Joab" (verse 4). His action became all the more rebellious in that he plunged ahead in spite of admonition. This was not a sin committed without calculation. David's example makes clear to us how easy it is to be blinded by pride, anger, greed, despair, or by some other powerful vice and strong emotion. The devil puts us in such a fog that the wrong actually appears right to us and the right wrong.

Someone might be surprised here at Joab's remark that David's sin would bring guilt on Israel. How could Israel be held accountable for something David did? There are numerous examples in the Old Testament of the unwitting community being involved in the guilt of one of its members. Achan's sin at Jericho is but one example (Joshua 7). The law of Moses even made provision for the sacrificial cleansing of the community if they sinned "unintentionally" (Leviticus 4:13-21). Part of our problem here is that we live at a time that no longer sees sin in its true nature as a horrid stain on God's good creation. Even one sin disturbs the harmony God intended for the world he made, a harmony that he desires especially for his people. In a broad sense, the sin of one member of the body of Christ brings harm to us all (1 Corinthians 12:26). Those who are one in Christ cannot take a detached attitude to a sin or problem involving a fellow member.

Even more than this, however, we know how easily people are caught up and swept away by the sins of others. If sin takes hold in the heart of one leader, it can quickly impose its mindset on others. One pastor or congregational leader can sway an entire group of God's people into doing what is clearly against God's Word. One pied piper can play a tune that will lead many children to destruction. Each member of a congregation has a responsibility to stand up and say "No!" when the line of God's will is being crossed. If they don't, they share the guilt. Joab warned, but he did not refuse. "Joab left and went throughout Israel" (verse 4) to do the king's bidding. Israel submitted to the census. Thus they shared the guilt of the one who commanded it.

There is a discrepancy between the numbers reported in 2 Samuel and the ones we see here. 2 Samuel lists 800,000 swordsmen in Israel with Judah numbering 500,000. Here we have 1,100,000 for Israel, "including" 470,000 for Judah (verse 5). Even if the NIV's interpretative translation "including" is correct here, the numbers don't add up. We can either chalk up this difference to a copyist's mistake, or we can ascribe it to Joab's apparent reluctance to include "all Israel" in the census. He did not count the tribe of Levi (an act forbidden by the Law, see Numbers 1:49), nor did he include the Benjaminites (for reasons more obscure). We do know that the task "was repulsive to him" (verse 6). So he may not have been overly concerned with the strictest precision in bookkeeping. In addition, the outbreak of plague as the census was winding down led to a holy fear of entering the final results in the annals of the king (see 1 Chronicles 27:24). There may well have been in existence several different versions of the count in various stages of completeness. The discrepancy, then, between Chronicles and 2 Samuel would accurately reflect Joab's carelessness and these somewhat confused conditions.

Once his sin was there for all to see, the king had an attack of conscience, "I have sinned greatly . . . take away the guilt of your servant. I have done a very foolish thing" (verse 8). What had brought about the king's change of heart? Had the Lord expressed his displeasure in some way, indicating through a prophet, perhaps, that he intended to punish Israel for the king's pride (verse 7)? We really don't know. We can only assume that the Spirit somehow reasserted his control of David's heart and helped him realize what he had done. Seldom do we know the precise chain of events that leads to a person's repentance. Sometimes trials humble a person and make him more open to the Word. Sometimes a fellow-Christian's loving rebuke, delivered in a timely way, will reclaim a brother on the spot. Sometimes the fog of sinful thinking and feeling and wanting simply lifts, and we see clearly the mess we're in. All we know for sure is that God has given us his Word and sacraments and promised that the Spirit works through these means to create in us a clean heart and renew in us a steady spirit. But God gives us no timetable telling us exactly when he will do that in the individual cases we deal with.

⁹The LORD said to Gad, David's seer, ¹⁰"Go and tell David, 'This is what the LORD says: I am giving you three options. Choose one of them for me to carry out against you.'"

¹¹So Gad went to David and said to him, "This is what the LORD says: 'Take your choice: ¹²three years of famine, three months of being swept away before your enemies, with their swords overtaking you, or three days of the sword of the LORD—days of plague in the land, with the angel of the LORD ravaging every part of Israel.' Now then, decide how I should answer the one who sent me."

¹³David said to Gad, "I am in deep distress. Let me fall into the hands of the LORD, for his mercy is very great; but do not let me fall into the hands of men."

The Lord replied to David's confession by sending Gad, the seer. The word "seer" means much the same thing as "prophet" (2 Kings 17:13). It refers to someone who brings to men messages he has received from God by direct inspiration. Prophets were also called "seers" because God often communicated with them in the form of waking dreams or visions. They "saw" things others did not see. One of the striking features of the kingdom of God in the Old Testament was the way God sent prophets to his people to warn, to instruct, to rebuke, and to encourage them. Their words were regarded as the words of God. There could be a number of prophets serving God at any one time. We already met Nathan in 1 Chronicles 17. The fact that Gad is called "David's seer" implies that he enjoyed some sort of official status in David's court.

The message he brought to his king was grim. God laid before David three "three's": three years of famine, three months of being defeated by enemies in battle, or three days of a mortal plague ravaging the land. David was free to select which chastisement he and his people would bear for the pride he had shown in tallying up his troop strength. Although God's agency is implied in all three options, it is directly mentioned only in the case of the third. This plague, should David choose it, would not be a sword carried by David's enemies, but the sword of the Lord carried by his angel (verse 12).

It was this consideration that led David to select it as the best of the three "threes." In his great distress he found one consolation: the sword would be carried by the angel of the Lord. We recognize the covenant name of God (see comments on 1 Chronicles 10:13,14). In the third option, David knew he would be dealing directly with the Savior-God. That is why he said, "Let me fall into the hands of the LORD" (verse 13). Men's hearts are hard. They show no mercy for an enemy and have precious little to spare even for a friend. But God's mercies are everlasting and new every morning. God may chasten, but he will not utterly consume. All must serve the interests of his love. Even if we are suffering the bitter consequences of a sin, it is by far the better thing to put ourselves into God's hands rather than to run away from him.

¹⁴So the LORD sent a plague on Israel, and seventy thousand men of Israel fell dead. ¹⁵And God sent an angel to destroy Jerusalem. But as the angel was doing so, the LORD saw it and was grieved because of the calamity and said to the angel who was destroying the people, "Enough! Withdraw your hand." The angel of the LORD was then standing at the threshing floor of Araunah the Jebusite.

¹⁶David looked up and saw the angel of the LORD standing between heaven and earth, with a drawn sword in his hand extended over Jerusalem. Then David and the elders, clothed in sackcloth, fell facedown.

¹⁷David said to God, "Was it not I who ordered the fighting men to be counted? I am the one who has sinned and done

wrong. These are but sheep. What have they done? O LORD my God, let your hand fall upon me and my family, but do not let this plague remain on your people."

There are a number of thematic parallels in this whole account that serve to hold it together as a unit. When David numbered the men who could handle a sword in his kingdom, he succeeded only in bringing on himself the sword of the Lord and the depletion of his fighting strength by seventy thousand men. When David decided to number his men in pride, he later changed his mind and confessed his sin. Then God decided to "number" David's men with a plague but later changed his mind and relented from inflicting complete destruction on Jerusalem. David's confidence in the Lord's mercy proved to be well founded. The expression "the LORD . . . was grieved" (verse 15) is simply a strong figure of speech that ascribes human emotions to a changeless God. From man's earthbound point of view, it appeared as if God had a sudden change of heart and decided instead to adopt a different course of action.

This "change of heart" was brought about by God's seeing what the angel was doing to Jerusalem. God would not permit the city where his ark was located to be destroyed. He had chosen Jerusalem as the place where his house would be built, the place where he would live among his people. His saving grace moved him to say to his messenger, "Enough! Withdraw your hand" (verse 15). In much the same way, Jesus assures us that the terrible last days will be shortened "for the sake of (God's elect)" (Matthew 24:22). We know that God will permit days of unparalleled distress to overtake the world as a consequence of sin. Just when it seems as if evil has reached its crescendo and there is no hope left, God will tell his destroying angels, "Enough!" and ring the curtain down on history. He will do this for the sake of his people, his church, the temple in which he lives by his Spirit (Ephesians 2:22).

This "change of heart" had occurred before David even began to utter his prayer of intercession for his people. Even so, David could not see into God's heart and know his plan. What he and the elders saw was the angel standing on top of the threshing floor of Araunah, the Jebusite. What they saw was the angel's sword still drawn and stretched out menacingly over the city. Once again, God gave David the heart to believe that death and destruction were not his final words to his people. He saw the fearsome aspect of God's avenging angel acting in judgment; yet he dared to hope in God's mercy. Such faith could have been based only on God's Word and promise, and not on anything David was experiencing at the time.

David and the elders fell facedown in worship of the God "whose judgments are unsearchable, and whose paths are beyond tracing out" (Romans 11:33). They were dressed in sackcloth as a sign of repentant grieving over sin. With his heart in his mouth, David turned to God in prayer on behalf of his people. As a true shepherd of his flock, he did not run away and let the people bear alone the consequence of God's anger on sin. Rather, he took full responsibility for what he had done and asked God "Let your hand fall upon me and my family, but do not let this plague remain on your people" (verse 17). It's as if he were saying, "Strike the shepherd, and let the sheep go free."

What courage it gives us in all circumstances to know that we, too, have a king who "pleads in our defense" (1 John 2:1,2). He is the Good Shepherd. He laid his life down for the sheep (John 10:11). This greater Son of the great king David answers our need far better than David could. After all, he does not need to plead in his own defense. He has no personal guilt to forgive. The Righteous One pleads our case before God by pointing to the undeniable evidence of his innocent life and the perfect atonement of his bitter death.

[18]Then the angel of the LORD ordered Gad to tell David to go up and build an altar to the LORD on the threshing floor of Araunah the Jebusite. [19]So David went up in obedience to the word that Gad had spoken in the name of the LORD.

[20]While Araunah was threshing wheat, he turned and saw the angel; his four sons who were with him hid themselves. [21]Then David approached, and when Araunah looked and saw him, he left the threshing floor and bowed down before David with his face to the ground.

[22]David said to him, "Let me have the site of your threshing floor so I can build an altar to the LORD, that the plague on the people may be stopped. Sell it to me at the full price."

[23]Araunah said to David, "Take it! Let my lord the king do whatever pleases him. Look, I will give the oxen for the burnt offerings, the threshing sledges for the wood, and the wheat for the grain offering. I will give all this."

[24]But King David replied to Araunah, "No, I insist on paying the full price. I will not take for the LORD what is yours, or sacrifice a burnt offering that costs me nothing."

[25]So David paid Araunah six hundred shekels of gold for the site.

In answer to David's prayer of intercession, the angel of the Lord instructed him to set up an altar of sacrifice at a threshing floor nearby. The threshing floor itself belonged to Araunah, a descendant of the original Jebusite inhabitants of Jerusalem. Before we go any further, it is probably helpful to have a few facts at our disposal on what *threshing floors* are. They were usually located on the tops of hills, places where one could expect the breezes to be blowing. Wind was helpful in the final part of the threshing process called *winnowing*. To winnow, a farmer would take a winnowing fork in hand (much like our modern pitchfork, with longer and more curved tines) and toss the threshed wheat up into the air. The heavier grains of wheat would fall straight down to the threshing floor, while the useless hulls and chaff would be carried off by the wind (see Psalm 1:4 and Luke 3:17).

But before grain could be winnowed, it first had to be *threshed*. This means that the husks of the grain had to be broken apart so that the grain itself could be separated from its non-edible hulls. Small quantities of grain could be threshed by rubbing the hands together (Luke 6:1). To take care of an entire harvest, however, a threshing floor was needed. The chief distinguishing feature of a threshing floor (besides the top-of-the-hill advantage described above) was a hard surface on which the grain could be crushed and the husks loosened. The farmer would put his grain on that hard surface, and there he could beat it with flails or have it trodden by oxen. State-of-the-art technology at the time employed a threshing sledge (verse 23). This was a wooden sled with stones or iron fragments embedded on its underside. Oxen would drag this sled over the grain until threshing was complete.

When we put all this information together with our text, we may draw the conclusion that Araunah had one of the finest threshing floors around. He had a flat rocky outcropping on top of a hill located near the capital city of the kingdom of Israel. He had oxen and threshing sledges and sons to work his threshing business along with him. God had other plans in mind for this threshing floor, however.

While David was en route to do the Lord's bidding, Araunah turned away from his work for a moment and caught sight of the angel. What a terrifying vision that must have been! An angel standing aloft above his threshing floor, sword of destruction outstretched in his hand. It proved too much for his sons. They hid themselves in fright. No doubt Araunah had it in mind to do the same, when he heard the sound of David approaching. He turned, saw his king, and bowed to the ground.

What follows next is an interesting example of working a deal, ancient near-eastern style. It bears some similarity to the negotiation Abraham carried out with Ephron the Hittite for purchase of the burial cave at Machpelah (Genesis 23:10-20). David states his purpose in coming (verse 22) and offers to buy the threshing floor "at the full price" (verse 22). Araunah then "counteroffers" by saying he will give it away for nothing. In addition he offers to throw in the oxen for the burnt offering, the threshing sledges for the wood, and the wheat for the grain offering! David insists again on paying the full price. They finally settle on six hundred shekels of gold (verse 25). For those who may be troubled with the difference between this amount and the fifty shekels of silver mentioned in 2 Samuel 24:24, we need only point out that 1 Chronicles talks about the purchase price for the entire "site"—threshing floor with its surroundings—whereas 2 Samuel mentions the price paid only for the threshing floor itself and the oxen for the sacrifice. No doubt the reason why Araunah was so willing to sell the family business was the vision of the angel he had just seen. God has his own ways of negotiating.

We are especially stirred by David's words to Araunah, "No, I insist on paying the full price. I will not take for the LORD what is yours, or sacrifice a burnt offering that costs me nothing" (1 Chronicles 21:24). Sin incurs a debt; that debt is called guilt. Guilt is more than just the internal feeling I have when I do something wrong. It is the objective reality that describes my standing before God after I sin. Put simply: I owe. What I owe, of course, is my life, since I have rebelled against the holy and infinite God who demands that I be holy. Under the Old Covenant, God graciously accepted the blood of bulls and goats as a substitute payment for the debt. David recognizes here that he cannot take from someone else to pay to God the debt he owes, nor can he offer a sacrifice that costs him nothing. That would be no sacrifice at all.

What David could not do, God did. Even the costliest bull could not serve as a substitute payment for the debt incurred by a moral creature. We owed God an infinite debt that we were utterly unable to repay, "could my zeal no respite know, could my tears forever flow" (TLH 376:2). Even if we, following some sin of ours, pledged to give God a perfect love and even if we succeeded in giving it, we would only be giving him what he already had coming. It would do nothing to erase the debt incurred by sin. Therefore, God gave us what was his—his only Son Jesus. Jesus offered up a sacrifice that cost him everything, though it cost us nothing. "The master pays the debt his servants owe him who would not know him" (TLH 143, verse 4). Those whose hearts find rest in his love cannot rest until they pay their neighbor the one debt still left outstanding: "Love one another" (Romans 13:8).

[26]David built an altar to the LORD there and sacrificed burnt offerings and fellowship offerings. He called on the LORD, and the LORD answered him with fire from heaven on the altar of burnt offering.

[27]Then the LORD spoke to the angel, and he put his sword back into its sheath. [28]At that time, when David saw that the LORD had answered him on the threshing floor of Araunah the Jebusite, he offered sacrifices there. [29]The tabernacle of the LORD, which Moses had made in the desert, and the altar of burnt offering were at that time on the high place at Gibeon. [30]But David could not go before it to inquire of God, because he was afraid of the sword of the angel of the LORD.

22

Then David said, "The house of the LORD God is to be here, and also the altar of burnt offering for Israel."

David fully obeyed the angel's command (see 1 Chronicles 21:18). After the threshing floor had been purchased, he built an altar there and offered sacrifice. His heart was seeking the reassurance that God had pardoned his sin and that his relationship with the Lord had been fully restored. "The LORD answered him with fire from heaven on the altar of burnt offering" (verse 26). In this striking way the Lord made it clear that he had accepted David's sacrifice and wanted to give him the reassurance he was seeking. As further confirmation David saw "the angel put his sword back into its sheath" (verse 27). At the threshing floor of Araunah, God accepted David's sacrifice, answered prayer, and came to the aid of his people.

David realized something more had happened than simply that a plague had been halted in its tracks. Prior to this event, the Israelites were bound by God's law to offer sacrifice at the high place in Gibeon, where the tabernacle of Moses was located along with the altar of burnt offering Moses had built (verse 29). When the plague was at its height, all movement in the country had stopped. David himself was afraid to make the journey there to "inquire of God" (verse 30). Only when God himself gave the command did David think to offer sacrifice elsewhere. Once God had given that command, however, and David had seen how God received his sacrifice from Araunah's threshing floor, David then realized that this new site and this new altar, too, had God's approval. After the plague David continued to sacrifice there (verse 28). Even more than this, he realized that God had selected the place where his house would be built (1 Chronicles 28:1).

"The LORD will provide." Through righteous David, the Lord had given his people rest from their enemies. Through

David's pride, the Lord had chosen a site for his temple to be built. The Chronicler points this out to us, not to encourage us to sin, but to magnify God's grace in overruling evil and turning it to good. God can work through our strength. God can also work through our weakness. Because "his mercy is very great" (1 Chronicles 21:13), we can be sure that at the same moment the devil is present to destroy us, our loving God is also right there, present to preserve us. He can turn our greatest defeats into the most astounding victories of his grace.

David Prepares for the Building of God's House Under Solomon

C. David Personally Commissions His Son Solomon to Build the Temple

One might have expected David to show a certain lack of enthusiasm for a project he would never live to see completed. But that's not how things work in the kingdom of God. In the kingdom, a believer's chief concern is making God's name great, not in enhancing his own reputation. In the following chapters we learn how David did everything within his power to prepare the ground for Solomon to build the temple.

²So David gave orders to assemble the aliens living in Israel, and from among them he appointed stonecutters to prepare dressed stone for building the house of God. ³He provided a large amount of iron to make nails for the doors of the gateways and for the fittings, and more bronze than could be weighed. ⁴He also provided more cedar logs than could be counted, for the Sidonians and Tyrians had brought large numbers of them to David.

⁵David said, "My son Solomon is young and inexperienced, and the house to be built for the LORD should be of great magnificence and fame and splendor in the sight of all the nations.

Therefore I will make preparations for it." So David made extensive preparations before his death.

David vigorously set about gathering the resources necessary for carrying out such a tremendous task. The most obvious needs were for manpower, materials, and money. Aliens living within the borders of Israel were pressed into the service of the one true God. Some of them David had trained as stonecutters; their job was to "prepare dressed stone for building the house of God" (verse 2). These "aliens" were probably descended from the original inhabitants of the land who had survived Joshua's conquest of Palestine (see Joshua 9).

The gathering of materials the Chronicler describes for us in verses three and four. Other empire builders may have preserved adequate supplies of bronze and iron for making weapons. David stockpiled them for the house of his God. The timbers needed for the roof and the paneling were gathered together in number greater "than could be counted" (verse 4). These cedar logs were one of the benefits gained from the alliance with Hiram of Tyre, as we remember also from 1 Chronicles 14:1. From that same verse we learn David received skilled craftsmen from Tyre as well, men who knew how to work with stone and wood. It seems reasonable to conclude that David made use of these technicians from Tyre to train his own "home-grown" work force of non-Israelites. David's financial preparations will be described later on in this chapter.

Before anyone can consider himself ready to take on a project, he must give some thought to the people-factor. Many a job has failed, not because there wasn't enough materiel or money to complete it, but because not enough time was spent considering the gifts and abilities of those involved in it. David demonstrated here that he had good "people skills" in addition to his organizational genius. He recognized that his son Solomon was "young and inexperienced" (verse 5). No criticism of Solomon was intended. It was simply that David would not allow even a father's love to blind him to the fact that his son was young and the job before him was immense. That was why he was determined to do all he could to prepare the way for Solomon.

What made the task so huge was that God's house had to be a place of "great magnificence and fame and splendor" (verse 5). And this magnificence was not for its own sake, still less for the glory of those involved in the project. God's house had to be striking in its beauty, arresting in its glory "in the sight of all nations" (verse 5). Under the Old Covenant, Israel was God's "city set on a hill" (Matthew 5:14-16), a beacon of faith by which God intended to beckon to the heathen nations round about. The temple was Israel's beating heart. There God was present among his people as their Savior. In David's perception of the future magnificence of God's house we see his missionary zeal.

There is something very useful the church can learn from David's example here. Whenever a congregation begins to consider a large project, it is not unusual for two groups to form. There are the "practical" ones who ask questions like, "Who, what, where, when, and how much is this all going to cost?" Then there are the "visionaries" who gaze far ahead, seeing no obstacles, only opportunities. Often tension develops between the two groups. Tempers may flare; accusations may fly. The practical ones accuse the visionaries of not counting the cost. The visionaries accuse the practical ones of not having enough faith. David teaches us here that vision and practicality can walk hand in hand. He clearly saw God's house being built after his death. Yet he also made careful preparations. May we all learn in our life of discipleship both to count the cost and yet live from the vision of our Savior's love!

⁶Then he called for his son Solomon and charged him to build a house for the LORD, the God of Israel. ⁷David said to Solomon: "My son, I had it in my heart to build a house for the Name of the LORD my God. ⁸But this word of the LORD came to me: 'You have shed much blood and have fought many wars. You are not to build a house for my Name, because you have shed much blood on the earth in my sight. ⁹But you will have a son who will be a man of peace and rest, and I will give him rest from all his enemies on every side. His name will be Solomon, and I will grant Israel peace and quiet during his reign. ¹⁰He is the one who will build a house for my Name. He will be my son, and I will be his father. And I will establish the throne of his kingdom over Israel forever.'

¹¹"Now, my son, the LORD be with you, and may you have success and build the house of the LORD your God, as he said you would. ¹²May the LORD give you discretion and understanding when he puts you in command over Israel, so that you may keep the law of the LORD your God. ¹³Then you will have success if you are careful to observe the decrees and laws that the LORD gave Moses for Israel. Be strong and courageous. Do not be afraid or discouraged.

¹⁴"I have taken great pains to provide for the temple of the LORD a hundred thousand talents of gold, a million talents of silver, quantities of bronze and iron too great to be weighed, and wood and stone. And you may add to them. ¹⁵You have many workmen: stonecutters, masons and carpenters, as well as men skilled in every kind of work ¹⁶in gold and silver, bronze and iron—craftsmen beyond number. Now begin the work, and the LORD be with you."

Continuing in his preparations, David called in Solomon to commission him for the job personally. David's action sets a fine example of how Christian encouragement can be carried out. By way of prologue, David reminded his son that originally he himself had intended to build the house for the Lord. God's will had overruled David's, however, and David had learned through prophecy that his son would build the temple in his stead. David rehearsed the prophecy once again for his son. This way, Solomon would know that the words of encouragement that followed contained not only a father's pious wish, but the Lord's sure promise.

God had denied David the privilege of building him a house because "(he) had shed much blood on the earth in (God's) sight" (verse 8). It was far more expressive of the true intent of the temple to have a "man of peace and rest" (verse 9) build it. At the temple God would restore harmony once again between himself and his people, a harmony they disrupted by sin. At the temple a gracious God would hear the prayers of his people and bless them with his peace. As we learned in 1 Chronicles 12:1-22, the Hebrew concept of peace is far richer than the one suggested by the English word used to translate it. It is not merely an absence of war, but a positive state of well-being brought about when God is in heaven and all is right between him and the world.

Solomon is described here as the one who will usher in that era of peace and rest. Verse nine in the original contains a lovely little play on words, complete with punning, alliteration, and assonance. It is impossible to reproduce in English; a person can only read it in transliteration to get some feel for it: *Shelomoh yiyeh shemoh va shalom va sheker* (etc). Literally rendered those words read, "Solomon will be his name and peace and tranquility . . . (etc.)" The basis for the word-play is the similarity between Solomon's name and the word for peace in Hebrew. As the man is named, so is he. The man called "Peace" will bring peace upon Israel by building God's house of peace.

Solomon, of course, could only bring provisionally what Jesus brought perfectly. The tranquility every human heart longs for is found only in Jesus. He is the Prince of Peace and the great restgiver. He pledges to give peace and rest to all who look for it in him (Matthew 11:28). This promised rest has nothing to do with doing nothing. It has everything to do with sweet freedom from pain and fear, dread and duty, toil and trouble—freedom from all the present plagues upon the children of Adam. It starts with the forgiveness of sins and the restoration of our relationship with God. It ends in the perfect city whose gates are never closed, where death and sorrow and pain are not even memories (Revelation 21).

On the basis of the sure mercies promised to him, David spoke these words of encouragement to his son, "Now . . . the LORD be with you . . . build the house of the LORD your God, *as he said you would*" (verse 11). Assurance of success in this matter would not come from David's ardent desire, his careful preparations, or his son's skill. Solomon could be certain that he would build the house only because the Lord had said he would. We notice, too, that the specific portion of David's speech to his son in which he exhorts him to build is held together—top and bottom—by the words "The LORD be with you" (verse 11 and verse 16). These are not throwaway lines. Building on God's promise, David could pronounce this blessing on his son. The vast scale of the enterprise he was about to undertake might be daunting to Solomon. He had to remember he would not be working alone. God would be with him—with him, not as a block of stone, a piece of wood or as some rabbit's foot for good luck—but with him with all his power, the infinite resources of heaven, to see him through his task.

Knowing this, David went on to say, "Be strong and courageous. Do not be afraid or discouraged" (verse 13). With God at his side, Solomon could advance against a whole troop of enemies. With God at his side, he had no need to be afraid. What could man do to him?

Lastly, we notice that David reminded Solomon to hold fast to the law of Moses. He prayed that the Lord would give his son the "discretion and understanding" to prize this word from God as his most precious possession (verse 12). Then—provided he looked first to God's commands and observed them carefully (verse 13)—he would find the success he was looking for. The standard by which a king was judged under the Old Covenant was his faithfulness to the law of Moses. God never intended that a king should enjoy absolute power over his people. The king himself was bound by the *Torah,* the Mosaic law code, which served as the constitution for the kingdom of Israel. This standard was reaffirmed as part of the special promise David had received concerning his house. There God had said, "When (one of your sons) does wrong, I will punish him" (2 Samuel 7:14). God's love was not conditional; it would remain with the house of David. But if an individual king in David's line ignored God's law, he would suffer the consequences. Only by keeping the law could a king of Israel enjoy God's approval in his office and find success.

In a sense, what David said to his son Solomon was meant to be a word of encouragement to all his successors, however many there might be. The man after the Lord's own heart told them, "Trust in the LORD, hold fast to his Word, observe the law given by Moses. Then you will be successful." Throughout the rest of his book, this standard will be the one the Chronicler uses to evaluate a particular king's reign and the one that will explain the reason for a king's success—or lack of it—in his office as shepherd over God's people.

David's words are an echo of what God himself had instructed Moses to tell his successor Joshua (Deuteronomy

3:27,28; 31:6,7). David knew his Moses and had studied his writings carefully. Moses, like David, had been a leader who had not been permitted to see a task through to its logical conclusion. He had led Israel out of Egypt, and guided them through forty years of wandering in the wilderness. But he himself was not permitted to enter the land of promise. So he died—in sight of, but not actually reaching—the goal of all his work. The task of leading the Israelites into the land he had to leave to Joshua. By the example of these great men, God makes it clear that the mere achievement of goals—even godly goals—is not our main objective in life as children of God. Our main objective is to remain faithful to our gracious God and to make his name great by serving him in whatever way he sees fit. Whatever we accomplish, we leave to him.

David concluded his personal words of encouragement to Solomon by pointing to the resources he had secured to carry out the project (verses 14-16). In addition to the manpower and the materials already mentioned, we see that David's victorious campaigning had also taken care of the temple building fund. It contained "a hundred thousand talents of gold and a million talents of silver" (verse 14). These were huge amounts by any man's measure, but only fitting in view of the exalted use to which they would be put. Truly, the Lord's house would be one of "great magnificence and fame and splendor" (verse 5). While Solomon was free to add to these resources if he wished, it was clear that he would not have to begin his task by organizing a fund drive. David already had that matter well in hand.

"Encourage one another" the writer to the Hebrews urges us (Hebrews 10:25). We may do this on an informal basis or in a formal worship service. In either case, the church grows and is strengthened by "the mutual conversation and consolation of brethren" (Part III, Article IV, Smalcald Articles). As

243

we speak to one another, we learn from David to offer encouragement on the basis of God's promises and to remind each other of God's will. What better way is there to induct congregational officers into their office than to remind them of what God has promised concerning those who serve his people? What does a Christian, confused by the sinful world and his own flesh, more need to hear than the clear guidance offered by God's Word? What does a brother or sister overcome with despair need by way of consolation more than the assurance that "God is with you in Christ," in spite of how he may feel? The necessity for such mutual support becomes even greater as we "see the Day approaching" (Hebrews 10:25). Let's not give up offering encouragement to each other and (what is perhaps more difficult at times) receiving it from one another!

[17]Then David ordered all the leaders of Israel to help his son Solomon. [18]He said to them, "Is not the LORD your God with you? And has he not granted you rest on every side? For he has handed the inhabitants of the land over to me, and the land is subject to the LORD and to his people. [19]Now devote your heart and soul to seeking the LORD your God. Begin to build the sanctuary of the LORD God, so that you may bring the ark of the covenant of the LORD and the sacred articles belonging to God into the temple that will be built for the Name of the LORD."

As we know from the second book of Samuel, David had to deal with the jealousy and the infighting that come from one man's having many sons by several different wives. He had been forced to weather the outright rebellion of his son Absalom, who nearly toppled him from the throne. This, no doubt, provides the background for our understanding of these verses. David did not want the leaders of his people to be caught up in palace intrigue following his death. He wanted them to be perfectly aware that the Lord had chosen Solomon to be his successor. He also wanted them to know what the Lord intended to accomplish through Solomon. There was to be no unclarity either as to the person of his successor or as to the goal of his rule.

As he had done with Solomon, David encouraged his leaders with the thought that the Lord was with them. There could be no doubt of that. The evidence was clear: God had granted them victory after victory over their enemies so that they enjoyed "rest on every side." Pockets of heathen resistance within the promised land had also been mopped up, so that it could be said, "The land is subject to the LORD and to his people" (verse 18). It was also clear that the necessary prerequisites for building a permanent house for the Lord's name, as outlined by Moses, had been fully met.

"Now devote your heart and soul to seeking the LORD your God" (verse 19). Let your whole inner life be completely directed to the one true God. This comes even before carrying out the goals he may lay before you in this life. Yet where the inner focus of the heart is on the Savior God, the outward life will show evidence of this. God does not just convert our heart, but our mouths, our feet, and our hands as well. David had every right to expect of Israel's princes that their devotion to God would lead them directly into building his house.

The Lutheran church rightly emphasizes that we are saved through faith alone in Christ Jesus. It is perfectly correct to exclude any thought of our good deeds winning us a place in God's good graces. Sometimes, however, we act as if the only thing God had a right to expect of anyone was faith alone and the only thing the congregation could ask of us is that we believe. But true faith is never alone. Devotion of the heart leads to the devotion of the whole person, who offers to God his entire life. We have every right to expect that the leaders of God's people will lead by their example. After all, those whom they lead cannot see the faith in their hearts; but they can see how that faith leads a congregational officer to live his life. They can observe him listening to God's Word in Bible class and supporting the Lord's work with his time, his money, and his abilities. David was not shy in expressing what he expected from those who led God's people. Nor should we be. Is not the Lord our God with us? He has given us victory and rest in Christ our Lord!

David Prepares for the Building of God's House Under Solomon

D. David Organizes Israel in Support of God's House

Once again we come to a section in Chronicles that is of vital interest to the holy writer's original readers, but that is somewhat less exciting to us. Chapters 23 through 27 of 1 Chronicles deal with David's efforts to organize his people around the temple and its services. First on the Chronicler's list come the Levites, or temple workers, then the priests, the singers, the gatekeepers, the Levite trustees, the army, tribal chieftains, trustees of the crown and, finally, the royal advisors. Many of these groups we have met before in our study of chapters 6, 9, and 15 of 1 Chronicles. Judging from the amount of space he gives them in his book, these are people close to our writer's heart! Yet we need not trouble ourselves by repeating remarks made previously.

Our concern will be to understand in broad detail the major emphases of these chapters and to clear up difficulties along the way. The most important question for us to answer is this: "What message from God was the Chronicler speaking to his people by means of this information? What was he trying to tell them?" When we know that, we will better be able to see what God is saying to us today through these ancient lists.

We can say a couple of things already before we even begin looking for the answers to those questions. In these chapters we see David's drive to organize all Israel as the "kingdom of priests and . . . holy nation" (Exodus 19:6) that God intended them to be. Every public aspect of Israelite society was to be put in orbit around the temple and to find its focus there. We also learn a great deal from this passage about the complexity and the magnificence of the worship of God's people as it was conducted in that first temple.

1. David Organizes the Levites

23 When David was old and full of years, he made his son Solomon king over Israel.

²He also gathered together all the leaders of Israel, as well as the priests and Levites. ³The Levites thirty years old or more were counted, and the total number of men was thirty-eight thousand. ⁴David said, "Of these, twenty-four thousand are to supervise the work of the temple of the LORD and six thousand are to be officials and judges. ⁵Four thousand are to be gatekeepers and four thousand are to praise the LORD with the musical instruments I have provided for that purpose."

⁶David divided the Levites into groups corresponding to the sons of Levi: Gershon, Kohath and Merari.

⁷Belonging to the Gershonites:
    Ladan and Shimei.
    ⁸The sons of Ladan:
    Jehiel the first, Zetham and Joel—three in all.
    ⁹The sons of Shimei:
    Shelomoth, Haziel and Haran—three in all.
    These were the heads of the families of Ladan.

¹⁰And the sons of Shimei:

Jahath, Ziza, Jeush and Beriah. These were the sons of Shimei—four in all.

¹¹Jahath was the first and Ziza the second, but Jeush and Beriah did not have many sons; so they were counted as one family with one assignment.

¹²The sons of Kohath:

Amram, Izhar, Hebron and Uzziel—four in all.

¹³The sons of Amram:

Aaron and Moses.

Aaron was set apart, he and his descendants forever, to consecrate the most holy things, to offer sacrifices before the LORD, to minister before him and to pronounce blessings in his name forever. ¹⁴The sons of Moses the man of God were counted as part of the tribe of Levi.

¹⁵The sons of Moses:

Gershom and Eliezer.

¹⁶The descendants of Gershom:

Shubael was the first.

¹⁷The descendants of Eliezer:

Rehabiah was the first.

Eliezer had no other sons, but the sons of Rehabiah were very numerous.

¹⁸The sons of Izhar:

Shelomith was the first.

¹⁹The sons of Hebron:

Jeriah the first, Amariah the second, Jahaziel the third and Jekameam the fourth.

²⁰The sons of Uzziel:

Micah the first and Isshiah the second.

²¹The sons of Merari:

Mahli and Mushi.

The sons of Mahli:

Eleazar and Kish.

²² Eleazar died without having sons: he had only daughters. Their cousins, the sons of Kish, married them.
²³The sons of Mushi:

Mahli, Eder and Jerimoth—three in all.

We are told that, towards the end of his life, David called together an assembly of "all the leaders of Israel, as well as the priests and Levites" (verse 2). David's purpose for gathering this assembly was to announce publicly Solomon's ascent to the throne as his co-regent over Israel (verse 1) and to make official the organizational plans he had for Israel. More than likely he had been in the process of putting all of this in place for some time already. Now he announced the final results. Apparently David realized the need for such a meeting after Adonijah's abortive attempt to take over the reins of power, as described in 1 Kings chapters 1 and 2.

The Levites who responded to David's summons were counted (verse 3). David wanted to know how many Levites there were "thirty years old or more." Later the cut-off point was lowered to those who were twenty or older (see verse 27). This census did not incur God's wrath as the previous one had. The motives for doing it were different. The previous one had arisen out of David's desire to find security in the numbers of fighting men he had. This one was to organize the Levites for their work in the temple. The previous one had been for the glory of David; this one was for the glory of God.

After the poll had been taken, David used the information to divide up the Levites into working groups (verses 3-5). Twenty-four thousand would serve in the temple itself, directly assisting the priests in the work of offering sacrifice. Six thousand would serve as officials of the temple and servants of the crown. Further details on their responsibilities will be given later (see 1 Chronicles 26:20-32). Four thousand would make up the gate keepers of the temple, and the final four thousand would provide musical accompaniment for the temple services. Details of their organization and duties will be given in chapters 25 and 26 respectively.

David did not invent his organizational chart out of whole cloth; he worked with the tribal and clan structure that was already in place. In David's division of the Levites we note the major (and by now familiar) clan divisions of Gershon, Kohath, and Merari (verse 6). We must pause awhile at Gershon's list to unravel a couple of difficulties. In other lists of the Gershonite clans, the two sons of Gershon are named Libni and Shimei, not Ladan and Shimei as we find here. This is best explained either by way of the "one-man-with-two-names" phenomenon that we have encountered before or as being an alteration of the spelling of the clan-father's name. This could easily have occurred with the passing of years. The second difficulty involves the plethora of Shimei's. The name appears three times in this short list: first, as Gershon's son (verse 7), as part of Ladan's clan (verse 9), and finally as a clan father in his own right (verse 10). Just how many Shimei's are there? It seems clear enough that the Shimei of verse 10 is the son of Gershon mentioned in verse 7. But what about the Shimei of verse 9? Is he an otherwise unmentioned son of Ladan? Or is it the same Shimei in all three cases? To hazard a guess, we might say that this list is just the Chronicler's way of informing us that, somehow, some of Shimei's descendants became associated with Ladan's clan. We have no way of knowing how rigid these clan divisions were. The exact understanding remains unclear.

Beginning with verse 12, the sons of Kohath are listed according to their major subdivisions: Amram, Izhar, Hebron, and Uzziel. Once again the Chronicler points out the distinct nature of the office held by Aaron and his descendants. God had set him apart as a priest "to consecrate the most holy things, to offer sacrifices . . . to minister before [the LORD] and to pronounce blessings in his name." This was God's permanent arrangement for Israel (verse 13). Even though this one clan in Israel was distinguished by having this particular responsibility, no slight was intended for any of the other sons of Levi. After all, the sons of Moses were counted as Levites, not as priests; and Moses was the great man of God, the fundamental prophet of Israel (verse 14)!

Levi's third son Merari receives his own listing in verses 21 to 23. Those who are familiar with genealogies notice a familiar phrase tacked onto Eleazar's line of descent. We are told that Eleazar "died without sons: he had only daughters" (verse 22). Their cousins, the sons of Kish, married them in order to preserve the rights of inheritance. For more information on this practice see Numbers 36:8 and the comments made on 1 Chronicles 7:14-19.

24These were the descendants of Levi by their families— the heads of families as they were registered under their names and counted individually, that is, the workers twenty years old or more who served in the temple of the LORD. 25For David had said, "Since the LORD, the God of Israel, has granted rest to his people and has come to dwell in Jerusalem forever, 26the Levites no longer need to carry the tabernacle or any of the articles used in its service." 27According to the last instructions of David, the Levites were counted from those twenty years old or more.

28The duty of the Levites was to help Aaron's descendants in the service of the temple of the LORD: to be in charge of the courtyards, the side rooms, the purification of all sacred things and the performance of other duties at the house of God. 29They were in charge of the bread set out on the table, the

flour for the grain offerings, the unleavened wafers, the baking and the mixing, and all measurements of quantity and size. [30]They were also to stand every morning to thank and praise the LORD. They were to do the same in the evening [31]and whenever burnt offerings were presented to the LORD on Sabbaths and at New Moon festivals and at appointed feasts. They were to serve before the LORD regularly in the proper number and in the way prescribed for them.

[32]And so the Levites carried out their responsibilities for the Tent of Meeting, for the Holy Place and, under their brothers the descendants of Aaron, for the service of the temple of the LORD.

As he had done with the princes of Israel (1 Chronicles 22:17-19), so now David took the time to explain to the Levites the reason for all this restructuring. He wanted them to have their goal clearly in mind. "The LORD, the God of Israel, has granted rest to his people and has come to dwell in Jerusalem forever" (verse 25). Reading between the lines of his remarks, we see that he was informing the Levites of the new way of things. From that point on, there would be only one central place of worship, as God had predicted in Deuteronomy. That central place would be Jerusalem. The ark and all the articles of Israel's worship would soon be housed in a permanent temple. The era of the moveable tabernacle was swiftly drawing to a close. It might seem as if the Levites would be left with no official worship duties to carry out, if they "no longer need[ed] to carry the tabernacle or any of [its] articles" (verse 26). This, however, was not the case. Their presence was even more necessary in the new era "to help Aaron's descendants in the service of the temple of the LORD" (verse 28). What those duties were to be with respect to the daily sacrificial routine, David spelled out for them in what follows.

In keeping with the sacred nature of the temple precincts, the Levites—as those set apart for the service of the Lord—were to have charge over "the courtyards, the side rooms, and the purification of all sacred things" (verse 28). By recounting this instruction of David's, the Chronicler was trying to deal with a problem that existed in the time of the return from exile. The priests had a predilection, apparently, for letting out rooms in the temple for the use of non-Israelites (see Nehemiah 13). This shocking disregard for the way things ought to be was an insult to the Lord, and a flagrant usurpation of the rights given by David to the Levites. Everything in the temple betokened a holy God who was set apart from sinners. He could be approached only in the prescribed way. The Levites played a crucial role in maintaining the purity of God's house. They were to be in charge of those rooms.

The other duties that the Chronicler lists have to do with the regular worship activities of God's house. We looked at some of those duties before under 1 Chronicles 9:28-34. There the Chronicler was discussing the Levitical responsibilities as they were reestablished following the return from exile. Here he traces the origin of those temple duties back to David and the first temple. It was vital for God's people, discouraged as they were following the return to Judah, to recognize the validity of their present institutions by seeing their connection with the sacred past. The Chronicler makes that link explicit in these verses.

Our writer concludes this section with the words, "And so the Levites carried out their responsibilities . . . under their brothers, the descendants of Aaron, for the service of the temple of the LORD" (verse 32). In emphasizing the importance of the work of the Levites, the Chronicler makes it clear that he does not want to transgress the proper order of things prescribed by God. Levites were to serve "under their

253

brothers, the descendants of Aaron." He needed to encourage the Levites of his day to report for duty at the temple in numbers larger than they had previously (see 1 Chronicles 6). But he refused to do so in a way that would erase or alter what God had ordained through Moses. Their work was important. Yet it was different from that of the priests. Priests were not to take away the prerogatives of the Levites. Levites were not to pretend they were priests. Let them hold this thought before their eyes: whatever they did, they did "for the service of the temple of the LORD."

As the church nears the end of the twentieth century, it has had to grapple with questions of ministry and the various roles to be carried out as we serve our God together. What is a pastor? What is a teacher? What is a staff-minister? What is the distinction between the public ministry, into which the church calls qualified candidates, and the personal ministry belonging to each one of us as priests of God anointed by baptism? Complicating these questions still further is the worldly rhetoric coming from radical feminists as well as mindless male-chauvinists. When Christians speak of these things, it is far too easy to let our sinful nature dictate. We frame the debate in terms of worldly conceptions of power. The whole issue degenerates into invalid value judgments ("This job is important; this job is not so important") and turf battles (Here's what I can do; here's what you can't do; here's what we'll let you do).

What God caused the Chronicler to write so long ago can help us keep our head on straight today. He reframes the question for us by presenting us with three vital points we must consider with respect to service offered to God. The first is: all service to God has infinite worth, not because of what it is in itself. It can be the scouring of a pot, the cleaning of a worship implement, or the singing of a song. It derives its value from the fact that it is done according to God's command and offered to him. Not the offerer, not what he offers, but the one to whom he offers it, is the consideration that gives value to service. The second point is that such service cannot go against God's Word and still be service to God. Simply giving something the name of a rose will not make it smell as sweet. The third point is that different groups may have different responsibilities, but they are no less loved by God for that. And if they are loved by God, we, too, will hold them in high regard as worthy of our love and respect. The church has no need for prima donnas and grandstanders. It has great need for Christians who are ruled by a spirit of humility and who "consider others better than themselves" (Philippians 2:3). The congregation where such a spirit prevails will work in harmony as they offer a united worship to God in all they do. These ideas are still further developed in what follows.

2. David Organizes the Priests

24 These were the divisions of the sons of Aaron:
The sons of Aaron were Nadab, Abihu, Eleazar and Ithamar. ²But Nadab and Abihu died before their father did, and they had no sons; so Eleazar and Ithamar served as the priests. ³With the help of Zadok a descendant of Eleazar and Ahimelech a descendant of Ithamar, David separated them into divisions for their appointed order of ministering. ⁴A larger number of leaders were found among Eleazar's descendants than among Ithamar's, and they were divided accordingly: sixteen heads of families from Eleazar's descendants and eight heads of families from Ithamar's descendants. ⁵They divided them impartially by drawing lots, for there were officials of the sanctuary and officials of God among the descendants of both Eleazar and Ithamar.

⁶The scribe Shemaiah son of Nethanel, a Levite, recorded their names in the presence of the king and of the officials:

Zadok the priest, Ahimelech son of Abiathar and the heads of families of the priests and of the Levites—one family being taken from Eleazar and then one from Ithamar.

> [7]The first lot fell to Jehoiarib,
>   the second to Jedaiah,
> [8]the third to Harim,
>   the fourth to Seorim,
> [9]the fifth to Malkijah,
>   the sixth to Mijamin,
> [10]the seventh to Hakkoz,
>   the eighth to Abijah,
> [11]the ninth to Jeshua,
>   the tenth to Shecaniah,
> [12]the eleventh to Eliashib,
>   the twelfth to Jakim,
> [13]the thirteenth to Huppah,
>   the fourteenth to Jeshebeab,
> [14]the fifteenth to Bilgah,
>   the sixteenth to Immer,
> [15]the seventeenth to Hezir,
>   the eighteenth to Happizzez,
> [16]the nineteenth to Pethahiah,
>   the twentieth to Jehezkel,
> [17]the twenty-first to Jakin,
>   the twenty-second to Gamul,
> [18]the twenty-third to Delaiah
>   and the twenty-fourth to Maaziah.

[19]This was their appointed order of ministering when they entered the temple of the LORD, according to the regulations prescribed for them by their forefather Aaron, as the LORD, the God of Israel, had commanded him.

God clearly spelled out the division of labor between priest and Levite at the time of Moses, when he said to

Aaron, "Only you and your sons may serve as priests in connection with everything at the altar and inside the curtain. I am giving you the service of the priesthood as a gift. Anyone else who comes near the sanctuary must be put to death" (Numbers 18:7). Priests were the mediators between the Israelites and their God. For the Old Testament believer the only way to God was through the priest. This office was a gift of God's grace, not a reward given to those who had earned it by good behavior. The Chronicler also gave a reminder to anyone who wished to go against God's order in verse 2. Let them consider Nadab and Abihu and what their self-prescribed worship led to in their case. For more background, the reader can consult the comments made in connection with 1 Chronicles 9:1-14.

To prepare for the temple services, David organized the priesthood into twenty-four divisions. These twenty-four divisions came from the two great priestly houses of Israel, named after the two remaining sons of Aaron, Eleazar and Ithamar. At the time of David, the house of Eleazar had come to be the more dominant of the two, because they had "a larger number of leaders" among them (verse 4). For this reason, sixteen of the priestly divisions came from Eleazar's line, and only eight from Ithamar's. We are surely not wrong in seeing this lopsided strength of Eleazar's line as being evidence of the working out of God's curse upon Eli, a descendant of Ithamar. Again the reader is encouraged to consult the commentary at 1 Chronicles 9:1-14 for more information.

Our writer is eager to point out the impartial way in which this division of priests was made. Representatives from both priestly houses helped David in arriving at the final disposition (verse 3). The divisions themselves were made by lot, since all recognized that there were leading priests to be found in both houses (verse 5). Casting lots

257

was an Old Testament way of leaving the decision up to God (see Leviticus 16:7,8). The whole process was done out in the open, in front of the king and his top officials. Shemaiah the scribe kept a public record of the results (verse 6). Finally, to ensure complete impartiality, the choosing alternated back and forth between the house of Eleazar and the house of Ithamar (verse 6).

Why this scrupulosity? Isn't it possible for children of the kingdom to trust one another? Certainly! But we recognize we still live in the world and not in heaven, and we still have a sinful nature. Love wants to give no base from which the flesh can operate, nor room in which the devil can maneuver. In matters that concern everyone, we want to give no one reason to accuse us of unfairness or impropriety. A child of God in the New Testament may not feel he has to adopt the same methods to ensure impartiality, but he shares the same concerns.

We see the actual list of the divisions in verses 7 to 18. Of these, it seems that only those of Jedaiah, Harim, and Immer (verses 7, 8, and 14) survived both the exile and the return intact (see Ezra 2:36-39). Somewhere along the line another clan by the name of Pashhur arose to prominence among the priestly houses and was counted as one of the twenty-four by the time of the restoration (see 1 Chronicles 9:12). Descendants of Hakkoz (verse 10) also came back from exile, but since they were unable to prove their descent, they were deemed unfit to serve as priests (Ezra 2:61,62).

From the New Testament we learn that this method of organizing the priests had worked out so well that it was still in effect at the time of Christ. Luke introduces the father of John the Baptist to us as Zechariah, a member of the "the priestly division of Abijah" (Luke 1:5). The gospel-writer also gives additional information on the way it all functioned in practice. Apparently, men from the twenty-four groups took turns in providing the regular priestly service in the temple. It does not seem too far-fetched to suppose that two divisions were responsible for each month of the year, much as the army division given later (see 1 Chronicles 27). The distribution of the particular duties was portioned out by lot (Luke 1:8-10). This leads us to conclude that it was a rare occasion when a priest from the rank-and-file would have an opportunity to perform some priestly service in the temple. When Zechariah learned that he had been chosen to burn incense in the sanctuary, he must have felt as if he had attained the high point of his career!

20As for the rest of the descendants of Levi:
  from the sons of Amram: Shubael;
    from the sons of Shubael: Jehdeiah.
   21As for Rehabiah, from his sons:
    Isshiah was the first.
22From the Izharites: Shelomoth;
  from the sons of Shelomoth: Jahath.
23The sons of Hebron: Jeriah the first, Amariah the second, Jahaziel the third and Jekameam the fourth.
24The son of Uzziel: Micah;
  from the sons of Micah: Shamir.
  25 The brother of Micah: Isshiah;
    from the sons of Isshiah: Zechariah.
26The sons of Merari: Mahli and Mushi.
  The son of Jaaziah: Beno.
27The sons of Merari:
  from Jaaziah: Beno, Shoham, Zaccur and Ibri.
28From Mahli: Eleazar, who had no sons.
29From Kish: the son of Kish:
  Jerahmeel.
30And the sons of Mushi: Mahli, Eder and Jerimoth.

These were the Levites, according to their families. [31]They also cast lots, just as their brothers the descendants of Aaron did, in the presence of King David and of Zadok, Ahimelech, and the heads of families of the priests and of the Levites. The families of the oldest brother were treated the same as those of the youngest.

The Chronicler concludes chapter 24 with some additional genealogical information on Levitical families he introduced to us in chapter 23. In chapter 23 we were told that Kohath had four sons: Amram, Izhar, Hebron, and Uzziel (verse 12). Here he delineates how those clans developed further and continued to subdivide into the prominent families listed in verses 20 to 25. Our writer also gives us further information on the major clan of Merari in verses 26 to 30. Since these families are listed right after the priests, we might well suppose that these particular Levites worked under the supervision of the priests in all the duties connected with sacrifice. As we shall see in the two chapters to come, other Levites were assigned duties as singers and gatekeepers.

We observe once again the impartial way in which David portioned out the various assignments and duty-rosters among these Levites. "Just as their brothers" the priests did, the Levites publicly cast lots to determine when and who was to do what (verse 31). No age-bias was shown. "The families of the oldest brother were treated the same as those of the youngest" (verse 31). In our days we may sometimes grow weary of people clamoring for their rights. Accusations of prejudice, ageism, sexism, and racial bias are easily made and not soon forgotten. Very often a reputation may be smeared for life by an unsubstantiated allegation. At the same time may we never grow weary in doing what is right! The church should not be the last in line to see to it that peo-

ple are treated fairly in its midst. The church ought not need
the government or the threat of lawsuits to force it into elimi-
nating bias, if it exists. David wanted to be impartial in the
way temple workers were treated. So do we wish to be unbi-
ased as we deal with one another in God's household.

3. David Organizes the Levitical Singers

25 David, together with the commanders of the army, set
apart some of the sons of Asaph, Heman and Jeduthun
for the ministry of prophesying, accompanied by harps, lyres
and cymbals. Here is the list of the men who performed this
service:

²From the sons of Asaph:

Zaccur, Joseph, Nethaniah and Asarelah. The sons of
Asaph were under the supervision of Asaph, who
prophesied under the king's supervision.

³As for Jeduthun, from his sons:

Gedaliah, Zeri, Jeshaiah, Shimei, Hashabiah and
Mattithiah, six in all, under the supervision of their
father Jeduthun, who prophesied, using the harp in
thanking and praising the LORD.

⁴As for Heman, from his sons:

Bukkiah, Mattaniah, Uzziel, Shubael and Jerimoth;
Hananiah, Hanani, Eliathah, Giddalti and Romamti-
Ezer; Joshbekashah, Mallothi, Hothir and Mahazioth. ⁵All these were sons of Heman the king's seer.
They were given him through the promises of God to
exalt him. God gave Heman fourteen sons and three
daughters.

⁶All these men were under the supervision of their fathers
for the music of the temple of the LORD, with cymbals, lyres
and harps, for the ministry at the house of God. Asaph, Jeduthun and Heman were under the supervision of the king.
⁷Along with their relatives—all of them trained and skilled in

music for the LORD—they numbered 288. ⁸Young and old alike, teacher as well as student, cast lots for their duties.

⁹ The first lot, which was for Asaph,
>   fell to Joseph,
>   his sons and relatives,   12*
>   the second to Gedaliah,
>   he and his relatives and sons,   12
¹⁰the third to Zaccur,
>   his sons and relatives,   12
¹¹the fourth to Izri,
>   his sons and relatives,   12
¹²the fifth to Nethaniah,
>   his sons and relatives,   12
¹³the sixth to Bukkiah,
>   his sons and relatives,   12
¹⁴the seventh to Jesarelah,
>   his sons and relatives,   12
¹⁵the eighth to Jeshaiah,
>   his sons and relatives,   12
¹⁶the ninth to Mattaniah,
>   his sons and relatives,   12
¹⁷the tenth to Shimei,
>   his sons and relatives,   12
¹⁸the eleventh to Azarel,
>   his sons and relatives,   12
¹⁹the twelfth to Hashabiah,
>   his sons and relatives,   12
²⁰the thirteenth to Shubael,
>   his sons and relatives,   12
²¹the fourteenth to Mattithiah,
>   his sons and relatives,   12
²²the fifteenth to Jerimoth,
>   his sons and relatives,   12

---

*See the total in verse 7; the Hebrew does not have 12

[23]the sixteenth to Hananiah,
his sons and relatives,   12
[24]the seventeenth to Joshbekashah,
his sons and relatives,   12
[25]the eighteenth to Hanani,
his sons and relatives,   12
[26]the nineteenth to Mallothi,
his sons and relatives,   12
[27]the twentieth to Eliathah,
his sons and relatives,   12
[28]the twenty-first to Hothir,
his sons and relatives,   12
[29]the twenty-second to Giddalti,
his sons and relatives,   12
[30]the twenty-third to Mahazioth,
his sons and relatives,   12
[31]the twenty-fourth to Romamti-Ezer,
his sons and relatives,   12

David could not consider his preparations for the temple complete without paying attention to the music. We have already noted David's lifelong interest in the worship of God through song. He was a composer of psalms, a maker of instruments, and an accomplished musician and singer in his own right. We see it as entirely within his character that at the end of his life he would want to ensure that musical worship would continue in the temple his son would build.

Leaders among God's people have always been aware of the power of music and have been eager to press it into service of the Word. Luther once remarked, "I would certainly like to praise music with all my heart as the excellent gift of God which it is and commend it to everyone . . . let this noble, wholesome, and cheerful creation of God be commended to you. . . . At the same time may you by this creation accustom yourself to *recognize and praise the Creator.*" As the spiritual heirs of men like David and Luther, may we, too, regard music as one of the best gifts God has to give to his church and see to it that musicians and their music are given the honor and respect they deserve, as they serve us in our worship of God. Let's pay attention to the music!

The NIV gives us what is most probably an incorrect translation when it tells us that David appointed singers in consultation with "the commanders *of the army*" (verse 1). The Hebrew for this phrase means simply, "the leaders of the host." "The host," in this case, could refer just as well to the tribal "host" of Levi as it could to the army "host." It is hard to see why David would have involved the army in the organization of the temple singers. When he prepared the singers to bring the ark up to Jerusalem, David had consulted "the leaders of the Levites" (1 Chronicles 15:16). It seems likely that he is doing the same thing here.

By now Asaph, Heman, and Jeduthun (also known as Ethan) are old friends to us (verse 1). David organized the three great guilds of temple singers around them and their families. The holy writer's purpose in including the list here is to remind the exiles who returned to serve in the second temple about their glorious past. We remember how few of the Levites responded to the call to return and rebuild. The list of Levites given in 1 Chronicles 9:14-16 seems rather pitiful when compared with the ones given here. The houses of Asaph, Heman, and Jeduthun had fallen on hard times! We can hardly fault those Levites, humanly speaking, for wondering if their service still had any value, or if they were still the ones God had chosen to do this work. After all, even if they were too young to remember the glories of the first temple, they had been exposed to all the pomp and circumstance of the false worship conducted in heathen lands. What went on in the second temple must have seemed shabby to them by comparison.

That is why the Chronicler patiently takes the time to remind them of how they had received their ministry of music in the house of God. Their families had received a divine call to serve! "David . . . set apart Asaph, Heman, and Jeduthun for the ministry of prophesying, accompanied by harps, lyres, and cymbals" (verse 1). And when David did it, it was the same as God doing it. For it was the Lord, the God of Israel, who had chosen David to be the shepherd and ruler over his people (1 Chronicles 11:2,3). Furthermore, David's actions—particularly with respect to the temple and its services—had an enduring significance, as enduring as the dynasty God had promised to establish from David's descendants. "Don't you see?" the holy writer is telling his Levite contemporaries, "You cannot find assurance in your calling on the basis of how big a temple you serve in or in how many serve with you or how splendid the services are in which you participate. The true glory of your calling is found in the fact that God has set you apart through righteous king David to serve in this way."

In a similar way, the public ministry has fallen on hard times lately. Nearly every week the media brings us another barrage of reports of venality, corruption, and lust among public servants of the Word. It is no great surprise that people have less and less respect for the ministry, and it's no great wonder that those still in the ministry struggle with the legitimacy of their vocation. "This is so hard! Not at all what I expected. Is this really what God wants me to be doing?" These and other thoughts plague the minds of our called workers. Where can they receive assurance in their work? Where but in the same place the Chronicler wanted his contemporaries to find renewal! Acting through his church that assembles in his name, our righteous King Jesus has set apart his servants to proclaim his gospel message (Matthew 18:19,20; Acts

20:28). They are gifts our victorious Lord gives to his church (Ephesians 4:11). Do not be deceived by mega-temples, media charmers or crystal cathedrals into believing that there is a better way of proving the validity of one's vocation. Christ has called us. There is no greater legitimacy than that.

Since we understand the main thrust of the Chronicler's message, we can now devote a little time to uncover a few of the lesser truths to be found in chapter 25. It is interesting to note that skill in music and the gift of prophecy went hand in hand at the time of David. The ability to prophesy (proclaim messages inspired from God) is mentioned three times in connection with the ministry of these singing guilds (verse 1, 2, and 3). In addition, Heman was accorded the title of "the king's *seer*," another word for prophet. A brief glance at the book of Psalms confirms what the holy writer is telling us here. The names of Asaph, Ethan, Jeduthun, and Heman appear in the titles of sixteen psalms. God worked through these singers to proclaim his message to Israel. In connection with this prophesying, we are told that it was either done "under the king's supervision" or under the supervision of one of the guild leaders (verses 2 and 6). Prophecy did not have to be accompanied by some wild, ecstatic display before it could qualify as true prophecy. It was subject to and carried out under the supervision of legitimate authority. Even in the Old Testament "the spirits of the prophets (were) subject to the control of the prophets" (1 Corinthians 14:32).

As we proceed with our overview of the chapter, we see the Chronicler's continued concern in pointing out the impartiality of the selection process. This time he also adds the fact that a singer's status as a teacher did not cause him to be chosen over a student for a round of temple duties (verse 8). Notice, too, that those chosen all had to have the basic qualifications necessary to carry out their ministry. Not only were they people "skilled in music" (verse 7), but they also were those who were willing to hone their skills by further training. There were teachers to teach and students willing to learn (verse 8). In other words, the selection by lot was carried out only after David and the Levites had exercised their own common sense in picking out the ones who had the qualifications to do the work. They did not expect a mere casting of a lot suddenly to supply people with skills they did not previously possess. So, too, in selecting people to carry out various roles and ministries in the church, we ought not take the "least common denominator" approach and simply lay hands suddenly on those who volunteer for everything, or on people whom we know will not refuse us when we ask for help. First look for those who possess the requisite skills for the ministry to which we are calling them. Then ask them to serve.

As the priests had been divided into 24 groups, so, too, the temple singers were now divided into 24 groups of 12, bringing the total of those selected to 288 (verses 9-31; verse 7). Again we surmise that these divisions were to serve on a rotating basis, with each division being given responsibility for half a month out of every year. The recurrence of the number twelve and its multiples is a reminder that priest and Levite were to represent *all* Israel—each one of the twelve tribes—in the worship of God.

Finally we close our study of 1 Chronicles 25 with another little excursion into the meaning of Hebrew names. In this case, we wish to look at the names Heman gave to his sons (verse 4). What is not apparent to the English reader is something that would have been easily discerned by someone who could read this account in the original. God had marked Heman out as an object of special favor. He had given him "fourteen sons and three daughters" (verse 5). In return, Heman gave his last nine sons names, which, when reeled off one after the other, formed a psalm of praise to the God who had so graciously kept his promise to exalt him. Let the following table demonstrate what I mean:

HEBREW NAME	*ENGLISH TRANSLATION*
Hananiah	Have mercy, O LORD!
Hanani	Have mercy on me!
Eliathah	You are my God,
Giddalti	whom I magnify
Romamti	and exalt.
Ezer(J)oshbekashah	My Helper when in difficulty,
Mallothi	He has endowed me
Hothir	by an abundance
Mahazioth	of (prophetic) visions

So Heman gives glory back to God in these names for his sons, just as God had given glory to Heman by blessing him with so many children and such a fruitful ministry! It is not hard for any pious parent to grasp what the Chronicler wants to tell us here. We also wish to give thanks to God for his blessing of children, and we pray that—whatever their names might be—their lives may form a song of praise to the God who has so graciously redeemed us in Christ.

26 **The divisions of the gatekeepers:**

From the Korahites: Meshelemiah son of Kore, one of the sons of Asaph.

²Meshelemiah had sons:
Zechariah the firstborn,
Jediael the second,
Zebadiah the third,
Jathniel the fourth,

³Elam the fifth,
Jehohanan the sixth
and Eliehoenai the seventh.
⁴Obed-Edom also had sons:
Shemaiah the firstborn,
Jehozabad the second,
Joah the third,
Sacar the fourth,
Nethanel the fifth,
⁵Ammiel the sixth,
Issachar the seventh
and Peullethai the eighth.
(For God had blessed Obed-Edom.)

⁶His son Shemaiah also had sons, who were leaders in their father's family because they were very capable men. ⁷The sons of Shemaiah: Othni, Rephael, Obed and Elzabad; his relatives Elihu and Semakiah were also able men. ⁸All these were descendants of Obed-Edom; they and their sons and their relatives were capable men with the strength to do the work—descendants of Obed-Edom, 62 in all.

⁹Meshelemiah had sons and relatives, who were able men—18 in all.

¹⁰Hosah the Merarite had sons: Shimri the first (although he was not the firstborn, his father had appointed him the first), ¹¹Hilkiah the second, Tabaliah the third and Zechariah the fourth. The sons and relatives of Hosah were 13 in all.

¹²These divisions of the gatekeepers, through their chief men, had duties for ministering in the temple of the LORD, just as their relatives had. ¹³Lots were cast for each gate, according to their families, young and old alike.

¹⁴The lot for the East Gate fell to Shelemiah. Then lots were cast for his son Zechariah, a wise counselor, and the lot for the North Gate fell to him. ¹⁵The lot for the South Gate fell to

Obed-Edom, and the lot for the storehouse fell to his sons. [16]The lots for the West Gate and the Shalleketh Gate on the upper road fell to Shuppim and Hosah.

Guard was alongside of guard: [17]There were six Levites a day on the east, four a day on the north, four a day on the south and two at a time at the storehouse. [18]As for the court to the west, there were four at the road and two at the court itself.

[19]These were the divisions of the gatekeepers who were descendants of Korah and Merari.

In the section before us now, the Chronicler spells out how David organized the four thousand Levites he had chosen to serve as gatekeepers in the temple (1 Chronicles 23:5). Again our writer wants to link up the work of the Levites who returned to serve in the second temple (see 1 Chronicles 9:17-27) with the foundation for it laid under David. Unless a believer is sure that what he does is pleasing to God, he can have no joy in doing it. With these words the holy writer assures the gatekeepers of his day, "You are where you are and you do what you do because God has called you and your clans through David to perform this vital service for him."

The gatekeepers traced their descent from the two major Levite clans of Kohath and Merari. Meshelemiah (verse 2), as well as all the other "sons of Korah" (verse 1), were from *Kohath*. Obed-Edom (verse 4) and Hosah (verse 10) both could trace their lineage back to *Merari* (see 1 Chronicles 16:38 and 6:44). Gershon, Levi's other major clan, was not represented among the gatekeepers. It is helpful in making sense of these lists to note that the "Shelemiah" of verse 14 is the same man as the "Meshelemiah" of verses 2 and 9. And as long as we're clearing away things that might confuse us, we should also take note that the "Asaph" of verse 1 is *not* the same man as the great musician and psalm composer. Other passages in 1 Chronicles give this man's name to us as

"Ebiasaph" (1 Chronicles 6:23 and 9:19). By now, we are able to take in stride alternate spellings of the same name.

In line with his basic purpose, our writer demonstrates in several ways that this office enjoyed God's special favor and required men of the highest calibre to serve in it. The number of sons given to Meshelemiah and Obed-Edom was a sign of God's blessing (verse 5). Obed-Edom's sons are further described as being "leaders," "very capable men" who possessed the "strength to do the work" (verses 6 and 8). Zechariah, the son of Meshelemiah, is held up for special comment as a "wise counselor" (verse 14). We know from the earlier account of the ark being brought up to Jerusalem that Obed-Edom himself was a man of many talents. Not only was he a gatekeeper, he was also an accomplished musician (1 Chronicles 15:21 and 16:5). The point is that these men were not given the task of gatekeeper because David could think of nothing else to do with them. They were talented men, and it was precisely because of their gifts that David selected them to occupy their high office.

When we combine this account with 1 Chronicles 9:23-27, we get a fair idea of what was entailed in being a gatekeeper. Their chief mission was to preserve the outward purity of God's house. To do this they would guard the entrances (1 Chronicles 9:23) so that no one unfit or unclean according to the law of Moses could enter (see Exodus 12:48 and Psalm 15:1-5). They were the first ones there to open up the gates at daybreak and the last ones there to close things down at night. Some were posted at various stations around the temple courts to keep watch throughout the hours of darkness (1 Chronicles 9:27). During the day others were, no doubt, responsible for keeping the temple courtyards free from disturbances. Worshipers of God had a right to expect a peaceful and orderly environment in which to offer their praises to the

Most High. Conflict and fighting would defile God's house. Charge of guarding the temple storerooms was also given to these men (verses 14 and 17). This concern for keeping God's house free from things that defile arose out of a deep reverence for the holy God. In his presence no sinner could stand unless he had first been cleansed and pardoned. The order and peace within the house of prayer was to reflect the character of the God whose dwelling place it was.

As consciences become dulled these days, it seems that a sense of sin is largely absent from the heart of modern man. When he lay dying, Heinrich Heine, the German poet, is reported to have said, *"Dieu me pardonnera. C'est son metier!"* "Of course God will forgive me. That's what he's good at!" To people who more and more take God's grace for granted, Christians need to reaffirm the holiness of God and say with David, "You are not a God who takes pleasure in evil; with you the wicked cannot dwell. The arrogant cannot stand in your presence; you hate all who do wrong" (Psalm 5:4,5). The Spirit must continually strive in Christians, too, so that they make their own the heartfelt cry of Isaiah, "Woe is me for I am a man of unclean lips and I live among a people of unclean lips and my eyes have seen the King, the LORD Almighty" (Isaiah 6:5).

When people fail to grasp the depth of sin, then they have no understanding of the depth of our Savior's love for sinners. The true solution for guilt will elude them as well. Modern man, for all his therapies, can never quite seem to rid himself of that nasty, nagging problem. The problem remains simply because people fail to connect their guilty feelings with their estrangement from the righteous God. Only through Christ does the restless heart gain entrance into the peaceable kingdom. He is "the way, the truth and the life" (John 14:6). By faith in him "we have gained access into this grace in which we now stand" (Romans 5:2). He is the gate-keeper, the one who guards the entrance to the temple, his church. No one may enter into God's presence except through him. Believers know this, and so they worship God with a deep sense of reverence, and a keen understanding of what a privilege it is—an amazing grace—to be able to stand before the Savior God. They conduct themselves accordingly when they gather in his name.

With verse 12 the Chronicler begins to tell us how the individual duties were portioned out. Again we see the same desire at work to keep the selection process as "clean" as possible. Lots are cast to leave the final choice up to the Lord; no bias is shown in any respect. The future entryways to the temple are divided among the various families, with two posts being given to the family of Meshelemiah (verse 14). The gates are identified by the points of the compass and by other geographical features that are somewhat obscure to us now. The "Shalleketh Gate," for example, and "the upper road" (verse 16) are otherwise unknown. The basic organizational framework, however, is clear, as the following table demonstrates:

FAMILY NAME	LOCATION	NUMBER OF GUARDS
(Me)Shelemiah	East Gate	six
Zechariah	North Gate	four
Obed-Edom	South Gate	four
Obed Edom's sons	Storehouse	four
Shuppim and Hosah	West Gate	four
Shuppim and Hosah	Court at West Gate	two
Total on Duty		**Twenty-Four**

Since the temple grounds were going to face east, the East Gate would serve as the main entrance, hence the additional guards. The South Gate would have been the king's entrance, for the simple reason that the king's palace lay directly to the south of the temple complex. It was, therefore, a mark of special honor to Obed-Edom and his clan to receive that post. Although the NIV translation would give a person to understand that there were only two of Obed-Edom's sons on guard at any one time at the storehouse (verse 17), another and equally legitimate understanding of the Hebrew would give us two *contingents* of two guards apiece for the storehouse. This brings the total of guards on duty at one time to the number twenty four, a recurring number in this section of Chronicles, as we have seen.

[20] Their fellow Levites were in charge of the treasuries of the house of God and the treasuries for the dedicated things.

[21] The descendants of Ladan, who were Gershonites through Ladan and who were heads of families belonging to Ladan the Gershonite, were Jehieli, [22] the sons of Jehieli, Zetham and his brother Joel. They were in charge of the treasuries of the temple of the LORD.

[23] From the Amramites, the Izharites, the Hebronites and the Uzzielites:

[24] Shubael, a descendant of Gershom son of Moses, was the officer in charge of the treasuries. [25] His relatives through Eliezer: Rehabiah his son, Jeshaiah his son, Joram his son, Zicri his son and Shelomith his son. [26] Shelomith and his relatives were in charge of all the treasuries for the things dedicated by King David, by the heads of families who were the commanders of thousands and commanders of hundreds, and by the other army commanders. [27] Some of the plunder taken in battle they dedicated for the repair of the temple of

the LORD. [28]And everything dedicated by Samuel the seer and by Saul son of Kish, Abner son of Ner and Joab son of Zeruiah, and all the other dedicated things were in the care of Shelomith and his relatives.

[29]From the Izharites: Kenaniah and his sons were assigned duties away from the temple, as officials and judges over Israel.

[30]From the Hebronites: Hashabiah and his relatives—seventeen hundred able men—were responsible in Israel west of the Jordan for all the work of the LORD and for the king's service. [31]As for the Hebronites, Jeriah was their chief according to the genealogical records of their families. In the fortieth year of David's reign a search was made in the records, and capable men among the Hebronites were found at Jazer in Gilead. [32]Jeriah had twenty-seven hundred relatives, who were able men and heads of families, and King David put them in charge of the Reubenites, the Gadites and the half-tribe of Manasseh for every matter pertaining to God and for the affairs of the king.

We have seen David give the Levites many responsibilities as he organized Israel for worship around the temple. They were to play an assisting role to the priests as they served in the sanctuary (1 Chronicles 23:28-32). They provided the service of music and song in God's house (1 Chronicles 25). They were to guard the purity of God's house and keep order within it (1 Chronicles 26). The Chronicler winds up the Levitical job-description here by adding two more duties to the list. Some Levites were given charge over the temple treasuries, and others served "away from the temple, as officials and judges over Israel" (1 Chronicles 26:29). In keeping with his desire to speak an encouraging word to the Levites of his day, the Chronicler has demonstrated in these chapters how important the tribe of Levi was to the orderly worship of

Israel. They were not merely useful; they were essential. Without them, Israel could not function as the "kingdom of priests and . . . nation" holy to the LORD (Exodus 19:6) in the way God had intended.

Verse 20 mentions two kinds of treasuries in which Levites served. The first was called "treasuries of the house of God." The money collected in a census, money received from personal vows, redemption money for the firstborn male, and the money given in freewill offerings would be stored in a facility like this. For more information on the different types of offerings, the reader is directed to Exodus 30:11ff, Numbers 18:14 ff, and Leviticus 27:1ff. It is reasonable to suppose that the precious implements of worship would also find a resting place there when they were not in use. The other kind of treasury was for "the dedicated things." From the discussion in verses 27-29, we get the impression that it served as a storehouse for precious plunder taken in battle, as well as other valuable objects turned over to the Lord by the kings and leaders of Israel.

Though passed over in the lists of gatekeepers, descendants of Gershon, the last major clan of Levi, were given the responsibility of managing "the treasuries of the temple of the LORD" (verse 23). They served under Shubael (verse 24) who is identified as having descended from Moses' son Gershom. This would make Shubael a Kohathite. The rest of the chapter is filled with names of Levites from the clans and sub-clans of Kohath who served in the various capacities mentioned. Shelomith and his family were put in charge of the "treasuries for the things dedicated" (verse 26). Kenaniah and his family were entrusted with duties away from the temple itself, "as officials and judges over Israel" (verse 29). West of the Jordan river, Hashabiah and his relatives were to serve as representatives of the Lord and of his anointed king (verses 30 & 32). Apparently the duties became greater than they could manage. This would explain why, late in David's reign, a search was made for more Levites who were qualified to do the work. As a result of the genealogical research "Jeriah and twenty-seven hundred relatives" (verse 32) became king's men and temple representatives for the tribes of Reuben, Gad, and half of Manasseh. In the kingdom of God under David and his successors, there was no distinction between church and state as we know it today. Israel of old was intended to be a true theocracy, where God ruled through his chosen leaders.

Somehow blind to the message of the holy writer, one commentator on Chronicles has remarked that the officials described in chapter 26 served in duties of "a more or less peripheral nature." Clearly thinking in worldly categories, that commentator evaluates service in God's kingdom in terms of how prestigious, how central, and how prominent a particular duty may be. This is a problem we all share, because of our sinful nature. Our attention is drawn to the service of the worship leader; but we seldom note the person sitting two pews back who is "merely" singing hymns. We are impressed by meeting someone who boasts a corporate title, but are less enthusiastic about someone who is "just a homemaker." We are told by church growth experts that people need to be given work that is "meaningful" if they are to remain vitally linked to a congregation's ministry. But how is one to define what is "meaningful"? Is it meaningful labor— or a menial task—to put flowers on the altar, to fix a sprinkler-head, or to shovel a sidewalk?

Let every Christian heart be impressed with the truth the Chronicler wishes to teach here. By devoting all this space to the names and the duties of various Levites, the holy writer is saying, "What these people did mattered. It was important. It was necessary. All Israel would have suffered had they not done their assigned tasks. This work was given to them by God, and was carried out to his glory. That is what makes them meaningful." For us Jesus reiterates the same truth when he says, "If anyone gives even a cup of cold water to one of these little ones because he is my disciple, I tell you the truth, he will certainly not lose his reward" (Matthew 10:42). To know that he serves his Lord and that his Lord honors his service is all the reassurance a disciple ever needs about the value of his work.

27 **This is the list of the Israelites—heads of families, commanders of thousands and commanders of hundreds, and their officers, who served the king in all that concerned the army divisions that were on duty month by month throughout the year. Each division consisted of 24,000 men.**

²In charge of the first division, for the first month, was Jashobeam son of Zabdiel. There were 24,000 men in his division. ³He was a descendant of Perez and chief of all the army officers for the first month.

⁴In charge of the division for the second month was Dodai the Ahohite; Mikloth was the leader of his division. There were 24,000 men in his division.

⁵The third army commander, for the third month, was Benaiah son of Jehoiada the priest. He was chief and there were 24,000 men in his division. ⁶This was the Benaiah who was a mighty man among the Thirty and was over the Thirty. His son Ammizabad was in charge of his division.

⁷The fourth, for the fourth month, was Asahel the brother of Joab; his son Zebadiah was his successor. There were 24,000 men in his division.

⁸The fifth, for the fifth month, was the commander Shamhuth the Izrahite. There were 24,000 men in his division.

⁹The sixth, for the sixth month, was Ira the son of Ikkesh the Tekoite. There were 24,000 men in his division.

¹⁰The seventh, for the seventh month, was Helez the Pelonite, an Ephraimite. There were 24,000 men in his division.

¹¹The eighth, for the eighth month, was Sibbecai the Hushathite, a Zerahite. There were 24,000 men in his division.

¹²The ninth, for the ninth month, was Abiezer the Anathothite, a Benjamite. There were 24,000 men in his division.

¹³The tenth, for the tenth month, was Maharai the Netophathite, a Zerahite. There were 24,000 men in his division.

¹⁴The eleventh, for the eleventh month, was Benaiah the Pirathonite, an Ephraimite. There were 24,000 men in his division.

¹⁵The twelfth, for the twelfth month, was Heldai the Netophathite, from the family of Othniel. There were 24,000 men in his division.

By drawing circles radiating outward from a central point, the Chronicler has been describing the great organization of Israel as completed by David towards the end of his reign. The central point, of course, was to be the sanctuary housing the ark of the covenant. The first circle was comprised of the priests and Levites most directly associated with worship. The second arc took in the singers who filled the temple courts with God's Word set to music. The third circle described the gatekeepers who guarded the entrances to God's house. The fourth brought in the Levitical treasurers and other Levites whose duties took them out of the temple precincts into the other towns and villages of Israel. Away from the temple courts, they worked for God and king among the people, even among those who lived on the far side of the Jordan. With chapter 27, the Chronicler draws in the final circles, ending where he began in chapter 23 with the king and his officials.

While the first fifteen verses give us David's blueprint for organizing the army, we do well to take note of the first words of the chapter, "This is the list of the Israelites." It is obvious the Chronicler wanted this chapter to represent more than a military flow chart, giving David's command structure. This was Israel—the people of God—organized for worship, set in systematic array around the house of God, where the Lord lived among his people.

So that God's people could worship in peace and without fear, the army was organized to protect the holy land. David created twelve divisions of 24,000 apiece, one for each month of the year and one for each of the original tribes of Israel. Each division had a tour of active duty one month per year. The divisional leaders (verses 2-15) were the capable men who had proven themselves in combat and so had earned themselves a place among David's "mighty men" (see chapter 11:10-47).

We also thank God for our governments and for the lawful exercise of the power of the state for much the same reason. Paul encourages us to pray for those in authority so that "we may live peaceful and quiet lives in all godliness and holiness" (1 Timothy 2:2).

¹⁶The officers over the tribes of Israel:

over the Reubenites: Eliezer son of Zicri;
over the Simeonites: Shephatiah son of Maacah;
¹⁷over Levi: Hashabiah son of Kemuel;
over Aaron: Zadok;
¹⁸over Judah: Elihu, a brother of David;
over Issachar: Omri son of Michael;

¹⁹over Zebulun: Ishmaiah son of Obadiah;
   over Naphtali: Jerimoth son of Azriel;
²⁰over the Ephraimites: Hoshea son of Azaziah;
   over half the tribe of Manasseh: Joel son of Pedaiah;
²¹over the half-tribe of Manasseh in Gilead: Iddo son of
      Zechariah;
   over Benjamin: Jaasiel son of Abner;
²²over Dan: Azarel son of Jeroham.
These were the officers over the tribes of Israel.
²³David did not take the number of the men twenty years old
or less, because the LORD had promised to make Israel as numerous as the stars in the sky. ²⁴Joab son of Zeruiah began to
count the men but did not finish. Wrath came on Israel on account of this numbering, and the number was not entered in
the book of the annals of King David.

Here we have the tribal organization of Israel. Some have
called it the "civil" authority as opposed to the military au-
thorities listed above. A brief glance over the names of the
tribes reveals something unusual. The tribes of Gad and Asher
are simply dropped. Whether this reflects their political state
or relative strength at the time is uncertain. There have been
other times already when we have seen tribal names dropped
from the twelve (e.g., Zebulun in the listing of the first eight
chapters) or added twice (e.g., Manasseh in that same and in
other listings.) What is utterly unique about this tribal list is
the appearance of Aaron in verse 17. A descendant of Levi,
Aaron is never counted as a tribe anywhere else. No doubt he
is elevated to this status here to remind all in Israel that they
are a nation of priests, whose life is dedicated to the worship
of the one true God. To bring the number of tribes to an even
twelve, the two halves of Manasseh must be counted as one.

We are reminded of the disastrous census that David un-
dertook and the wrath of God that came upon Israel as a

consequence of it (verses 23,24). But we are also reminded of the great covenantal promise made to Abraham "to make Israel as numerous as the stars in the sky" (verse 23; see also Genesis 22:17,18). Because of that promise—and the promise of the Savior that stands at the heart of it—all who by faith regard Abraham as their father may be sure of a number of things. "(God) will not always accuse, nor will he harbor his anger forever. . . . For as high as the heavens are above the earth, so great is his love for those who fear him" (Psalm 103:9,11). However the earthly number of God's people may dwindle (and they certainly seem to have dwindled in the Chronicler's time and in ours) we can be sure that the full number of God's elect will be gathered into his kingdom.

²⁵Azmaveth son of Adiel was in charge of the royal storehouses.

Jonathan son of Uzziah was in charge of the storehouses in the outlying districts, in the towns, the villages and the watchtowers.

²⁶Ezri son of Kelub was in charge of the field workers who farmed the land.

²⁷Shimei the Ramathite was in charge of the vineyards. Zabdi the Shiphmite was in charge of the produce of the vineyards for the wine vats.

²⁸Baal-Hanan the Gederite was in charge of the olive and sycamore-fig trees in the western foothills. Joash was in charge of the supplies of olive oil.

²⁹Shitrai the Sharonite was in charge of the herds grazing in Sharon.

Shaphat son of Adlai was in charge of the herds in the valleys.

³⁰Obil the Ishmaelite was in charge of the camels. Jehdeiah the Meronothite was in charge of the donkeys.

³¹Jaziz the Hagrite was in charge of the flocks.

All these were the officials in charge of King David's property.

[32]Jonathan, David's uncle, was a counselor, a man of insight and a scribe. Jehiel son of Hacmoni took care of the king's sons.

[33]Ahithophel was the king's counselor.

Hushai the Arkite was the king's friend. [34]Ahithophel was succeeded by Jehoiada son of Benaiah and by Abiathar.

Joab was the commander of the royal army.

The final two lists are comprised of "the king's men," men who either served at David's side or were put in charge of his personal interests. From verses 25 to 31 we have the list of the trustees, managers, and administrators of crown property. At the top of the list are the men who were given the management of the king's "storehouses." Azmaveth (verse 25) was put in charge of "royal storehouses," which were probably located in Jerusalem. These are distinguished from the "storehouses in the outlying districts," overseen by Jonathan son of Uzziah. What was put into these storehouses is told to us in what follows. David had extensive landholdings: farms, vineyards, olive and sycamore-fig groves, and lands for grazing livestock. Many of David's storehouses must have been barns in which the harvests from his lands were kept. In addition David owned herds of cattle, camels, donkeys, and sheep (verses 29-31). Truly God had blessed the one he had taken from "following the flock" (1 Chronicles 17:7). Now he needed managers to tend to his personal property. When God blesses someone, there are no half-measures. We note that the king had a total of twelve officials in charge of his wealth.

The king's advisors are listed in verses 32-34. We note the names of Ahithophel and Hushai the Arkite, both of whom figured so prominently in the rebellion of David's son Absalom. Ahithophel betrayed his king while Hushai saved him (see 2 Samuel 15:32-37 and 16:15—17:14). Hushai truly earned his official title as "the king's friend" (verse 33). We also see Joab, the fiery and sometimes violent commander of David's troops. Against the king's direct orders, he killed the helpless Absalom as he hung from a tree, caught by his hair (2 Samuel 18:5 and 14). During the course of David's long life, he had known trouble and sorrow, heartache and betrayal. As a righteous king he had experienced how "the LORD (had) delivered him from them all" (Psalm 34:19). So the circles are complete, the circles that began with the king summoning the leaders of all Israel to organize for worship around the temple (1 Chronicles 23:1,2), and ending with all Israel standing at the ready to serve the one true God under the rule of its righteous king (1 Chronicles 27).

Concluding reflections on chapters 23-27

In the Chronicler's description of Israel's worship forms under King David, we can detect certain ideals and attitudes worth looking at more closely. For one thing, we see a love of order and organization. Perhaps for some the idea of organization connotes impersonal office buildings occupied by the grey shadows of robotic men and women. Not for Israel. We recall that the Hebrew word for "peace"—*shalom*—means more than an absence of war. It means a state of harmony and symmetry, where everything is right and in its right place. David organized his people in this orderly way because he wanted to do things right, so that priest and gatekeeper, singer and treasurer, counselor and army officer, all would fit together to form a pleasing whole. Each had his own particular role to play. Each role was important and necessary. But the whole was much greater than any individual part. We see this same spirit reflected in Paul's exalted words concerning the church in the letter to the Ephesians, "From

(Christ) the whole body, joined and held together by every supporting ligament, grows and builds itself up in love, as each part does its work" (4:16).

This detailed description by the Chronicler is his way of conveying this same truth to the people of his era. It's an Old Testament method of saying, "Let each one of us work together in love, accepting with joy the service God has assigned to us. Let no one be puffed up with pride. Let no one who serves in such a kingdom feel dejected. We all serve to the glory of God!" This ideal of peaceful order is clearly a reflection, not of the mind of man, but of the mind of God. "For God is not a God of disorder but of peace" (1 Corinthians 14:33). The descriptions of heaven and of the redeemed in the book of Revelation all resonate with the same sense of beauty and perfection. Everything is right. Each one is in his place. Every tongue and tribe is able to unite in one harmonious song to the one who sits on the throne.

We live at a time when scandals and divisions rock the church, when people wander from one fellowship to the next, hoping in each one to find in some external way the true church of God. "Do the people love each other here? Is the Spirit evident here?" We live at a time when it's easy to become discouraged about the church, so marred by sin does it appear to our eyes.

This is precisely why we need to see things the way the Chronicler sees them. He knew there was more to say about David's reign. He could have recounted the divisions and the scandals that rocked the people of God after Bathsheba took her bath, or Absalom tried to win the hearts of Israel away from their king. But he does not, for the simple reason that God's people do not need to hear that message when they are at the brink of giving up. What they need to win again for themselves is the truth that God loves them, in spite of their sin, and counts them holy, in spite of the imperfection of their lives. What they need to hear is how "Christ loved the church and gave himself up for her, to make her holy, cleansing her by the washing with water through the word, and to present her to himself as a radiant church, without stain or wrinkle or any other blemish, but holy and blameless" (Ephesians 5:24-27).

We, too, need to hear this message, or else we will never have the hope and courage that comes when a person sees the church the way God sees it! We find the true church wherever the word of forgiveness is proclaimed, and it must be perceived through the prism of forgiveness, or it won't be seen at all. But when we do detect it through the Word, then our sight is true. Then we see things with God's eyes.

David Prepares for the Building of God's House Under Solomon

E. David Publicly Commissions Solomon to Build

The last two chapters of 1 Chronicles complete the description of David's careful preparations for building a temple he would never see. The Chronicler sets before us a magnificent scene. David summons all the leaders of all the various groups within his kingdom to a great assembly. This is the congregation of Israel. In chapter 28 the holy writer records the public commissioning David gave to his son at that assembly. Chapter 29 sets down the story of an extraordinary outpouring of freewill offerings from the king and his leaders, an outpouring that would ensure that Solomon would have the financial resources to complete the task. In response to God's grace in moving hearts to give so generously, David lifts up his heart in a matchless prayer of praise to the Lord. In the prayer, the keynote of the book is sounded, "Yours, O LORD, is the kingdom!" The chapter concludes with the coronation of Solomon and the death of David "at a good old age."

Some make too much of the differences in the description we have of David's final days in the book of 1 Kings and the account we have here. In 1 Kings, they say, the picture is of an aged king who can barely rouse himself from bed to bring under control a kingdom become chaotic and riddled with intrigue. In Chronicles, on the other hand, we see a man in full possession of his faculties calmly passing on to his son his kingdom and his life's work. While both accurately describe conditions toward the end of David's life, the account we have before us in 1 Chronicles must have occurred just prior to David's death, well after Adonijah's abortive *coup d'etat*. The rebellion of Adonijah had moved David to establish a co-regency with his son Solomon immediately (see 1 Kings 1 for details). Now David wanted to hand over the reins of power completely, and so he had Solomon anointed king "a second time" (1 Chronicles 29:22). As for David being bedridden, anyone who has had experience with the aged knows that, if there is a pressing need, they can suddenly summon the strength to do things they had previously found difficult or almost impossible to do. David here literally rose to the occasion.

There is another interesting feature to the two chapters before us. In them we find many similarities in language and in incident to the scriptural account of Moses handing over power to his successor Joshua. For someone who knows the living God, this is hardly surprising. God's dealings with his people form patterns that are repeated as history moves along. As the plucking of one string on a harp might cause another one to vibrate, so one Bible passage resonates with another in playing the song of God's love. We also know that David was familiar with the prophetic writings of Moses. As such, he must have noticed the similarities between his life and the life of that great prophet. Since he had studied the life and the language of Moses, he made the language his own when he spoke to his son.

28 David summoned all the officials of Israel to assemble at Jerusalem: the officers over the tribes, the commanders of the divisions in the service of the king, the commanders of thousands and commanders of hundreds, and the officials in charge of all the property and livestock belonging to the king and his sons, together with the palace officials, the mighty men and all the brave warriors.

²King David rose to his feet and said: "Listen to me, my brothers and my people. I had it in my heart to build a house as a place of rest for the ark of the covenant of the LORD, for the footstool of our God, and I made plans to build it. ³But God said to me, 'You are not to build a house for my Name, because you are a warrior and have shed blood.'

⁴"Yet the LORD, the God of Israel, chose me from my whole family to be king over Israel forever. He chose Judah as leader, and from the house of Judah he chose my family, and from my father's sons he was pleased to make me king over all Israel. ⁵Of all my sons—and the LORD has given me many—he has chosen my son Solomon to sit on the throne of the kingdom of the LORD over Israel. ⁶He said to me: 'Solomon your son is the one who will build my house and my courts, for I have chosen him to be my son, and I will be his father. ⁷I will establish his kingdom forever if he is unswerving in carrying out my commands and laws, as is being done at this time.'

⁸"So now I charge you in the sight of all Israel and of the assembly of the LORD, and in the hearing of our God: Be careful to follow all the commands of the LORD your God, that you may possess this good land and pass it on as an inheritance to your descendants forever."

David solemnly summoned the assembly of Israel to Jerusalem to hear what he had to say. All Israel was present (see verse 8), represented by their leaders. David had organized Israel for worship, and now he was going to give them their marching orders. The Chronicler notes that the aged king rose to his feet (verse 2) to speak to the congregation. He prefaced his remarks by reminding all how God's will had overruled his heart's desire, and yet how God's grace had proceeded to give him more than his heart could have imagined: "I had wanted to build a house for the ark; God instead built an eternal house for me, and chose my son Solomon to be his own and to build his house."

These words were the mature reflections of a man who looked back at his life and saw it whole as a revelation of God's love—not only for himself, but for all who ever hoped for God to deliver them from sin. By his sure promise God had caused Israel's hopes first to center in Judah (verse 4; see also Genesis 49:10), then to rest in David (verse 4; see also 1 Chronicles 17). The Savior would be born from David's line, "to be king over Israel forever" (verse 4). Out of all David's sons, God had settled his saving will on Solomon as the one who would "sit upon the throne of the kingdom of the LORD" (verse 5) and build a house for God (verse 6). For the full significance of this Messianic language, the reader is urged to consult the commentary at 1 Chronicles 17:10-15.

The Lord had chosen Solomon to be his son and had promised to make his dynasty a permanent one over Israel "if he [was] unswerving in carrying out my commands and laws" (verse 7). As far as the earthly kingdom and earthly dynasty of David was concerned, the promises of God were conditional, just as the promise to adopt the people of Israel as his own had been conditional under the covenant that God made with them on Sinai (Exodus 19:5). "If you obey," said God, "then you will enjoy my favor." Obedience brought great earthly blessings; disobedience brought God's wrath and earthly disaster. This becomes a theme David will repeat in this exhortation, and a theme the Chronicler will develop in the second part of his book. "Be careful to follow all the commands of the LORD . . . then you may possess this good land" (verse 8). The fortunes of God's people in the promised land would rise and fall depending on their loyalty to the true God and their faithful adherence to the law of Moses.

It is also clear from this same passage that the unconditional covenant of God's grace forms the underlying bedrock of David's exhortation. David could claim that God's commands were being carried out "at this time" (verse 7). Certainly David could not say such a thing because his entire life had been lived in perfect harmony with the will of God. Only God's grace enabled David to make such a claim. David had found his righteousness first in God's pardon; then he had demonstrated his faith by the way he walked before the Lord. David had found the strength to make "preparations to build" a house for God (verse 2, Hebrew) only because God had first "prepared for him an everlasting kingdom" (verse 7, Hebrew). David's confidence in the power of God's pardoning love was such that he could urge his son Solomon to imitate his life of faith.

The Hebrew indicates that David directed his initial exhortation not only to Solomon, but to the entire assembly of Israel. All the verbs in verse eight are set in the plural. David wanted all of God's people to be faithful, not just Israel's king. True, the king could have a great influence for good or ill upon the rest of the nation, as the book of 2 Chronicles makes clear. Bad leaders would lead them astray; good leaders would bring them into the green pastures of God. But the people could not look at their king as being solely responsible for their spiritual state. They, too, had a charge from God to "be careful to follow all the commands of the LORD" (verse 8).

Faithful people can also be a powerful influence on a less than ideal spiritual leader. And even if a shepherd is strong in his personal faith, he will not be able to accomplish much if his people's hearts are becoming hardened to the Word.

What did the Chronicler intend to say to his original audience with this account? Though David's earthly throne was gone, God's promise to David remained. Though the first temple had been destroyed, a second temple had been built in its place. The Chronicler wanted David's words to ring down through the centuries and touch his people's hearts, "Be faithful to your faithful God. Obey him and keep his commandments. Imitate David, the righteous king. Live in God's grace as he did. God will not let his promise of a Savior fail. He will send you another Son of David to be your King forever. He will restore the glory of God's house." Similarly the holy writer urges us who live in these evil last days, "Do not falter in your faith. Hold fast to the promise of the King's appearing. Pursue righteousness. Walk in his love!"

⁹"And you, my son Solomon, acknowledge the God of your father, and serve him with wholehearted devotion and with a willing mind, for the LORD searches every heart and understands every motive behind the thoughts. If you seek him, he will be found by you; but if you forsake him, he will reject you forever. ¹⁰Consider now, for the LORD has chosen you to build a temple as a sanctuary. Be strong and do the work."

¹¹Then David gave his son Solomon the plans for the portico of the temple, its buildings, its storerooms, its upper parts, its inner rooms and the place of atonement. ¹²He gave him the plans of all that the Spirit had put in his mind for the courts of the temple of the LORD and all the surrounding rooms, for the treasuries of the temple of God and for the treasuries for the dedicated things. ¹³He gave him instructions for the divisions of the priests and Levites, and for all the work of serving in the

temple of the LORD, as well as for all the articles to be used in its service. ¹⁴He designated the weight of gold for all the gold articles to be used in various kinds of service, and the weight of silver for all the silver articles to be used in various kinds of service: ¹⁵the weight of gold for the gold lampstands and their lamps, with the weight for each lampstand and its lamps; and the weight of silver for each silver lampstand and its lamps, according to the use of each lampstand; ¹⁶the weight of gold for each table for consecrated bread; the weight of silver for the silver tables; ¹⁷the weight of pure gold for the forks, sprinkling bowls and pitchers; the weight of gold for each gold dish; the weight of silver for each silver dish; ¹⁸and the weight of the refined gold for the altar of incense. He also gave him the plan for the chariot, that is, the cherubim of gold that spread their wings and shelter the ark of the covenant of the LORD.

¹⁹"All this," David said, "I have in writing from the hand of the LORD upon me, and he gave me understanding in all the details of the plan."

²⁰David also said to Solomon his son, "Be strong and courageous, and do the work. Do not be afraid or discouraged, for the LORD God, my God, is with you. He will not fail you or forsake you until all the work for the service of the temple of the LORD is finished. ²¹The divisions of the priests and Levites are ready for all the work on the temple of God, and every willing man skilled in any craft will help you in all the work. The officials and all the people will obey your every command."

With verse nine, David began to direct his words of encouragement specifically to his son. In the first place, he wanted his son to "acknowledge (better: know) the God of your father" (verse 9). More important than knowing yourself, more important than knowing what you are to do is for you to know your God. These words seem so simple, and yet they are so charged with meaning. To know God means to know him as he truly is: a just God who "does not leave the guilty unpunished," and yet a God who is above all merciful and compassionate, "forgiving wickedness, rebellion and sin" (Exodus 34:6,7). To know God is not merely to know of him, as a person might know and be aware of someone famous. The Hebrew word implies a knowing that is based on personal experience, a knowing that can only come about when there is a living relationship between the individual and his God. Luther once suggested that true religion lies in the pronouns. To know God in this biblical sense is not just to know that there is a God, a Savior, a Judge, a Helper—existing somewhere out there beyond the vast reaches of space. Rather it means we can say that he is my God, my Savior, my Judge, and my helper in every need. This kind of knowledge comes about when we consider what God has done for his people. David exhorted Solomon to know the God "of your father." The record of David's life, far more than telling us who David was and what David did, is a record of the God of Israel and tells us who he is and what he will do for all who trust in his name.

When a person knows God in this way, he has the power to serve God "with wholehearted devotion and with a willing mind" (verse 9). God has a right to expect the undivided loyalty of a believer's heart. This is exactly what the believer wants to give to the God he now knows as his Savior. When God comes to man, the beggar, and fills his hands with the good things of salvation, that man's heart is possessed by joy and becomes wholly set on serving this gracious God. David could speak from experience on this point. Not only did he know the Lord as his Rock and his Redeemer, but God had taken him from following a flock of sheep and graciously made him the shepherd of his people. God had given him the grace to be his own and the grace to serve him only. Taking God's promise firmly in hand, David now said to his son,

293

"Consider . . . the LORD has chosen you to build a temple" (verse 10). Not only was God pleased to call Solomon his son, he was also pleased to give him the privilege of demonstrating his sonship in a life of meaningful service. Solomon would build the temple, the sanctuary where the holy God would live among his people!

The believer's service is marked by a holy awe and a reverent heart. The God with whom we have to do is the God of all power, the God of all knowledge. He "searches the heart and understands every motive behind the thoughts" (verse 9). We can hide nothing from him: no godless impulse, no loveless thought. We do well, therefore, to walk in his presence "with fear and trembling" (Philippians 2:12). Yet there is something we possess that transforms the raw terror of the sinner into the reverent awe of a believer. It is the consoling knowledge that "If you seek him, he will be found by you" (verse 9). In spite of our personal sin and unworthiness, God does not conceal himself from us. He is there to be found by the lowly. He is there to be found by the broken-hearted. He is there to be found by those overwhelmed by want. He is there to be found by the poor sinner seeking pardon. He revealed himself to Abraham, to Moses, and to David. He reveals himself to us in Jesus. Anyone who sees Jesus is looking into the heart of God (John 14:9). Looking at Jesus, we know that God's heart is a boundless ocean of love for us. This knowledge sets us free from our guilty fears and gives us eternal life (John 17:3).

Apart from the knowing that comes from God's revelation, there can be no knowledge of God. There is only a hopeless groping after something uncertain. The true God remains unknown (Acts 17:23). Anyone who tries to find him by pursuing his own thoughts will never succeed. Anyone who abandons God as he graciously reveals himself to us in Scripture can never hope to find him anywhere else. "If you forsake him, he will reject you forever" (verse 9). We hear David's words resound again in the New Testament's stern declaration, "Whoever does not believe will be condemned" (Mark 16:16).

We have spent time unfolding the meaning of verses 9 and 10 because they form the core of David's exhortation to his son. After reminding him where true strength can be found, David told his son, "Be strong and do the work" (verse 10). In addition, David equipped his son for the work by giving him not only a detailed plan for all the buildings of the temple complex, but also the "instructions for the divisions of the priests and Levites, and for all the work of serving in the temple of the LORD" (verse 13).

From verses 14 to 17 we get some idea of the detail into which David went in his planning. It included specifications for the amount of silver and gold to be used to make the various articles and furnishings of the temple. The cherubim (angels) of gold, whose wings would overshadow the ark of the covenant, came last on the list, but they were clearly first in importance. In referring last to the ark (the visible place where the invisible God was then to be found on earth), David gave his son a final reminder whose house he was about to build. We may assume that David's instructions for organizing the priests, etc., were given to us at least in part in what we have read in 1 Chronicles 23 - 28. We may also assume that David's plans for the temple and its furnishings will be further described for us in 2 Chronicles 3 and 4. For the first time we learn here that all these plans had God's approval. David specifically claimed for his blueprints—in all their details—the authority of being divinely inspired. "All this I have in writing from the hand of the LORD upon me" (verse 19). That was why Solomon could be confident that he was pleasing God when he put the plans into effect.

David concluded the public commissioning of Solomon by saying once again, "Be strong and courageous and do the work" (verse 20). Nothing on the outside should hinder Solomon from carrying out his assignment from the Lord. The preparations had all been made; the people had all been organized and mobilized for service. They stood ready "to obey your every command" (verse 21). Nothing on the inside should cause Solomon to hesitate, either. No doubts or fears ought to plague him or prevent him from doing the work at hand. "The LORD God, my God, is with you. He will not fail you or forsake you" (verse 20). Whatever fears he had he could overcome with the thought that God was with him. And when God is with you, he is not there as a lifeless block of wood or stone, but with all his power—put at your disposal according to his gracious promise.

The art of encouragement to service is one we will do well to learn from David here. No preacher or teacher of God's Word can consider his job done if he speaks of sin and then of God's grace in forgiving sin, but of nothing more. God's pardoned people also want to be pointed in a direction. They want to know where and how they can serve this gracious God whom they now know. There is no better way of doing this than the way we see David use in encouraging his son. Remind God's people where their strength comes from. Remind them of God's promises. Then remind them of God's will for their lives. Here is what God says about being a disciple, a mother, a father, a child, a friend, an employer, a worker. You can be sure that what you are doing is pleasing to God, because these callings in life are established by him and spoken of clearly in his Word. "Be strong and do the work," whatever work it is the Lord has set before you!

In finding God's message for ourselves today in this chapter of 1 Chronicles, we also note that David took the time at the end of his life to call this public assembly of all God's people. He wanted to solemnly charge them and his son to see the mission of God's kingdom as being one of holding up before all the world the saving name of the one true God. That was really the point of building the magnificent temple, the point behind all the planning and giving— to make God's name great. We certainly need to hear David speak to our church today. There are so many claims made upon the time, energy, and money of God's people that the claim of the kingdom and the mission of the church somehow gets lost in the shuffle. There are so many things to do that little time is left for the one thing only the church can do. Jesus gave us our marching orders, "Preach the good news" (Mark 16:15). That is why the church exists. That is why Jesus left us here. It is important for the leaders of God's people to remind the saints of their mission, to hold it before them as the one unalterable goal we all share. Let us make the saving name of Jesus great!

We conclude our study of this chapter by pointing out some of the specific similarities between David's commissioning of Solomon and Moses' commissioning of Joshua. It seems clear enough that the Chronicler wanted us to draw this parallel. As David was prevented from building the temple, so God prohibited Moses from experiencing the goal of his life's work. When he commissioned Joshua "in the presence of all Israel" (Deuteronomy 31:7; compare 1 Chronicles 28:8), he reminded him of what the Lord had said to him, "You shall not cross the Jordan" (verse 2). It would be left to Joshua to lead the people into the promised land. In encouraging Joshua to carry out his commission, Moses used almost the exact words that David used with Solomon, "Be strong and courageous. Do not be afraid or terrified. . . . The Lord himself will be with you; he will never leave you nor forsake you. Do not be afraid; do not be discouraged" (Deuteronomy 31:6-8; compare 1 Chronicles 28:20).

As Moses received the plans for the tabernacle from the hand of God (Exodus 25:9), so David also could claim divine inspiration for his plans to build the temple (1 Chronicles 28:12,19). There are other parallels between David and Moses, Solomon and Joshua. We may take note of some of them as they come up in our reading. The question that remains for us now is this: what significance, if any, can these parallels have for us today?

As the events of life unfold before us, it is often difficult to see the purpose of God or to detect his hand at work. Why is there famine here and plenty there? Why does war plague this country while peace prevails in that one? Why is my family member stricken with disease while so many others seem to live lives free from any trouble? Why is my life such a struggle for me, while others seem to have things so easy? Satan can at times insinuate himself into our thoughts and lead us to believe that God's dealings with the world lack justice—or worse, that there is no God at all, that everything happens in a random chaos. Parallels like these are patterns God weaves to demonstrate that he is at work in history. He is not aloof and uncaring, but near to us and involved. He works in all things "for the good of those who love him" (Romans 8:28). When we view events from close up, we may not see the pattern. No doubt when he was running from Saul, David, too, had his difficulties in detecting God's purpose. But time and distance may give us a truer perspective on even sad events. God's Word gives the truest perspective of all. Passages like these assure us that God is at work among us and in us "to will and to act according to his good purpose" (Philippians 2:13).

F. David's Final Appeal, Solomon's Ascent to the Throne, David's Death

Not content with what he had done already, David brought the public assembly of Israel to a close by appealing for offerings to build the Lord's house. In this final chapter of the first book of Chronicles, we can expect to learn a great deal, not only about how to make offerings to God, but also about the loving nature of our God and what it means to live a life in worshipful fellowship with him.

29 Then King David said to the whole assembly: "My son Solomon, the one whom God has chosen, is young and inexperienced. The task is great, because this palatial structure is not for man but for the LORD God. ²With all my resources I have provided for the temple of my God—gold for the gold work, silver for the silver, bronze for the bronze, iron for the iron and wood for the wood, as well as onyx for the settings, turquoise, stones of various colors, and all kinds of fine stone and marble—all of these in large quantities. ³Besides, in my devotion to the temple of my God I now give my personal treasures of gold and silver for the temple of my God, over and above everything I have provided for this holy temple: ⁴three thousand talents of gold (gold of Ophir) and seven thousand talents of refined silver, for the overlaying of the walls of the buildings, ⁵for the gold work and the silver work, and for all the work to be done by the craftsmen. Now, who is willing to consecrate himself today to the LORD?"**

David began by reminding his people of the salient facts. God had chosen Solomon to build the temple. But God's choice did not alter the fact that Solomon was "young and inexperienced" (verse 1). Nor did it lessen the magnitude of the task at hand—"this palatial structure is not for man but for the LORD God" (verse 1). David's words did not arise from a desire to humiliate his son publicly; Solomon himself would admit on a later occasion, "I am only a little child and do not know how to carry out my duties" (1 Kings 3:7). Rather, what David said came from his conviction that no one person could do the work by himself. No one individual possessed all the requisite skills, resources, and gifts to offer God such an act of worship as to build him a house. This was something all God's people needed to do together. In a similar way we know that man was not meant to worship God alone but in joyful fellowship with all God's people. Calling a pastor, teacher, or staff minister to serve a congregation—and recognizing God's choice in that call—does not mean the congregation thinks the one called has all the ability to do everything. The worship we offer in our united life as God's people requires the gifts of every member of the body (1 Corinthians 12:12-27).

David also reminded the people of the things he had already done to prepare for the work of building. In his official capacity as king and head of state, he had provided gold, silver, iron, wood, and precious stones—"all of these in large quantities" (verse 2). Now he added one thing more, "I . . . give my personal treasure . . ." (verse 3). In the ancient Near East, a ruler's personal fortune (as opposed to the official funds of the state) was his hedge against disaster and trouble. It was a financial security blanket, should war or intrigue deprive him of his throne. Once we grasp this, then we understand that David's action here is a public placing of his life and security into God's hands. It was a way of expressing with deeds the trust David had always affirmed in his psalms, "My God is my rock, in whom I take refuge" (Psalm 18:2; see also Psalm 31). Faith is willing to abandon all earthly guarantees and rely solely on God.

The public nature of David's gift was intended to provide leadership by example. What he said, he said as a prelude to his question, "Now who is willing to consecrate himself to-day to the LORD?" (verse 5). David felt he had a right to expect certain things from the leaders of God's people. Chief among the things he expected was that the leaders would be just as willing to serve God as he had been. When a person knows the Lord, he wants to serve him. It is as simple as that. For this reason, David simply assumed that the princes of Israel would demonstrate the consecration of their hearts in a concrete way by freely offering gifts for the building of the temple. The expression David employed for "consecrate himself" (verse 5) is a significant one. Literally it means "to fill his hand." It is used in Scripture for the way a priest is formally inducted into the priesthood as one who is willing to offer his life in service of God (Exodus 28:41; 32:29). David understood that offering gifts to God was one way of offering one's life in priestly service.

Some may wonder at the appropriateness of David declaring publicly what amount he was willing to give. "Isn't he taking pride in his good works?" a person may ask. More to the point: doesn't it go against our Savior's instruction to "give in secret" (Matthew 6:4)? A closer look at our Savior's words reveals that he is not giving us a command to observe absolute silence whenever it comes to almsgiving. Pushed to the extreme, we could turn the Lord's words into a prohibition of our public gathering of the offering every Sunday. That certainly does not happen "in secret," but before all. What Jesus is zeroing in on here is the motive for giving. Are people doing it for the praise and honor of men? Are they doing it just to have that "good feeling" that comes from knowing we've been good little boys and girls? Or are we doing it in the simplicity of our hearts to praise and honor and please God? If it is the latter, then whether we do it in public or in private, the action is pure since it comes from a pure heart.

Who can doubt that David's actions stemmed from such a pure heart? He knew that he stood in the presence of a God who "tests the heart and (is) pleased with integrity" (verse 17). The only reason he gave his offering publicly was to provide leadership for his people. He did not do it to procure applause for himself.

There are a whole host of practical applications we could make to our own lives from this passage. We will content ourselves with just a few. In the church we are so strange when it comes to money. We act as if it were a commodity too degraded to mention in a spiritual context. We tiptoe timidly around the thought of asking people to offer any. And then there are those who act as if it were a thoroughly ungodly thing for anyone else to know what they give to God! "That's between him and me, and sometimes, I don't even know about it. I just give whatever my hand happens to find in my suit pocket whenever I see the collection plate passed around." Contrast this attitude with David's actions. He publicly declares what he is willing to offer to his God. He is not boasting, this is not vainglory. In generosity born of faith, he wants to provide God's people with the encouragement of his own example. More than this, as one whose eyes see true because they are filled with a vision of God's grace, he can "see" the willingness of the leaders to offer their priestly service to God as well. Because of this, he does not hesitate to ask them also to "consecrate (themselves) today to the LORD."

⁶Then the leaders of families, the officers of the tribes of Israel, the commanders of thousands and commanders of hundreds, and the officials in charge of the king's work gave willingly. ⁷They gave toward the work on the temple of God five thousand talents*ᵈ* and ten thousand darics*ᵉ* of gold, ten thousand talents*ᶠ* of silver, eighteen thousand talents*ᵍ* of bronze and a hundred thousand talents*ʰ* of iron. ⁸Any who had precious

stones gave them to the treasury of the temple of the LORD in the custody of Jehiel the Gershonite. ⁹The people rejoiced at the willing response of their leaders, for they had given freely and wholeheartedly to the LORD. David the king also rejoiced greatly.

WEIGHT EQUIVALENTS

d	5,000 talents	about 190 tons (170 metric tons)
e	10,000 darics	about 185 pounds (84 kilograms)
f	10,000 talents	about 375 tons (345 metric tons)
g	10,000 talents	about 675 tons (610 metric tons)
h	100,000 talents	about 3,750 tons (3,450 metric tons)

David was not disappointed in his hope. The two key words in this passage are "willing" and "joy." David's mobilization of God's people for worship, as detailed in Chapters 22-27, was much more than a matter of mere outward organization. United under the Lord's anointed, enjoying the "rest" God had given them through him, the leaders of Israel willingly poured out their hearts to God. They offered him their worldly wealth. And what an offering it was! These were not the dregs, squeezed out of them by guilt, duty, or compulsion of any kind. The amounts offered were much more than princely sums, much more than a king's ransom. The total given was an amount so huge, only God could have enabled it. The accounting given in verse 7 is a stupendous amount by any form of calculation. Instead of this offering bringing grudging comments and mean-spirited remarks from the people, it gave them and their king great joy (verse 9), because they noted the freedom and enthusiasm with which their leaders gave. Joy begets joy, just as love begets love. The heart in which Christ rules is refreshed and encouraged when it sees the willing service our loving Lord inspires. In it, we see proof of the truth that we live in the presence of a God who "is able to make all grace abound to [us], so that in all things at all times, having all that [we] need, [we] will abound in every good work" (2 Corinthians 9:8).

¹⁰**David praised the LORD in the presence of the whole assembly, saying,**

"Praise be to you, O LORD,
God of our father Israel,
from everlasting to everlasting.
¹¹**Yours, O LORD, is the greatness and the power**
and the glory and the majesty and the splendor,
for everything in heaven and earth is yours.
Yours, O LORD, is the kingdom;
you are exalted as head over all.
¹²**Wealth and honor come from you;**
you are the ruler of all things.
In your hands are strength and power
to exalt and give strength to all.
¹³**Now, our God, we give you thanks,**
and praise your glorious name.

¹⁴**"But who am I, and who are my people, that we should be able to give as generously as this? Everything comes from you, and we have given you only what comes from your hand. ¹⁵We are aliens and strangers in your sight, as were all our forefathers. Our days on earth are like a shadow, without hope. ¹⁶O LORD our God, as for all this abundance that we have provided for building you a temple for your Holy Name, it comes from your hand, and all of it belongs to you. ¹⁷I know, my God, that you test the heart and are pleased with integrity. All these things have I given willingly and with honest intent. And now I have seen with joy how willingly your people who are here have given to you. ¹⁸O LORD, God of our fathers Abraham,**

Isaac and Israel, keep this desire in the hearts of your people forever, and keep their hearts loyal to you. ¹⁹And give my son Solomon the wholehearted devotion to keep your commands, requirements and decrees and to do everything to build the palatial structure for which I have provided."

²⁰Then David said to the whole assembly, "Praise the LORD your God." So they all praised the LORD, the God of their fathers; they bowed low and fell prostrate before the LORD and the king.

A worthwhile study in itself would be one that encompassed all the great prayers in Chronicles. Before us is one example. A magnificent offering for a magnificent building led David to express his own and his people's joy in a magnificent prayer of praise and thanksgiving. This prayer puts the offering of gifts to the Lord into its proper context. Giving is worship and worship is giving. The center of the giving is always God, not man. David and the leaders could only worship and give to God because they had first received from God. For David, the words "We give thee but thine own," (TLH 441, verse 1) were more than a trite phrase, they were the summation of his life.

David offered praise to God as the true possessor of all things: There is no greatness except that which comes from God. There is no power but what is given by God. "For everything in heaven and in earth is yours" (verse 11). God called the universe into being. It belongs to him. More than simply being the Creator of all things, God also is at work in all things for his saving, redemptive purposes. "Yours, O LORD, is the kingdom" (verse 11). This affirmation forms the theme of the entire book. David knew that all that he had been able to accomplish, he had been enabled to accomplish by the Savior-God who rules in love. In this phrase, great king David cast his crown before the Lord. "It is not my

305

kingdom, my throne, my glory, my people, my goals, my plans. Yours is the kingdom. Yours alone!"

Let David teach us all to pray these words. How the human heart longs for fulfillment, to be lifted up above the dreary dust of life! Yet how perversely it seeks that lifting up in some empty self-exaltation or in pursuit of creature comforts instead of resting in the consolation of its Creator. Only when the human heart is won over to the kingdom of Christ can it know the joy of being caught up into God's world-rule, a righteous, saving purpose at work in history and in the annals of our lives. When the kingdom of Christ our Lord comes to our heart, we know the joy of being part of something bigger than our puny selves. That's the joy expressed in David's song. His throne was not his own, but God's. What God did for him he did not for him alone, but for a world of hungry, hurting souls.

"Who am I?" David went on to ask, "And who are my people?" (verse 14). We remember David asking similar questions in 1 Chronicles 17. There they formed David's initial response to all God had done for him in making him king. There it was David's way of expressing his wonder at hearing the announcement that he would be the founder of an eternal dynasty and the forefather of the Messiah and Savior. Here the questions expressed his amazement that he and his people "should be able to give as generously as this" (verse 14). Grace defined David. Grace had enabled David to become great and to do great things. Now we see how God's grace to David overflowed also to his people. Grace enabled David's people to follow their anointed king, to be great in God's eyes, and to do great things also. When beggars like us catch a glimpse of the depth of God's love, we can only say, "Amazing! Who am I or what have I ever done to be worthy of such a wealth of compassion?"

Specifically, what David had witnessed in the willingness to give led him to say to God, "Everything comes from you, and we have given you only what comes from your hand" (verse 14). Not only did the wealth itself come from God (verse 16), but also the eager heart that wants to give (verses 14,18). Not only the means, but also the motive—all is God's gift to us. In the end, grace serves to frame a believer's entire life. When we understand it fully, we realize that we never truly give to God. We only receive. For even when we offer our service to God, our money to God, our worship to God, we are only returning to him what he has first given to us. So we worship God as God—the giver; we confess ourselves to be beggars who depend on his mercy for every good thing.

David confessed that truth with respect to the abundance they gave and the willing hearts that prompted it to be given. He confessed that truth with respect to the land of Israel in which they lived. "We are aliens and strangers"; God alone is the true possessor (verse 15). A person who knows the grace of God knows that he is not entitled to any possession by personal right. Call it a loan, call it trust, call it a gift. Do not treat it as your due, something owed you for services rendered. Lastly, David confessed it also with respect to his hope of salvation. "Our days on earth are like a shadow, without hope" (verse 15). We put no trust in anything we have done in this world; we do not derive our confidence from anything in this impermanent life. We do not expect man to save us. None of these things breed true hope. "Lord, you have been our dwelling place throughout all generations. Before the mountains were born or you brought forth the earth and the world, from everlasting to everlasting, you are God" (Psalm 90:1). *Here above all* man may not give, but only receive, putting his hope in God's promise. "For the wages of sin is death, but the gift of God is eternal life in Christ Jesus our Lord" (Romans 6:23).

They say that the final words Luther wrote before his death were these, "Wir sind Bettler. Das ist wahr!—We are beggars, that is true." After all the great reformer had accomplished and in spite of all the works he could have laid claim to, that remained his final confession. "All is from you, O Lord, and from you we have received whatever we have done." Long before Luther, David arrived at the same conclusion, "Everything is from you, and we have given you only what comes from your hand." What united both hearts across the millennia—and unites them still—is a heartfelt appreciation for God's amazing grace to us poor sinners.

In this entire section we see David, the Lord's anointed, serving as a sort of high priest for his people. We have seen him in this role before (1 Chronicles 15 and 16). As a mediator, he represented the congregation of Israel to the Lord, giving him thanks on their behalf (verse 13), interceding with him for their good (verses 18,19), and inviting them to praise their God (verse 20). It is well worth noting what David asked for when he interceded for his people, "Keep this desire in the hearts of your people forever, and keep their hearts loyal to you. . . . And give my son Solomon the wholehearted devotion to keep your commands." Also worth noting is the basis on which David made his request. He appealed to the LORD, the God who made a covenant of grace with their "fathers Abraham, Isaac and Israel" (verse 18).

We cannot help but hear in David's words of intercession an echo of our Lord's great prayer to the Father just before he laid down his life for the world. "Holy Father, protect [my disciples] by the power of your name—the name you gave me—so that they may be one as we are one" (John 17:11).

The Father is pleased to grant this request of his Son, the King anointed by the Spirit to save us. We know that God grants that request because Jesus is the fulfillment of the covenant made with Abraham, Isaac, and Israel. He is the Son of David who came to found the everlasting kingdom promised to his earthly ancestor. That is why we have every confidence in Christ that God will preserve in us a ready mind and a loyal will. He will keep us eager to serve the God who saved us and has gathered us together into the perfect unity of his love.

[21]The next day they made sacrifices to the LORD and presented burnt offerings to him: a thousand bulls, a thousand rams and a thousand male lambs, together with their drink offerings, and other sacrifices in abundance for all Israel. [22]They ate and drank with great joy in the presence of the LORD that day.

Then they acknowledged Solomon son of David as king a second time, anointing him before the LORD to be ruler and Zadok to be priest. [23]So Solomon sat on the throne of the LORD as king in place of his father David. He prospered and all Israel obeyed him. [24]All the officers and mighty men, as well as all of King David's sons, pledged their submission to King Solomon.

[25]The LORD highly exalted Solomon in the sight of all Israel and bestowed on him royal splendor such as no king over Israel ever had before.

The day after Solomon's commissioning and the great offering, the congregation gathered to rededicate themselves to the Lord. The completion of David's preparations for the temple, the ending of his reign, and the beginning of Solomon's, all these were good reasons to gather for such a purpose. By the thousands, bulls, rams, and male lambs were offered as whole burnt offerings (verse 21). These sacrifices expressed the desire of king and people to offer their whole lives completely to the Lord. It is clear that fellowship offerings also were made. Part of this sacrifice was burnt on the altar as an offering to God, and part was consumed by the worshippers who then "ate and drank . . . in the presence of the LORD" (verse 22). This intimate "table fellowship" with God was marked by joy, a precursor of that joy we will all experience in that great Messianic banquet to come. Then "people will come from east and west and north and south, and will take their places at the feast in the kingdom of God" (Luke 13:29). What a happy day that will be!

On the same occasion, "Solomon son of David" was acclaimed and anointed king for a second time. The first anointing had taken place in haste, of necessity, to take the steam out of Adonijah's coup (see 1 Kings 1). Now Solomon's ascent to the throne could be celebrated with proper solemnity, in the calmer days at the end of David's life. Now it could take place within the context of Solomon's public commissioning to build the temple, instead of being a mere reaction to the threat Adonijah posed to God's good order. God's people could now fully unite in freely pledging their submission to the son of David sitting "on the throne of the LORD" (verses 23,24). This unity even embraced "all of King David's sons" (verse 24), including the erstwhile rebel Adonijah. Even before he gives us the full account of Solomon's reign, the holy writer summarizes it for us by saying, "The LORD highly exalted Solomon . . . and bestowed on him royal splendor such as no king over Israel ever had before" (verse 25). "Solomon in all his splendor" will be a major theme of the second book of Chronicles.

The Chronicler brings his first book to a close by drawing this lovely picture of God's kingdom for us. Here is all Israel fully united under the glorious son of David and fully dedicated to the mission of building God's house. He does not do so for nostalgia's sake, simply to play a bit upon "the mystic chords of memory." Ultimately this description is not so much a look backward at what God did, as it is a look forward to what God intends still to do for his people. "There will yet come the Child to rule on David's throne," the Chronicler reminds those beleaguered believers of his day. "Of the increase of his government and peace, there will be no end. He will reign . . . with justice and righteousness . . . forever. The zeal of the LORD Almighty will accomplish this" (Isaiah 9:7).

God's people in every age have taken comfort from the knowledge that whatever their external state might be, their eternal fate has been determined by the words and promises of God. Those promises were fulfilled one dark day outside Jerusalem, where the Lord of all gave up his life for our sins. They were confirmed on Easter morning when our glorious King rose again to establish his victorious rule over all our enemies. Nothing in heaven and earth can keep him from bringing that rule to completion, so that we share his glory. Meanwhile, let us be about his business and carry out with joy the mission he has given us to build his temple, the holy Christian Church.

[26]David son of Jesse was king over all Israel. [27]He ruled over Israel forty years—seven in Hebron and thirty-three in Jerusalem. [28]He died at a good old age, having enjoyed long life, wealth and honor. His son Solomon succeeded him as king.

[29]As for the events of King David's reign, from beginning to end, they are written in the records of Samuel the seer, the records of Nathan the prophet and the records of Gad the seer, [30]together with the details of his reign and power, and the circumstances that surrounded him and Israel and the kingdoms of all the other lands.

So ended the reign of David. Forty years he had ruled Israel. During those years God had taken his people from being a loose confederation of tribes at the mercy of their enemies and made them into a unified kingdom, enjoying rest under God's kind of king. The ark had been restored to its rightful place at the heart of Israel's worship life. A site had been picked, and all the preparations had been made for the building of a temple to house it. David had organized the entire kingdom for the worship of the one true God and had left his people a legacy of inspired songs to praise him by. In recognition of his faithful service, God had bestowed on him the three great earthly blessings of "long life, wealth and honor" (verse 28). His son Solomon—and all his successors after him—would be evaluated according to the standard of faithfulness David had demonstrated. They would be blessed to the degree they "walked in the ways of . . . father David" (2 Chronicles 17:4).

There were other things the Chronicler could have written about, other "details of [David's] reign and power" (verse 30) he might have given. But his intent never had been to write about everything David did. His desire was to present David's life as God saw it, under grace, as an example and foreshadowing of the Righteous King who was yet to come. By the same token, there were other things the Chronicler could have said about "Israel and the kingdoms of all the surrounding lands" (verse 30). But again, it was not his purpose merely to trace the rise and fall of earthly kingdoms or give us the dry details of history emptied of faith. The holy writer wanted to hold before his readers the vision of the kingdom of God, the gracious and saving purpose of God working "in with and under" everything that happens. He wanted to build a spiritual wall around Zion, to protect God's people from the assaults of Satan who wanted to rob them of their hope. He wanted to teach them to see history from God's point of view.

May the Spirit train us in this point of view, too. However hard it may be at times to discern God's eternal purpose with our eyes, faith judges everything by the promise. By the promise God clears our vision to see things as they are. With faith renewed in God's promise through the Chronicler's message, may the Spirit teach us to sing even now in anticipation of history's consummation, "The kingdom of the world has become the kingdom of our Lord and of his Christ, and he will reign forever and ever" (Revelation 11:15).